2015 | World Development Indicators

 **WORLD BANK GROUP**

i 0074ᴜ40ᴜ0

Preface

The year 2015 is when the world aimed to achieve many of the targets set out in the Millennium Development Goals. Some have been met. The rate of extreme poverty and the proportion of people without access to safe drinking water were both halved between 1990 and 2010, five years ahead of schedule. But some targets have not been achieved, and the aggregates used to measure global trends can mask the uneven progress in some regions and countries. This edition of *World Development Indicators* uses the latest available data and forecasts to show whether the goals have been achieved and highlights some of the differences between countries and regions that underlie the trends. Figures and data are also available online at http://data.worldbank .org/mdgs.

But this will be the last edition of *World Development Indicators* that reports on the Millennium Development Goals in this way. A new and ambitious set of goals and targets for development—the Sustainable Development Goals—will be agreed at the UN General Assembly in September 2015. Like the Millennium Development Goals before them, the Sustainable Development Goals will require more and better data to monitor progress and to design and adjust the policies and programs that will be needed to achieve them. Policymakers and citizens need data and, equally important, the ability to analyze them and understand their meaning.

The need for a data revolution has been recognized during the framing of the Sustainable Development Goals by the UN Secretary-General's High-Level Panel on the Post-2015 Development Agenda. In response, a group of independent advisors—of which I was privileged to have been part—has called for action in several areas. A global consensus is needed on principles and standards for interoperable data. Emerging technology innovations need to be shared, especially in low-capacity countries and institutions. National capacities among data producers and users need to be strengthened with new and sustained investment. And new forms of public–private partnerships are needed to promote innovation, knowledge and data sharing, advocacy, and technology transfer. The World Bank Group is addressing all four of these action areas, especially developing new funding streams and forging public–private partnerships for innovation and capacity development.

This edition of *World Development Indicators* retains the structure of previous editions: *World view*, *People*, *Environment*, *Economy*, *States and markets*, and *Global links*. New data include the average growth in income of the bottom 40 percent of the population, an indicator of shared prosperity presented in *World View*, and an indicator of statistical capacity in *States and markets*. *World view* also includes a new snapshot of progress toward the Millennium Development Goals, and each section includes a map highlighting an indicator of special interest.

World Development Indicators is the result of a collaborative effort of many partners, including the UN family, the International Monetary Fund, the International Telecommunication Union, the Organisation for Economic Co-operation and Development, the statistical offices of more than 200 economies, and countless others. I wish to thank them all. Their work is at the very heart of development and the fight to eradicate poverty and promote shared prosperity.

Haishan Fu
Director
Development Economics Data Group

Acknowledgments

This book was prepared by a team led by Masako Hiraga under the management of Neil Fantom and comprising Azita Amjadi, Maja Bresslauer, Tamirat Chulta, Liu Cui, Federico Escaler, Mahyar Eshragh-Tabary, Juan Feng, Saulo Teodoro Ferreira, Wendy Huang, Bala Bhaskar Naidu Kalimili, Haruna Kashiwase, Buyant Erdene Khaltarkhuu, Tariq Khokhar, Elysee Kiti, Hiroko Maeda, Malvina Pollock, William Prince, Leila Rafei, Evis Rucaj, Umar Serajuddin, Rubena Sukaj, Emi Suzuki, Jomo Tariku, and Dereje Wolde, working closely with other teams in the Development Economics Vice Presidency's Development Data Group.

World Development Indicators electronic products were prepared by a team led by Soong Sup Lee and comprising Ying Chi, Jean-Pierre Djomalieu, Ramgopal Erabelly, Shelley Fu, Omar Hadi, Gytis Kanchas, Siddhesh Kaushik, Ugendran Machakkalai, Nacer Megherbi, Parastoo Oloumi, Atsushi Shimo, and Malarvizhi Veerappan.

All work was carried out under the direction of Haishan Fu. Valuable advice was provided by Poonam Gupta, Zia M. Qureshi, and David Rosenblatt.

The choice of indicators and text content was shaped through close consultation with and substantial contributions from staff in the World Bank's various Global Practices and Cross-Cutting Solution Areas and staff of the International Finance Corporation and the Multilateral Investment Guarantee Agency. Most important, the team received substantial help, guidance, and data from external partners. For individual acknowledgments of contributions to the book's content, see Credits. For a listing of our key partners, see Partners.

Communications Development Incorporated provided overall design direction, editing, and layout, led by Bruce Ross-Larson and Christopher Trott. Elaine Wilson created the cover and graphics and typeset the book. Peter Grundy, of Peter Grundy Art & Design, and Diane Broadley, of Broadley Design, designed the report. Staff from the World Bank's Publishing and Knowledge Division oversaw printing and dissemination of the book.

Table of contents

Introduction
Millennium Development Goals snapshot
MDG 1 Eradicate extreme poverty
MDG 2 Achieve universal primary education
MDG 3 Promote gender equality and
        empower women
MDG 4 Reduce child mortality
MDG 5 Improve maternal health
MDG 6 Combat HIV/AIDS, malaria, and
        other diseases
MDG 7 Ensure environmental sustainability
MDG 8 Develop a global partnership for
        development
Targets and indicators for each goal
World view indicators
About the data
Online tables and indicators
Poverty indicators
About the data
Shared prosperity indicators
About the data
Map

Introduction
Highlights
Map
Table of indicators
About the data
Online tables and indicators

Partners

Defining, gathering, and disseminating international statistics is a collective effort of many people and organizations. The indicators presented in *World Development Indicators* are the fruit of decades of work at many levels, from the field workers who administer censuses and household surveys to the committees and working parties of the national and international statistical agencies that develop the nomenclature, classifications, and standards fundamental to an international statistical system. Non-governmental organizations and the private sector have also made important contributions, both in gathering primary data and in organizing and publishing their results. And academic researchers have played a crucial role in developing statistical methods and carrying on a continuing dialogue about the quality and interpretation of statistical indicators. All these contributors have a strong belief that available, accurate data will improve the quality of public and private decisionmaking.

The organizations listed here have made *World Development Indicators* possible by sharing their data and their expertise with us. More important, their collaboration contributes to the World Bank's efforts, and to those of many others, to improve the quality of life of the world's people. We acknowledge our debt and gratitude to all who have helped to build a base of comprehensive, quantitative information about the world and its people.

For easy reference, web addresses are included for each listed organization. The addresses shown were active on March 1, 2015.

International and government agencies

Carbon Dioxide Information Analysis Center

http://cdiac.ornl.gov

Centre for Research on the Epidemiology of Disasters

www.emdat.be

Deutsche Gesellschaft für Internationale Zusammenarbeit

www.giz.de

Food and Agriculture Organization

www.fao.org

Institute for Health Metrics and Evaluation

www.healthdata.org

Internal Displacement Monitoring Centre

www.internal-displacement.org

International Civil Aviation Organization

www.icao.int

International Diabetes Federation

www.idf.org

International Energy Agency

www.iea.org

International Labour Organization

www.ilo.org

Partners

International
Monetary Fund

www.imf.org

International Telecommunication
Union

www.itu.int

Joint United Nations
Programme on HIV/AIDS

www.unaids.org

National Science
Foundation

www.nsf.gov

The Office of U.S. Foreign
Disaster Assistance

www.usaid.gov

Organisation for Economic Co-operation
and Development

www.oecd.org

Stockholm International
Peace Research Institute

sipri

www.sipri.org

Understanding
Children's Work

www.ucw-project.org

United Nations

www.un.org

United Nations Centre for Human
Settlements, Global Urban Observatory

www.unhabitat.org

**United Nations
Children's Fund**

www.unicef.org

**United Nations Conference on
Trade and Development**

www.unctad.org

**United Nations Department of
Economic and Social Affairs,
Population Division**

www.un.org/esa/population

**United Nations Department of
Peacekeeping Operations**

www.un.org/en/peacekeeping

**United Nations Educational, Scientific
and Cultural Organization, Institute
for Statistics**

www.uis.unesco.org

**United Nations
Environment Programme**

www.unep.org

**United Nations Industrial
Development Organization**

www.unido.org

**United Nations
International Strategy
for Disaster Reduction**

www.unisdr.org

**United Nations Office on
Drugs and Crime**

www.unodc.org

**United Nations Office
of the High Commissioner
for Refugees**

www.unhcr.org

Partners

United Nations
Population Fund

www.unfpa.org

Upsalla Conflict
Data Program

www.pcr.uu.se/research/UCDP

World Bank

http://data.worldbank.org

World Health Organization

www.who.int

World Intellectual
Property Organization

www.wipo.int

World Tourism
Organization

www.unwto.org

World Trade
Organization

www.wto.org

Private and nongovernmental organizations

**Center for International Earth
Science Information Network**

www.ciesin.org

**Containerisation
International**

Lloyd's List | CONTAINERISATION
INTERNATIONAL

www.ci-online.co.uk

DHL

www.dhl.com

**International Institute for
Strategic Studies**

IISS

www.iiss.org

**International
Road Federation**

IRF

www.irfnet.ch

Netcraft

http://news.netcraft.com

PwC

pwc

www.pwc.com

**Standard &
Poor's**

STANDARD
&POOR'S

www.standardandpoors.com

**World Conservation
Monitoring Centre**

www.unep-wcmc.org

**World Economic
Forum**

WORLD
ECONOMIC
FORUM

www.weforum.org

**World Resources
Institute**

www.wri.org

User guide to tables

World Development Indicators is the World Bank's premier compilation of cross-country comparable data on development. The database contains more than 1,300 time series indicators for 214 economies and more than 30 country groups, with data for many indicators going back more than 50 years.

The 2015 edition of *World Development Indicators* offers a condensed presentation of the principal indicators, arranged in their traditional sections, along with regional and topical highlights and maps.

- World view
- People
- Environment
- Economy
- States and markets
- Global links

Tables

The tables include all World Bank member countries (188), and all other economies with populations of more than 30,000 (214 total). Countries and economies are listed alphabetically (except for Hong Kong SAR, China, and Macao SAR, China, which appear after China).

The term *country,* used interchangeably with *economy,* does not imply political independence but refers to any territory for which authorities report separate social or economic statistics. When available, aggregate measures for income and regional groups appear at the end of each table.

Aggregate measures for income groups

Aggregate measures for income groups include the 214 economies listed in the tables, plus Taiwan, China, whenever data are available. To maintain consistency in the aggregate measures over time and between tables, missing data are imputed where possible.

Aggregate measures for regions

The aggregate measures for regions cover only low- and middle-income economies.

The country composition of regions is based on the World Bank's analytical regions and may differ from common geographic usage. For regional classifications, see the map on the inside back cover and the list on the back cover flap. For further discussion of aggregation methods, see *Statistical methods.*

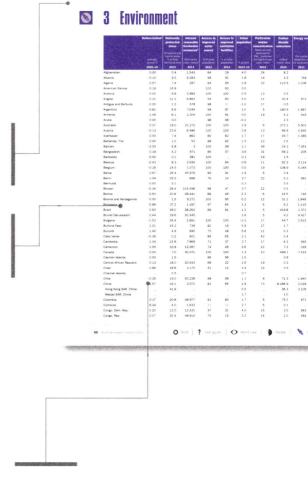

Data presentation conventions

- A blank means not applicable or, for an aggregate, not analytically meaningful.
- A billion is 1,000 million.
- A trillion is 1,000 billion.
- Figures in purple italics refer to years or periods other than those specified or to growth rates calculated for less than the full period specified.
- Data for years that are more than three years from the range shown are footnoted.
- The cutoff date for data is February 1, 2015.

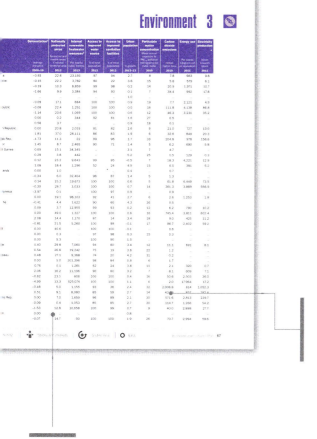

Symbols

..   means that data are not available or that aggregates cannot be calculated because of missing data in the years shown.

0 or 0.0   means zero or small enough that the number would round to zero at the displayed number of decimal places.

/   in dates, as in 2012/13, means that the period of time, usually 12 months, straddles two calendar years and refers to a crop year, a survey year, or a fiscal year.

$ means current U.S. dollars unless otherwise noted.

<   means less than.

Classification of economies

For operational and analytical purposes the World Bank's main criterion for classifying economies is gross national income (GNI) per capita (calculated using the *World Bank Atlas* method). Because GNI per capita changes over time, the country composition of income groups may change from one edition of *World Development Indicators* to the next. Once the classification is fixed for an edition, based on GNI per capita in the most recent year for which data are available (2013 in this edition), all historical data presented are based on the same country grouping.

Low-income economies are those with a GNI per capita of $1,045 or less in 2013. Middle-income economies are those with a GNI per capita of more than $1,045 but less than $12,746. Lower middle-income and upper middle-income economies are separated at a GNI per capita of $4,125. High-income economies are those with a GNI per capita of $12,746 or more. The 19 participating member countries of the euro area are presented as a subgroup under high income economies.

Statistics

Data are shown for economies as they were constituted in 2013, and historical data have been revised to reflect current political arrangements. Exceptions are noted in the tables.

Additional information about the data is provided in *Primary data documentation,* which summarizes national and international efforts to improve basic data collection and gives country-level information on primary sources, census years, fiscal years, statistical concepts used, and other background information. *Statistical methods* provides technical information on calculations used throughout the book.

Country notes

· Data for China do not include data for Hong Kong SAR, China; Macao SAR, China; or Taiwan, China.

· Data for Serbia do not include data for Kosovo or Montenegro.

· Data for Sudan exclude South Sudan unless otherwise noted.

User guide to WDI online tables

Statistical tables that were previously available in the *World Development Indicators* print edition are available online. Using an automated query process, these reference tables are consistently updated based on revisions to the World Development Indicators database.

How to access WDI online tables

To access the WDI online tables, visit http://wdi.worldbank.org/tables. To access a specific WDI online table directly, use the URL http://wdi.worldbank.org/table/ and the table number (for example, http://wdi.worldbank.org/table/1.1 to view the first table in the *World view* section). Each section of this book also lists the indicators included by table and by code. To view a specific indicator online, use the URL http://data.worldbank.org/indicator/ and the indicator code (for example, http://data.worldbank.org/indicator/SP.POP.TOTL to view a page for total population).

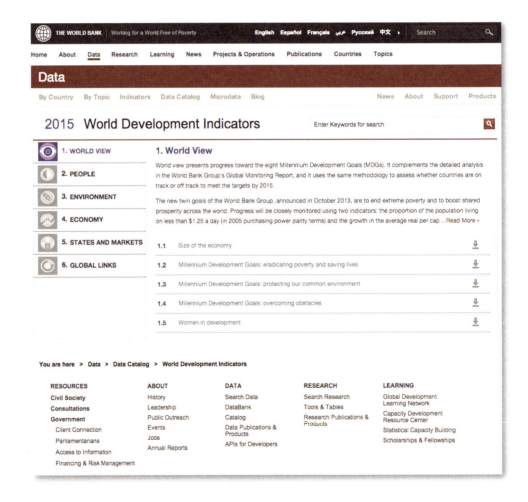

Breadcrumbs to show
where you've been

Click on an indicator
to view metadata

Click on a country
to view metadata

How to use DataBank

DataBank (http://databank.worldbank.org) is a web resource that provides simple and quick access to collections of time series data. It has advanced functions for selecting and displaying data, performing customized queries, downloading data, and creating charts and maps. Users can create dynamic custom reports based on their selection of countries, indicators, and years. All these reports can be easily edited, saved, shared, and embedded as widgets on websites or blogs. For more information, see http://databank.worldbank.org/help.

Actions

 Click to edit and revise the table in DataBank

 Click to download corresponding indicator metadata

 Click to export the table to Excel

 Click to export the table and corresponding indicator metadata to PDF

 Click to print the table and corresponding indicator metadata

 Click to access the WDI Online Tables Help file

 Click the checkbox to highlight cell level metadata and values from years other than those specified; click the checkbox again to reset to the default display

User guide to DataFinder

DataFinder is a free mobile app that accesses the full set of data from the World Development Indicators database. Data can be displayed and saved in a table, chart, or map and shared via email, Facebook, and Twitter.

DataFinder works on mobile devices (smartphone or tablet computer) in both offline (no Internet connection) and online (Wi-Fi or 3G/4G connection to the Internet) modes.

- Select a topic to display all related indicators.
- Compare data for multiple countries.
- Select predefined queries.
- Create a new query that can be saved and edited later.

- View reports in table, chart, and map formats.
- Send the data as a CSV file attachment to an email.
- Share comments and screenshots via Facebook, Twitter, or email.

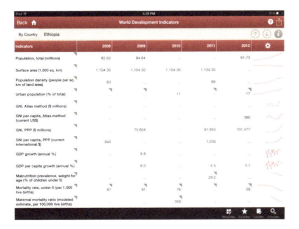

Table view provides time series data tables of key development indicators by country or topic. A compare option shows the most recent year's data for the selected country and another country.

Chart view illustrates data trends and cross-country comparisons as line or bar charts.

Map view colors selected indicators on world and regional maps. A motion option animates the data changes from year to year.

User guide to MDG Data Dashboards

The World Development Indicators database provides data on trends in Millennium Development Goals (MDG) indicators for developing countries and other country groups. Each year the World Bank's *Global Monitoring Report* uses these data to assess progress toward achieving the MDGs. Six online interactive MDG Data Dashboards, available at http://data.worldbank.org/mdgs, provide an opportunity to learn more about the assessments.

The MDG progress charts presented in the *World view* section of this book correspond to the *Global Monitoring Report* assessments (except MDG 6). Sufficient progress indicates that the MDG will be attained by 2015 based on an extrapolation of the last observed data point using the growth rate over the last observable five-year period (or three-year period in the case of MDGs 1 and 5). Insufficient progress indicates that the MDG will be met between 2016 and 2020. Moderately off target indicates that the MDG will be met between 2020 and 2030. Seriously off target indicates that the MDG will not be met by 2030. Insufficient data indicates an inadequate number of data points to estimate progress or that the MDG's starting value is missing.

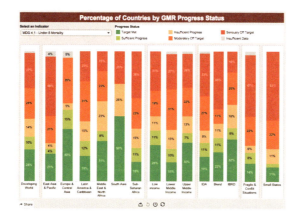

View progress status for regions, income classifications, and other groups by number or percentage of countries.

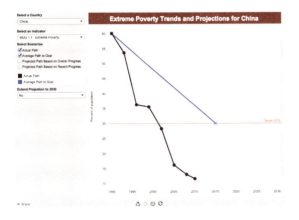

View details of a country's progress toward each MDG target, including trends from 1990 to the latest year of available data, and projected trends toward the 2015 target and 2030.

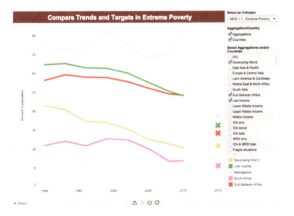

Compare trends and targets of each MDG indicator for selected groups and countries.

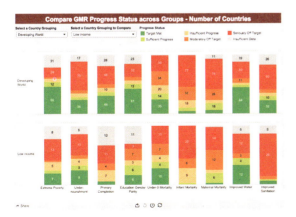

Compare the progress status of all MDG indicators across selected groups.

WORLD
VIEW

The United Nations set 2015 as the year by which the world should achieve many of the targets set out in the eight Millennium Development Goals. *World view* presents the progress made toward these goals and complements the detailed analysis in the World Bank Group's *Global Monitoring Report* and the online progress charts at http://data.worldbank.org/mdgs. This section also includes indicators that measure progress toward the World Bank Group's two new goals of ending extreme poverty by 2030 and enhancing shared prosperity in every country. Indicators of shared prosperity, based on measuring the growth rates of the average income of the bottom 40 percent of the population, are new for this edition of *World Development Indicators* and have been calculated for 72 countries.

A final verdict on the Millennium Development Goals is close, and the focus of the international community continues to be on achieving them, especially in areas that have been lagging. Attention is also turning to a new sustainable development agenda for the next generation, to help respond to the global challenges of the 21st century. An important step was taken on September 8, 2014, when the UN General Assembly decided that the proposal of the UN Open Working Group on Sustainable Development Goals, with 17 candidate goals and 169 associated targets, will be the basis for integrating sustainable development goals into the post-2015 development agenda. Final negotiations will be concluded at the 69th General Assembly in September 2015, with implementation likely

to begin in January 2016. This is thus the last edition of *World Development Indicators* to report on the Millennium Development Goals in their current form.

One important aspect of the Millennium Development Goals has been their focus on measuring and monitoring progress, which has presented a clear challenge in improving the quality, frequency, and availability of relevant statistics. In the last few years much has been done by both countries and international partners to invest in the national statistical systems where most data originate. But weaknesses remain in the coverage and quality of many indicators in the poorest countries, where resources are scarce and careful measurement of progress may matter the most.

With a new, broader set of goals, targets, and indicators, the data challenge will become even greater. The recent report, *A World That Counts* (United Nations 2014), discusses the actions and strategies needed to mobilize a data revolution for sustainable development—by exploiting advances in knowledge and technology, using resources for capacity development, and improving coordination among key actors. Both governments and development partners still need to invest in national statistical systems and other relevant public institutions, where much of the data will continue to originate. At the same time serious efforts need to be made to better use data and techniques from the private sector, especially so-called "big data" and other new sources.

Millennium Development Goals snapshot

MDG 1: Eradicate extreme poverty and hunger

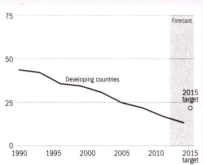

Developing countries as a whole met the Millennium Development Goal target of halving extreme poverty rates five years ahead of the 2015 deadline. Forecasts indicate that the extreme poverty rate will fall to 13.4 percent by 2015, a drop of more than two-thirds from the 1990 estimate of 43.6 percent. East Asia and Pacific has had the most astounding record of poverty alleviation; despite improvements, Sub-Saharan Africa still lags behind and is not forecast to meet the target by 2015.

People living on less than $1.25 a day (% of population)

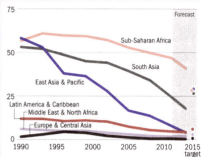

Source: World Bank PovcalNet (http://iresearch.worldbank.org/PovcalNet/).

MDG 2: Achieve universal primary education

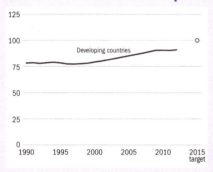

The primary school completion rate for developing countries reached 91 percent in 2012 but appears to fall short of the MDG 2 target. While substantial progress was made in the 2000s, particularly in Sub-Saharan Africa and South Asia, only East Asia and Pacific and Europe and Central Asia have achieved or are close to achieving universal primary education.

Primary completion rate (% of relevant age group)

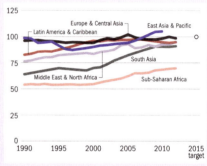

Source: United Nations Educational, Scientific and Cultural Organization Institute for Statistics.

MDG 3: Promote gender equality and empower women

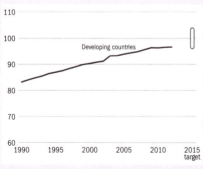

Developing countries have made substantial gains in closing gender gaps in education and will likely reach gender parity in primary and secondary education. In particular, the ratio of girls' to boys' primary and secondary gross enrollment rate in South Asia was the lowest of all regions in 1990, at 68 percent, but improved dramatically to reach gender parity in 2012, surpassing other regions that were making slower progress.

Ratio of girls' to boys' primary and secondary gross enrollment rate (%)

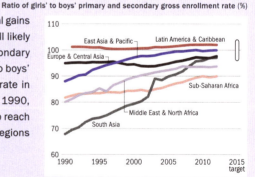

Source: United Nations Educational, Scientific and Cultural Organization Institute for Statistics.

MDG 4: Reduce child mortality

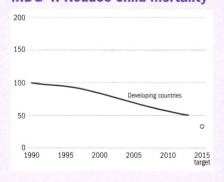

The under-five mortality rate in developing countries declined by half, from 99 deaths per 1,000 live births in 1990 to 50 in 2013. Despite this tremendous progress, developing countries as a whole are likely to fall short of the MDG 4 target of reducing under-five mortality rate by two-thirds between 1990 and 2015. However, East Asia and Pacific and Latin America and the Caribbean have already achieved the target.

Under-five mortality rate (per 1,000 live births)

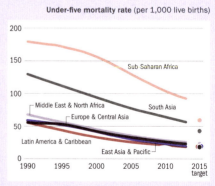

Source: United Nations Inter-agency Group for Child Mortality Estimation.

 Front | User guide | World view | People | Environment

Millennium Development Goals snapshot

MDG 5: Improve maternal health

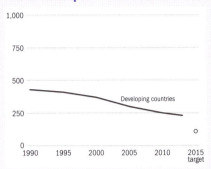

The maternal mortality ratio has steadily decreased in developing countries as a whole, from 430 in 1990 to 230 in 2013. While substantial, the decline is not enough to achieve the MDG 5 target of reducing the maternal mortality ratio by 75 percent between 1990 and 2015. Regional data also indicate large declines, though no region is likely to achieve the target on time. Despite considerable drops, the maternal mortality ratio in Sub-Saharan Africa and South Asia remains high.

Maternal mortality ratio, modeled estimate (per 100,000 live births)

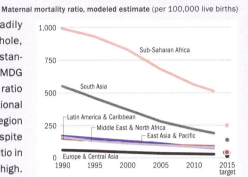

Source: United Nations Maternal Mortality Estimation Inter-agency Group.

MDG 6: Combat HIV/AIDS, malaria, and other diseases

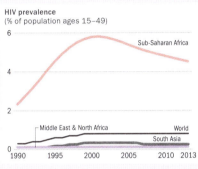

The prevalence of HIV is highest in Sub-Saharan Africa. The spread of HIV/AIDS there has slowed, and the proportion of adults living with HIV has begun to fall while the survival rate of those with access to antiretroviral drugs has increased. Global prevalence has remained flat since 2000. Tuberculosis prevalence, incidence, and death rates have fallen since 1990. Globally, the target of halting and reversing tuberculosis incidence by 2015 has been achieved.

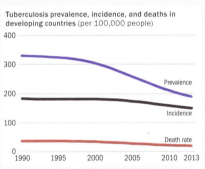

Source: Joint United Nations Programme on HIV/AIDS.

Source: World Health Organization.

MDG 7: Ensure environmental sustainability

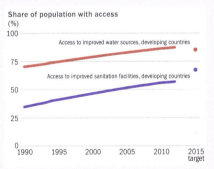

In developing countries the proportion of people with access to an improved water source rose from 70 percent in 1990 to 87 percent in 2012, achieving the target. The proportion with access to improved sanitation facilities rose from 35 percent to 57 percent, but 2.5 billion people still lack access. The large urban-rural disparity, especially in South Asia and Sub-Saharan Africa, is the principal reason the sanitation target is unlikely to be met on time.

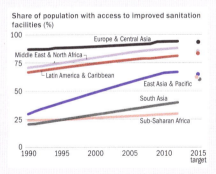

Source: World Health Organization–United Nations Children's Fund Joint Monitoring Programme for Water Supply and Sanitation.

MDG 8: Develop a global partnership for development

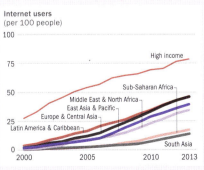

In 2000 Internet use was rapidly increasing in high-income economies but barely under way in developing countries. Now developing countries are catching up. Internet users per 100 people have grown 27 percent a year since 2000. The debt service–to-export ratio averaged 11 percent in 2013 for developing countries, half its 2000 level but with wide disparity across regions. It will likely rise, considering the 33 percent increase in their combined external debt stock since 2010.

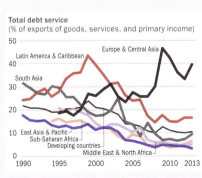

Source: International Telecommunications Union.

Source: World Development Indicators database.

For a more detailed assessment of each MDG, see the spreads on the following pages.

 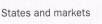

MDG 1 Eradicate extreme poverty

The poverty target has been met in nearly all developing country regions `1a`

Proportion of the population living on less than 2005 PPP $1.25 a day (%)

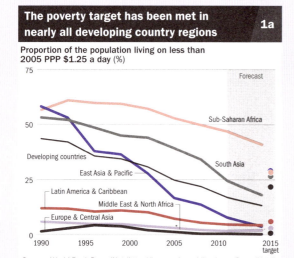

Source: World Bank PovcalNet (http://iresearch.worldbank.org/PovcalNet/).

A billion people were lifted out of extreme poverty between 1990 and 2015 `1b`

Number of people living on less than 2005 PPP $1.25 a day (billions)

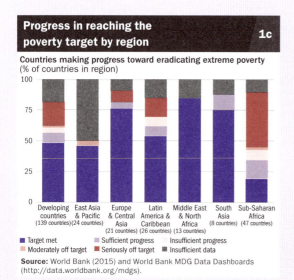

Source: World Bank PovcalNet (http://iresearch.worldbank.org /PovcalNet/).

Progress in reaching the poverty target by region `1c`

Countries making progress toward eradicating extreme poverty (% of countries in region)

Developing countries (139 countries) | East Asia & Pacific (24 countries) | Europe & Central Asia (21 countries) | Latin America & Caribbean (26 countries) | Middle East & North Africa (13 countries) | South Asia (8 countries) | Sub-Saharan Africa (47 countries)

■ Target met   ■ Sufficient progress   ■ Insufficient progress
■ Moderately off target   ■ Seriously off target   ■ Insufficient data

Source: World Bank (2015) and World Bank MDG Data Dashboards (http://data.worldbank.org/mdgs).

Developing countries as a whole (as classified in 1990) met the Millennium Development Goal target of halving the proportion of the population in extreme poverty five years ahead of the 2015 deadline. The latest estimates show that the proportion of people living on less than $1.25 a day fell from 43.6 percent in 1990 to 17.0 percent in 2011. Forecasts based on country-specific growth rates in the past 10 years indicate that the extreme poverty rate will fall to 13.4 percent by 2015 (figure 1a), a drop of more than two-thirds from the baseline.

Despite the remarkable achievement in developing countries as a whole, progress in reducing poverty has been uneven across regions. East Asia and Pacific has had an astounding record of alleviating long-term poverty, with the share of people living on less than $1.25 a day declining from 58.2 percent in 1990 to 7.9 percent in 2011. Relatively affluent regions such as Europe and Central Asia, Latin America and the Caribbean, and the Middle East and North Africa started with very low extreme poverty rates and sustained poverty reduction in the mid-1990s to reach the target by 2010. South Asia has also witnessed a steady decline of poverty in the past 25 years, with a strong acceleration since 2008 that enabled the region to achieve the Millennium Development Goal target by 2011. By contrast, the extreme poverty rate in Sub-Saharan Africa did not begin to fall below its 1990 level until after 2002. Even with the acceleration in the past decade, Sub-Saharan Africa still lags behind and is not forecast to meet the target by 2015 (see figure 1a).

The number of people worldwide living on less than $1.25 a day is forecast to be halved by 2015 from its 1990 level as well. Between 1990 and 2011 the number of extremely poor people fell from 1.9 billion to 1 billion, and according to forecasts, another 175 million people will be lifted out of extreme poverty by 2015. Compared with 1990, the number of extremely poor people has fallen in all regions except Sub-Saharan Africa, where population growth exceeded the rate of poverty reduction, increasing the number of extremely poor people from 290 million in 1990 to 415 million in 2011. South Asia has the second largest number of extremely poor people: In 2011 close to 400 million people lived on less than $1.25 a day (figure 1b).

Based on current trends, nearly half of developing countries have already achieved the poverty target of Millennium Development Goal 1. However, 20 percent are seriously off track, meaning that at the current pace of progress they will not be able to halve their 1990 extreme poverty rates even by 2030 (World Bank 2015). Progress is most sluggish among countries in Sub-Saharan Africa, where about 45 percent of countries are seriously off track (figure 1c). A large proportion of countries classified as International Development Association–eligible and defined by the World Bank as being in fragile and conflict situations are also among those seriously off track (figure 1d).

Millennium Development Goal 1 also addresses hunger and malnutrition. On average, developing countries saw the prevalence of undernourishment drop from 24 percent in 1990–92 to 13 percent in 2012–14. The decline has been steady in most developing country regions in the past decade, although the situation appears to have worsened in the Middle East and North Africa, albeit from a low base. The 2013 estimates show that East Asia and Pacific and Latin America and the Caribbean have met the target of halving the prevalence of undernourishment from its 1990 level by 2012–14. By crude linear growth prediction, developing countries as a whole will meet the target by 2015, whereas the Middle East and North Africa, South Asia, and Sub-Saharan Africa likely will not (figure 1e).

Another measure of hunger is the prevalence of underweight children (child malnutrition). Prevalence of malnutrition in developing countries has dropped substantially, from 28 percent of children under age 5 in 1990 to 17 percent in 2013. Despite considerable progress, in 2013 South Asia still had the highest prevalence, 32 percent. By 2013 East Asia and Pacific, Europe and Central Asia, and Latin America and the Caribbean met the target of halving the prevalence of underweight children under age 5 from its 1990 level. The Middle East and North Africa is predicted to be on track to meet the target by 2015. However, developing countries as a whole may not be able to meet the target by 2015, nor will South Asia or Sub-Saharan Africa (figure 1f).

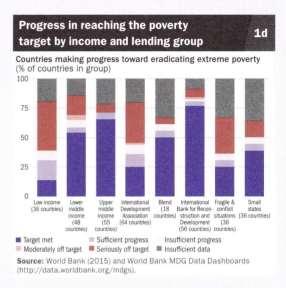

Progress in reaching the poverty target by income and lending group 1d

Countries making progress toward eradicating extreme poverty (% of countries in group)

■ Target met ■ Sufficient progress ■ Insufficient progress
■ Moderately off target ■ Seriously off target ■ Insufficient data

Source: World Bank (2015) and World Bank MDG Data Dashboards (http://data.worldbank.org/mdgs).

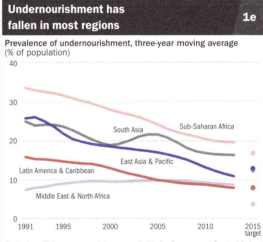

Undernourishment has fallen in most regions 1e

Prevalence of undernourishment, three-year moving average (% of population)

Note: Insufficient country data are available for Europe and Central Asia.
Source: FAO, IFAD, and WFP (2014).

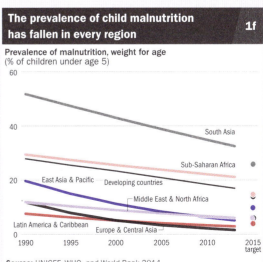

The prevalence of child malnutrition has fallen in every region 1f

Prevalence of malnutrition, weight for age (% of children under age 5)

Source: UNICEF, WHO, and World Bank 2014.

MDG 2 Achieve universal primary education

More children are completing primary school **2a**

Primary completion rate (% of relevant age group)

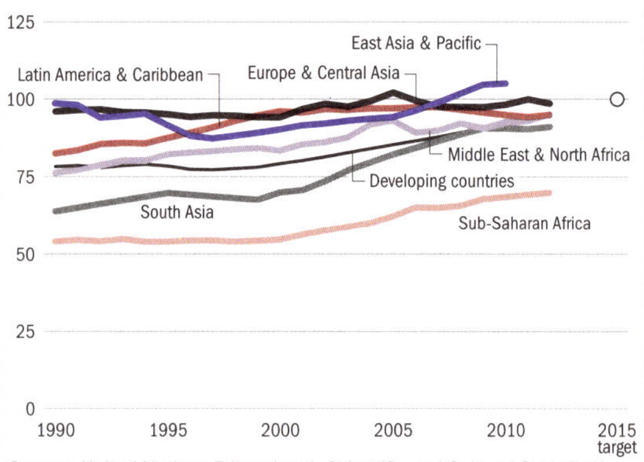

125
100
75
50
25
0
1990
1995
2000
2005
2010
2015 target
East Asia & Pacific
Latin America & Caribbean
Europe & Central Asia
Middle East & North Africa
Developing countries
South Asia
Sub-Saharan Africa

Source: United Nations Educational, Scientific and Cultural Organization Institute for Statistics.

Universal primary education remains elusive in many countries **2b**

Countries making progress toward universal primary education (% of countries in region)

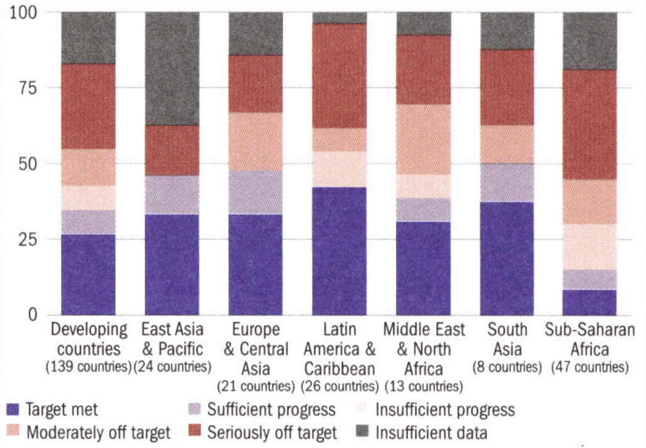

100
75
50
25
0
Developing countries (139 countries)
East Asia & Pacific (24 countries)
Europe & Central Asia (21 countries)
Latin America & Caribbean (26 countries)
Middle East & North Africa (13 countries)
South Asia (8 countries)
Sub-Saharan Africa (47 countries)
Target met
Sufficient progress
Insufficient progress
Moderately off target
Seriously off target
Insufficient data

Source: World Bank (2015) and World Bank MDG Data Dashboards (http://data.worldbank.org/mdgs).

Some 55 million children remain out of school **2c**

Primary school–age children not attending school (millions)

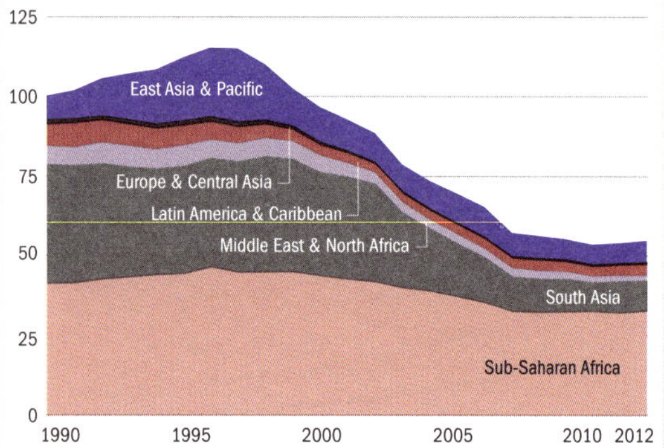

125
100
75
50
25
0
1990
1995
2000
2005
2010
2012
East Asia & Pacific
Europe & Central Asia
Latin America & Caribbean
Middle East & North Africa
South Asia
Sub-Saharan Africa

Source: United Nations Educational, Scientific and Cultural Organization Institute for Statistics.

After modest movement toward universal primary education in the poorest countries during the 1990s, progress has accelerated considerably since 2000, particularly for South Asia and Sub-Saharan Africa. But achieving full enrollment remains daunting. Moreover, enrollment by itself is not enough. Many children start school but drop out before completion, discouraged by cost, distance, physical danger, and failure to advance. An added challenge is that even as countries approach the target and the education demands of modern economies expand, primary education will increasingly be of value only as a stepping stone toward secondary and higher education.

Achieving the target of everyone, boys and girls alike, completing a full course of primary education by 2015 appeared within reach only a few years ago. But the primary school completion rate—the number of new entrants in the last grade of primary education divided by the population at the entrance age for the last grade of primary education—has been stalled at 91 percent for developing countries since 2009. Only two regions, East Asia and Pacific and Europe and Central Asia, have reached or are close to reaching universal primary education. The Middle East and North Africa has steadily improved, to 95 percent in 2012, the same rate as Latin America and the Caribbean. South Asia reached 91 percent in 2009, but progress since has been slow. The real challenge is in Sub-Saharan Africa, which lags behind at 70 percent in 2012 (figure 2a).

When country-level performance is considered, a more nuanced picture emerges: 35 percent of developing countries have achieved or are on track to achieve the target of the Millennium Development Goal, while 28 percent are seriously off track and unlikely to achieve the target even by 2030 (figure 2b). Data gaps continue to hinder monitoring efforts: In 24 countries, or 17 percent of developing countries, data availability remains inadequate to assess progress.

In developing countries the number of children of primary school age not attending school has been almost halved since 1996. A large reduction was made in South Asia in the early 2000s, driven by progress in India. Still, many children never attend school or start school but attend intermittently or drop out entirely; as many as 55 million children remained out of school in 2012. About 80 percent of out-of-school children live in South Asia and Sub-Saharan Africa (figure 2c). Obstacles such as the need for boys and girls to participate in the planting and harvesting of staple crops, the lack of suitable school facilities, the absence of teachers, and school fees may discourage parents from sending their children to school.

Not all children have the same opportunities to enroll in school or remain in school, and children from poorer households are particularly disadvantaged. For example, in Niger two-thirds of children not attending primary school are from the poorest 20 percent of households; children from wealthier households are three times more likely than children from poorer households to complete primary education (figure 2d). The country also faces an urban-rural divide: In 2012 more than 90 percent of children in urban areas completed primary education, compared with 51 percent of children in rural areas. And boys were more likely than girls to enroll and stay in school. Girls from poor households in rural areas are the most disadvantaged and the least likely to acquire the human capital that could be their strongest asset to escape poverty. Many countries face similar wealth, urban-rural, and gender gaps in education.

A positive development is that demand is growing for measuring and monitoring education quality and learning achievements. However, measures of quality that assess learning outcomes are still not fully developed for use in many countries. Achieving basic literacy is one indicator that can measure the quality of education outcomes, though estimates of even this variable can be flawed. Still, the best available data show that nearly 90 percent of young people in developing countries had acquired basic literacy by 2012, but the level and speed of this achievement vary across regions and by gender (figure 2e).

Access to education is inequitably distributed by income, area, and gender 2d

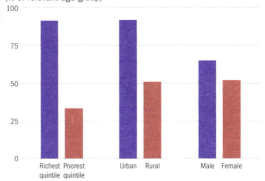

Primary completion rate by income, area, and gender, Niger, 2012 (% of relevant age group)

Source: United Nations Educational, Scientific and Cultural Organization Institute for Statistics and World Bank EdStats database.

Progress in youth literacy varies by region and gender 2e

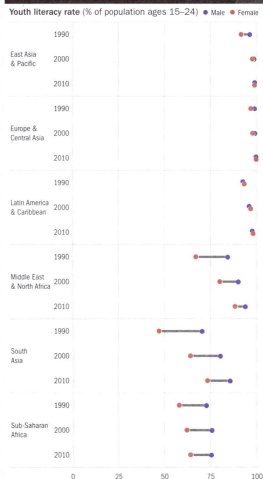

Youth literacy rate (% of population ages 15–24) ● Male ● Female

Source: United Nations Educational, Scientific and Cultural Organization Institute for Statistics.

MDG 3 Promote gender equality and empower women

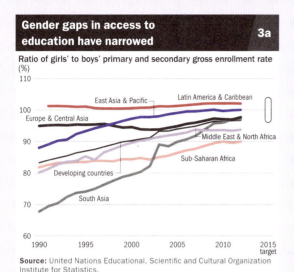

Gender gaps in access to education have narrowed 3a

Ratio of girls' to boys' primary and secondary gross enrollment rate (%)

- East Asia & Pacific
- Latin America & Caribbean
- Europe & Central Asia
- Middle East & North Africa
- Sub-Saharan Africa
- Developing countries
- South Asia

Source: United Nations Educational, Scientific and Cultural Organization Institute for Statistics.

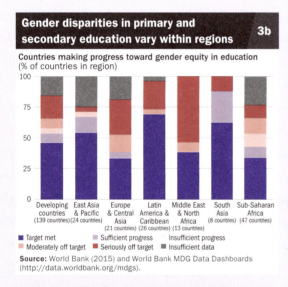

Gender disparities in primary and secondary education vary within regions 3b

Countries making progress toward gender equity in education (% of countries in region)

Developing countries (139 countries) · East Asia & Pacific (24 countries) · Europe & Central Asia (21 countries) · Latin America & Caribbean (26 countries) · Middle East & North Africa (13 countries) · South Asia (8 countries) · Sub-Saharan Africa (47 countries)

- Target met
- Moderately off target
- Sufficient progress
- Seriously off target
- Insufficient progress
- Insufficient data

Source: World Bank (2015) and World Bank MDG Data Dashboards (http://data.worldbank.org/mdgs).

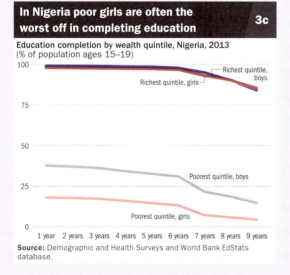

In Nigeria poor girls are often the worst off in completing education 3c

Education completion by wealth quintile, Nigeria, 2013 (% of population ages 15–19)

- Richest quintile, boys
- Richest quintile, girls
- Poorest quintile, boys
- Poorest quintile, girls

1 year 2 years 3 years 4 years 5 years 6 years 7 years 8 years 9 years

Source: Demographic and Health Surveys and World Bank EdStats database.

Millennium Development Goal 3 is concerned with boosting women's social, economic, and political participation to build gender-equitable societies. Expanding women's opportunities in the public and private sectors is a core development strategy that not only benefits girls and women, but also improves society more broadly.

By enrolling and staying in school, girls gain the skills they need to enter the labor market, care for families, and make informed decisions for themselves and others. The target of Millennium Development Goal 3 is to eliminate gender disparity in all levels of education by 2015. Over the past 25 years, girls have made substantial gains in school enrollment across all developing country regions. In 1990 the average enrollment rate of girls in primary and secondary schools in developing countries was 83 percent of that of boys; by 2012 it had increased to 97 percent (figure 3a). The ratio of girls to boys in tertiary education has also increased considerably, from 74 percent to 101 percent. Developing countries as a whole are likely to reach gender parity in primary and secondary enrollment (defined as having a ratio of 97–103 percent, according to UNESCO 2004).

However, these averages disguise large differences across regions and countries. South Asia made remarkable progress, closing the gender gap in primary and secondary enrollment more than 40 percent between 1990 and 2012. Sub-Saharan Africa and the Middle East and North Africa saw fast progress but continue to have the largest gender disparities in primary and secondary enrollment rates among developing country regions. Given past rates of change, the two regions are unlikely to meet the target of eliminating disparities in education by 2015. Furthermore, about half the countries in the Middle East and North Africa are seriously off track to achieve the target (figure 3b). Disparities across regions are larger in tertiary education: The ratio of girls' to boys' enrollment in tertiary education is 64 percent in Sub-Saharan Africa, compared with 128 percent in Latin America and the Caribbean. These high estimates tend to drive up the aggregate estimates for

 Front   User guide   World view   People   Environment

all developing countries, disguising some of the large disparities in other regions and countries.

There are also large differences within countries. Poor households are often less likely than wealthy households to enroll and keep children in school, and girls from poor households tend to be the worst off. In Nigeria only 4 percent of girls in the poorest quintile stay in school until grade 9, compared with 85 percent of girls in the richest quintile. Within the poorest quintile, 15 percent of boys complete nine years of schooling, compared with 4 percent for the poorest girls. (figure 3c).

Women work long hours and contribute considerably to their families' economic well-being, but many are unpaid for their labor or work in the informal sector. These precarious forms of work, often not properly counted as economic activity, tend to lack formal work arrangements, social protection, and safety nets and leave workers vulnerable to poverty. In many countries a far larger proportion of women than men work for free in establishments operated by families (according to the International Labour Organization's Key Indicators of the Labour Market 8th edition database; figure 3d). The share of women's paid employment in the nonagricultural sector is less than 20 percent in South Asia and the Middle East and North Africa and has risen only marginally over the years. The share of women's employment in the nonagricultural sector is highest in Europe and Central Asia, where it almost equals men's (figure 3e).

More women are participating in public life and decisionmaking at the highest levels than in 1990, based on the proportion of parliamentary seats held by women. Latin America and the Caribbean leads developing country regions in 2014, at 27 percent, followed closely by Sub-Saharan Africa at 23 percent. The biggest change has occurred in the Middle East and North Africa, where the proportion of seats held by women more than quadrupled between 1990 and 2014 (figure 3f). At the country level Rwanda leads the way with 64 percent in 2014, higher than the percentage for high-income countries, at 26 percent.

In many countries more women than men work as unpaid family workers — 3d

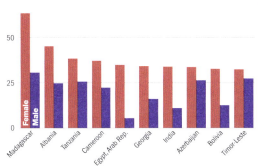

Unpaid family workers, national estimates, most recent year available during 2009–13 (% of employment)

Source: International Labour Organization Key Indicators of the Labour Market 8th edition database.

Fewer women than men are employed in nonagricultural wage employment — 3e

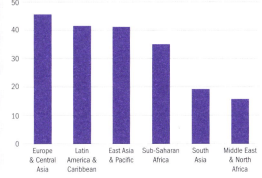

Female employees in nonagricultural wage employment, median value, 2008–12 (% of total nonagricultural wage employment)

Source: International Labour Organization Key Indicators of the Labour Market 8th edition database.

More women are in decisionmaking positions — 3f

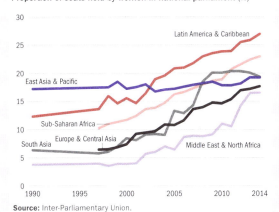

Proportion of seats held by women in national parliament (%)

Source: Inter-Parliamentary Union.

MDG 4 Reduce child mortality

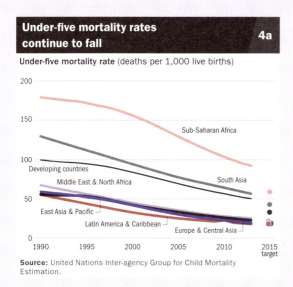

Under-five mortality rates continue to fall | **4a**

Under-five mortality rate (deaths per 1,000 live births)

Sub-Saharan Africa
Developing countries
Middle East & North Africa
South Asia
East Asia & Pacific
Latin America & Caribbean
Europe & Central Asia

1990 1995 2000 2005 2010 2015 target

Source: United Nations Inter-agency Group for Child Mortality Estimation.

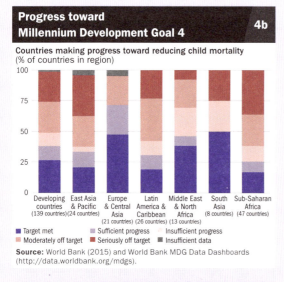

Progress toward Millennium Development Goal 4 | **4b**

Countries making progress toward reducing child mortality (% of countries in region)

Developing countries (139 countries)
East Asia & Pacific (24 countries)
Europe & Central Asia (21 countries)
Latin America & Caribbean (26 countries)
Middle East & North Africa (13 countries)
South Asia (8 countries)
Sub-Saharan Africa (47 countries)

■ Target met   ■ Sufficient progress   ■ Insufficient progress
■ Moderately off target   ■ Seriously off target   ■ Insufficient data

Source: World Bank (2015) and World Bank MDG Data Dashboards (http://data.worldbank.org/mdgs).

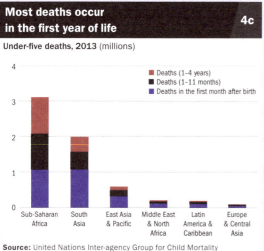

Most deaths occur in the first year of life | **4c**

Under-five deaths, 2013 (millions)

■ Deaths (1–4 years)
■ Deaths (1–11 months)
■ Deaths in the first month after birth

Sub-Saharan Africa
South Asia
East Asia & Pacific
Middle East & North Africa
Latin America & Caribbean
Europe & Central Asia

Source: United Nations Inter-agency Group for Child Mortality Estimation.

In the last two decades the world has witnessed a dramatic decline in child mortality, enough to almost halve the number of children who die each year before their fifth birthday. In 1990 that number was 13 million, by 1999 it was less than 10 million, and by 2013 it had fallen to just over 6 million. This means that at least 17,000 fewer children now die each day compared with 1990.

The target of Millennium Development Goal 4 was to reduce the under-five mortality rate by two-thirds between 1990 and 2015. In 1990 the average rate for all developing countries was 99 deaths per 1,000 live births; in 2013 it had fallen to 50—or about half the 1990 rate. This is tremendous progress. But based on the current trend, developing countries as a whole are likely to fall short of the Millennium Development Goal target. Despite rapid improvements since 2000, child mortality rates in Sub-Saharan Africa and South Asia remain considerably higher than in the rest of the world (figure 4a).

While 53 developing countries (38 percent) have already met or are likely to meet the target individually, 84 countries (61 percent) are unlikely to achieve it based on recent trends (figure 4b). Still, the average annual rate of decline of global under-five mortality rates accelerated from 1.2 percent over 1990–95 to 4 percent over 2005–13. If the more recent rate of decline had started in 1990, the target for Millennium Development Goal 4 would likely have been achieved by 2015. And if this recent rate of decline continues, the target will be achieved in 2026 (UNICEF 2014).

Although there has been a dramatic decline in deaths, most children still die from causes that are readily preventable or curable with existing interventions. Pneumonia, diarrhea, and malaria are the leading causes, accounting for 30 percent under-five deaths.

 Front | ? User guide | World view | People | Environment

Almost 74 percent of deaths of children under age 5 occur in the first year of life, and 60 percent of those occur in the neonatal period (the first month; figure 4c). Preterm birth (before 37 weeks of pregnancy) complications account for 35 percent of neonatal deaths, and complications during birth another 24 percent (UNICEF 2014). Because declines in the neonatal mortality rate are slower than declines in the postneonatal mortality rate, the share of neonatal deaths among all under-five deaths increased from 37 percent in 1990 to 44 percent in 2013. Tackling neonatal mortality will have a major impact in reducing under-five mortality rate.

Twenty developing countries accounted for around 4.6 million under-five deaths in 2013, or around 73 percent of all such deaths worldwide. These countries are mostly large, often with high birth rates, but many have substantially reduced mortality rates over the past two decades. Of these 20 countries, Bangladesh, Brazil, China, the Arab Republic of Egypt, Ethiopia, Indonesia, Malawi, Niger, and Tanzania achieved or are likely to achieve a two-thirds reduction in their under-five mortality rate by 2015. Had the mortality rates of 1990 prevailed in 2013, 2.5 million more children would have died in these 9 countries, and 3.6 million more would have died in the remaining 11 (figure 4d).

Measles vaccination coverage is one indicator used to monitor the progress toward achieving Millennium Development Goal 4. In developing countries measles vaccinations of one-year-old children reached about 83 percent in 2013. Both Sub-Saharan Africa and South Asia have seen the coverage of measles vaccinations increase since 1990, but the trend has recently slowed in both regions. This is concerning, as it might make further reductions in under-five mortality more challenging (figure 4e).

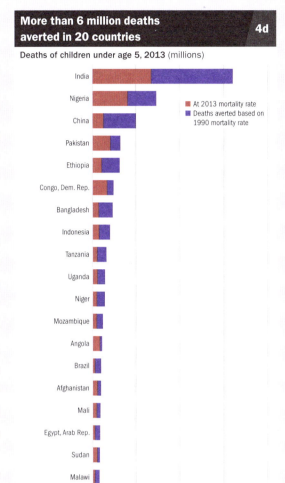

More than 6 million deaths averted in 20 countries **4d**

Deaths of children under age 5, 2013 (millions)

At 2013 mortality rate
Deaths averted based on 1990 mortality rate

Source: World Bank staff calculations.

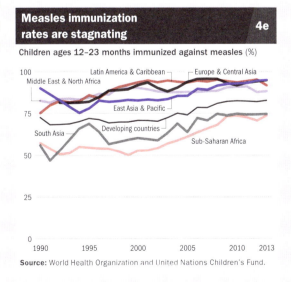

Measles immunization rates are stagnating **4e**

Children ages 12–23 months immunized against measles (%)

Source: World Health Organization and United Nations Children's Fund.

MDG 5 Improve maternal health

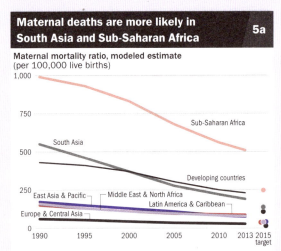

Maternal deaths are more likely in South Asia and Sub-Saharan Africa · **5a**

Maternal mortality ratio, modeled estimate
(per 100,000 live births)

Sub-Saharan Africa
South Asia
Developing countries
East Asia & Pacific   Middle East & North Africa
Latin America & Caribbean
Europe & Central Asia

1990 1995 2000 2005 2010 2013 2015 target

Source: United Nations Maternal Mortality Estimation Inter-agency Group.

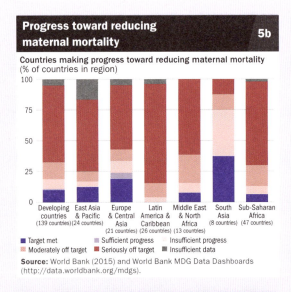

Progress toward reducing maternal mortality · **5b**

Countries making progress toward reducing maternal mortality
(% of countries in region)

Developing countries (139 countries) · East Asia & Pacific (24 countries) · Europe & Central Asia (21 countries) · Latin America & Caribbean (26 countries) · Middle East & North Africa (13 countries) · South Asia (8 countries) · Sub-Saharan Africa (47 countries)

■ Target met   ■ Sufficient progress   ■ Insufficient progress
■ Moderately off target   ■ Seriously off target   ■ Insufficient data

Source: World Bank (2015) and World Bank MDG Data Dashboards (http://data.worldbank.org/mdgs).

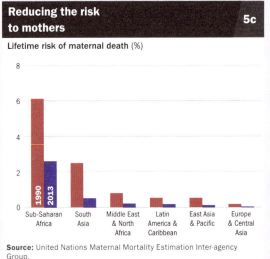

Reducing the risk to mothers · **5c**

Lifetime risk of maternal death (%)

1990   2013

Sub-Saharan Africa · South Asia · Middle East & North Africa · Latin America & Caribbean · East Asia & Pacific · Europe & Central Asia

Source: United Nations Maternal Mortality Estimation Inter-agency Group.

While many maternal deaths are avoidable, pregnancy and delivery are not completely risk free. Every day, around 800 women lose their lives before, during, or after child delivery (WHO 2014b). In 2013 an estimated 289,000 maternal deaths occurred worldwide, 99 percent of them in developing countries. More than half of maternal deaths occurred in Sub-Saharan Africa, and about a quarter occurred in South Asia.

However, countries in both South Asia and Sub-Saharan Africa have made great progress in reducing the maternal mortality ratio. In South Asia it fell from 550 per 100,000 live births in 1990 to 190 in 2013, a drop of 65 percent. In Sub-Saharan Africa, where maternal deaths are more than twice as prevalent as in South Asia, the maternal mortality ratio dropped almost 50 percent. And East Asia and Pacific, Europe and Central Asia, and the Middle East and North Africa have all reduced their maternal morality ratio by more than 50 percent (figure 5a).

These achievements are impressive, but progress in reducing maternal mortality ratios has been slower than the 75 percent reduction between 1990 and 2015 targeted by the Millennium Development Goals. No developing regions on average are likely to achieve the target. But the average annual rate of decline has accelerated from 1.1 percent over 1990–95 to 3.1 percent over 2005–13. This recent rate of progress is getting closer to the 5.5 percent that would have been needed since 1990 to achieve the Millennium Development Goal 5 target. According to recent data, a handful of developing countries (15 or about 11 percent) have already achieved or are likely to achieve the target (figure 5b).

The maternal mortality ratio is an estimate of the risk of a maternal death at each birth, a risk that is compounded with each pregnancy. And because women in poor countries have more children under riskier conditions, their lifetime risk of maternal death may be 100 or more times greater than that of women in high-income countries. Improved health care and lower fertility rates have reduced the lifetime risk in all regions, but in 2013 women ages 15–49 in Sub-Saharan Africa still faced a 2.6 percent chance of dying in childbirth, down from more than 6 percent in 1990 (figure 5c). In Chad and Somalia, both fragile states, lifetime risk is still more than 5 percent, meaning more than 1 woman in 20 will die in childbirth, on average.

Reducing maternal mortality requires a comprehensive approach to women's reproductive health, starting with family planning and access to contraception. In countries with data, more than half of women who are married or in union use some method of contraception. However, around 225 million women want to delay or conclude childbearing, but they are not using effective family planning methods (UNFPA and Guttmacher Institute 2014). There are wide differences across regions in the share of women of childbearing age who say they need but are not using contraception (figure 5d). More surveys have been carried out in Sub-Saharan Africa than in any other region, and many show a large unmet need for family planning.

Women who give birth at an early age are likely to bear more children and are at greater risk of death or serious complications from pregnancy. The adolescent birth rate is highest in Sub-Saharan Africa, and though it has been declining, the pace is slow (figure 5e). By contrast, South Asia has experienced a rapid decrease.

Many health problems among pregnant women are preventable or treatable through visits with trained health workers before childbirth. One of the keys to reducing maternal mortality is to provide skilled attendants at delivery and access to hospital treatments, required for treating life-threatening emergencies such as severe bleeding and hypertensive disorders. In South Asia and Sub-Saharan Africa only half of births are attended by doctors, nurses, or trained midwives (figure 5f).

A wide range of contraception needs 5d

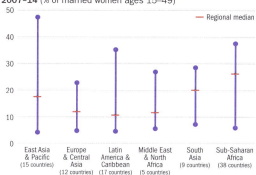

Unmet need for contraception, most recent year available during 2007–14 (% of married women ages 15–49)

Source: United Nations Population Division and household surveys (including Demographic and Health Surveys and Multiple Indicator Cluster Surveys).

Fewer young women are giving birth 5e

Adolescent fertility rate (births per 1,000 women ages 15–19)

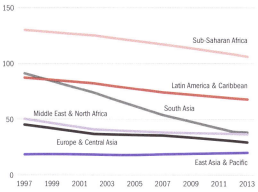

Source: United Nations Population Division.

Every mother needs care 5f

Births attended by skilled health staff, most recent year available, 2008–14 (%)

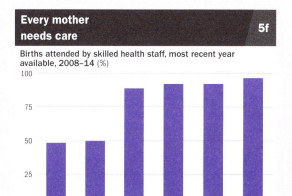

Source: United Nations Children's Fund and household surveys (including Demographic and Health Surveys and Multiple Indicator Cluster Surveys).

MDG 6 Combat HIV/AIDS, malaria, and other diseases

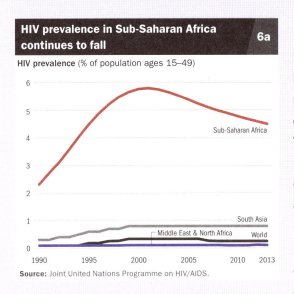

HIV prevalence in Sub-Saharan Africa continues to fall — 6a

HIV prevalence (% of population ages 15–49)

Sub-Saharan Africa
South Asia
Middle East & North Africa
World

Source: Joint United Nations Programme on HIV/AIDS.

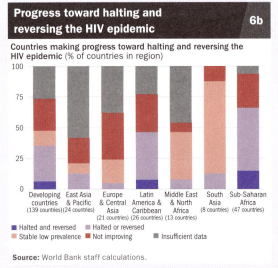

Progress toward halting and reversing the HIV epidemic — 6b

Countries making progress toward halting and reversing the HIV epidemic (% of countries in region)

Developing countries (139 countries)
East Asia & Pacific (24 countries)
Europe & Central Asia (21 countries)
Latin America & Caribbean (26 countries)
Middle East & North Africa (13 countries)
South Asia (8 countries)
Sub-Saharan Africa (47 countries)

- Halted and reversed
- Halted or reversed
- Stable low prevalence
- Not improving
- Insufficient data

Source: World Bank staff calculations.

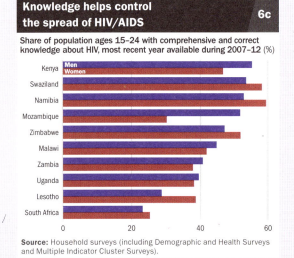

Knowledge helps control the spread of HIV/AIDS — 6c

Share of population ages 15–24 with comprehensive and correct knowledge about HIV, most recent year available during 2007–12 (%)

Men
Women

Kenya
Swaziland
Namibia
Mozambique
Zimbabwe
Malawi
Zambia
Uganda
Lesotho
South Africa

Source: Household surveys (including Demographic and Health Surveys and Multiple Indicator Cluster Surveys).

HIV/AIDS, malaria, and tuberculosis are among the world's deadliest communicable diseases. In Africa the spread of HIV/AIDS has reversed decades of improvement in life expectancy and left millions of children orphaned. Malaria takes a large toll on young children and weakens adults at great cost to their productivity. Tuberculosis killed 1.1 million people in 2013, most of them ages 15–45, and sickened millions more. Millennium Development Goal 6 targets are to halt and begin to reverse the spread and incidence of these diseases by 2015.

Some 35 million people were living with HIV/AIDS in 2013. The number of people who are newly infected with HIV is continuing to decline in most parts of the world: 2.1 million people contracted the disease in 2013, down 38 percent from 2001 and 13 percent from 2011. The spread of new HIV infections has slowed, in line with the target of halting and reversing the spread of HIV/AIDS by 2015. However, the proportion of adults living with HIV worldwide has not fallen; it has stayed around 0.8 percent since 2000. Sub-Saharan Africa remains the center of the HIV/AIDS epidemic, but the proportion of adults living with AIDS has begun to drop while the survival rate of those with access to antiretroviral drugs has increased (figures 6a and 6b). At the end of 2013, 12.9 million people worldwide were receiving antiretroviral drugs. The percentage of people living with HIV who are not receiving antiretroviral therapy has fallen from 90 percent in 2006 to 63 percent in 2013 (UNAIDS 2014).

Altering the course of the HIV epidemic requires changes in behavior by those already infected with the virus and those at risk of becoming infected. Knowledge of the cause of the disease, its transmission, and what can be done to avoid it is the starting point. The ability to reject false information is another important kind of knowledge. But wide gaps in knowledge remain. Many young people do not know enough about HIV and continue with risky behavior. In only 2 of the 10 countries (Namibia and Swaziland) with the highest HIV prevalence rates in 2013 did more than half the men and women ages 15–24 tested demonstrate knowledge of two ways to prevent HIV and reject three misconceptions about HIV (figure 6c). In Kenya and Mozambique men scored above 50 percent, but women fell short; the reverse was true in Zimbabwe.

In 2013 there were 9 million new tuberculosis cases and 1.5 million tuberculosis-related deaths, but incidence of, prevalence of, and death rates from tuberculosis are falling (figure 6d). Tuberculosis incidence fell an average rate of 1.5 percent a year between 2000 and 2013. By 2013 tuberculosis prevalence had fallen 41 percent since 1990, and the tuberculosis mortality rate had fallen 45 percent (WHO 2014a). Globally, the target of halting and reversing tuberculosis incidence by 2015 has been achieved.

An estimated 200 million cases of malaria occurred globally in 2013, which led to 600,000 deaths. An estimated 3.2 billion people are at risk of being infected with malaria and developing the disease, and 1.2 billion of them are at high risk. But there has been progress. In 2013, 2 countries reported zero indigenous cases for the first time (Azerbaijan and Sri Lanka) and 11 countries maintained zero cases (Argentina, Armenia, Egypt, Iraq, Georgia, Kyrgyz Republic, Morocco, Oman, Paraguay, Turkmenistan, and Uzbekistan; WHO 2014c). Although malaria occurs in all regions, the most lethal form of the malaria parasite is most abundant in Sub-Saharan Africa. Insecticide-treated nets have proven an effective preventative, and their use by children in the region is growing (figure 6e). Better testing and the use of combination therapies with artemisinin-based drugs are improving the treatment of at-risk populations. But malaria is difficult to control. There is evidence of emerging resistance to artemisinins and to pyrethroid insecticides used to treat mosquito nets.

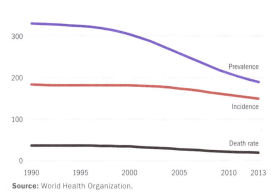

Fewer people are contracting, living with, and dying from tuberculosis 6d

Incidence of, prevalence of, and death rate from tuberculosis in developing countries (per 100,000 people)

Source: World Health Organization.

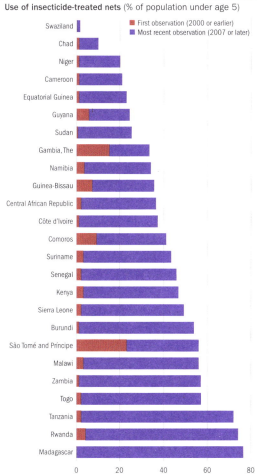

Use of insecticide-treated nets is increasing in Sub-Saharan Africa 6e

Use of insecticide-treated nets (% of population under age 5)

■ First observation (2000 or earlier)
■ Most recent observation (2007 or later)

Source: Household surveys (including Demographic and Health Surveys, Malaria Indicator Surveys, and Multiple Indicator Cluster Surveys).

MDG 7 Ensure environmental sustainability

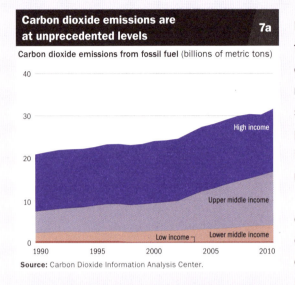

Carbon dioxide emissions are at unprecedented levels **7a**

Carbon dioxide emissions from fossil fuel (billions of metric tons)

High income

Upper middle income

Low income   Lower middle income

1990 1995 2000 2005 2010

Source: Carbon Dioxide Information Analysis Center.

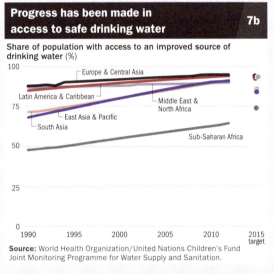

Progress has been made in access to safe drinking water **7b**

Share of population with access to an improved source of drinking water (%)

Europe & Central Asia

Latin America & Caribbean

Middle East & North Africa

East Asia & Pacific

South Asia

Sub-Saharan Africa

1990 1995 2000 2005 2010 2015 target

Source: World Health Organization/United Nations Children's Fund Joint Monitoring Programme for Water Supply and Sanitation.

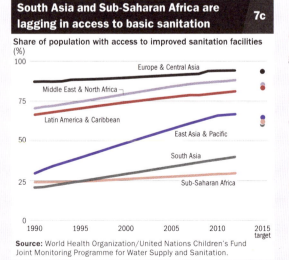

South Asia and Sub-Saharan Africa are lagging in access to basic sanitation **7c**

Share of population with access to improved sanitation facilities (%)

Europe & Central Asia

Middle East & North Africa

Latin America & Caribbean

East Asia & Pacific

South Asia

Sub-Saharan Africa

1990 1995 2000 2005 2010 2015 target

Source: World Health Organization/United Nations Children's Fund Joint Monitoring Programme for Water Supply and Sanitation.

Millennium Development Goal 7 has far-reaching implications for the planet's current and future inhabitants. It addresses the condition of the natural and built environments: reversing the loss of natural resources, preserving biodiversity, increasing access to safe water and sanitation, and improving the living conditions of people in slums. The overall theme is sustainability, an equilibrium in which people's lives can improve without depleting natural and manmade capital stocks.

The continued rise in greenhouse gas emissions leaves billions of people vulnerable to the impacts of climate change, with developing countries hit hardest. Higher temperatures, changes in precipitation patterns, rising sea levels, and more frequent weather-related disasters pose risks for agriculture, food, and water supplies. Annual emissions of carbon dioxide reached 33.6 billion metric tons in 2010, a considerable 51 percent rise since 1990, the baseline for Kyoto Protocol requirements (figure 7a). Carbon dioxide emissions were estimated at an unprecedented 36 billion metric tons in 2013, with an annual growth rate of 2 percent—slightly lower than the average growth of 3 percent since 2000.

One target of Millennium Development Goal 7 calls for halving the proportion of the population without access to improved water sources and sanitation facilities by 2015. In 1990 almost 1.3 billion people worldwide lacked access to drinking water from a convenient, protected source. By 2012 that had dropped to 752 million people—a 41 percent reduction. In developing countries the proportion of people with access to an improved water source rose from 70 percent in 1990 to 87 percent in 2012, achieving the target of 85 percent of people with access by 2015. Despite such major gains, almost 28 percent of countries are seriously off track toward meeting the water target. Some 52 countries have not made enough progress to reach the target, and 18 countries do not have enough data to determine whether they will reach the target by 2015. Sub-Saharan Africa is lagging the most, with 36 percent of its population lacking access (figure 7b). East Asia and Pacific made impressive improvements from a starting position of only 68 percent in 1990,

Front | User guide | World view | People | Environment

to 91 percent in 2012. In general, the other regions have managed to reach access rates of more than 89 percent.

In 1990 only 35 percent of the people in developing economies had access to a flush toilet or other form of improved sanitation. By 2012, 57 percent did. But 2.5 billion people in developing countries still lack access to improved sanitation. The situation is worse in rural areas, where only 43 percent of the population has access to improved sanitation, compared with 73 percent in urban areas. This large disparity, especially in South Asia and Sub-Saharan Africa, is the principal reason the sanitation target of the Millennium Development Goals is unlikely to be met on time (figure 7c).

The loss of forests threatens the livelihood of poor people, destroys the habitat that harbors biodiversity, and eliminates an important carbon sink that helps moderate the climate. Net losses since 1990 have been substantial, especially in Latin American and the Caribbean and Sub-Saharan Africa, and have been only partly compensated for by gains elsewhere (figure 7d). The rate of deforestation slowed over 2002–12, but on current trends zero net losses will not be reached for another two decades.

Protecting forests and other terrestrial and marine areas helps protect plant and animal habitats and preserve the diversity of species. By 2012 over 14 percent of the world's land and over 12 percent of its oceans had been protected, an improvement of 6 percent for both since 1990 (figure 7e).

Deforestation is a major cause of loss of biodiversity, and habitat conservation is vital for stemming this loss. Many species are under threat due to climate change, overfishing, pollution, and habitat degradation. As conservation efforts focus on protecting areas of high biodiversity, the number of threatened species becomes an important measure of the immediate need for conservation in an area. Among assessed species, the highest number of threatened plant species are in Latin America and the Caribbean, the highest number of threatened fish species are in Sub-Saharan Africa, and the highest number of threatened mammal and bird species are in East Asia and Pacific (figure 7f).

Forest losses and gains vary by region 7d

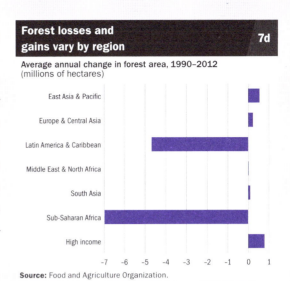

Average annual change in forest area, 1990–2012 (millions of hectares)

Source: Food and Agriculture Organization.

The world's nationally protected areas have increased substantially 7e

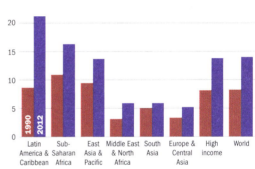

Territorial and marine protected areas (% of terrestrial area and territorial waters)

Source: United Nations Environment Programme–World Conservation Monitoring Centre.

The number of threatened species is an important measure of biodiversity loss 7f

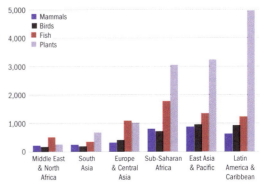

Threatened species, by taxonomic group, 2014

Source: International Union for the Conservation of Nature Red List of Threatened Species.

MDG 8 Develop a global partnership for development

Aid flows have increased — 8a

Official development assistance from Development Assistance Committee members (2012 $ billions)

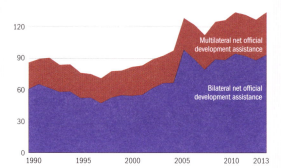

Multilateral net official development assistance

Bilateral net official development assistance

Source: Organisation for Economic Co-operation and Development StatExtracts.

Domestic subsidies to agriculture exceed aid flows — 8b

Agricultural support ($ billions)

European Union
United States
Japan
Korea, Rep.
Turkey

Source: Organisation for Economic Co-operation and Development StatExtracts.

More opportunities for exporters in developing countries — 8c

Goods (excluding arms) admitted free of tariffs from developing countries (% of total merchandise imports, excluding arms)

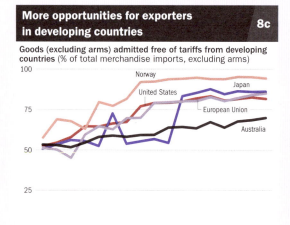

Norway
United States
Japan
European Union
Australia

Source: World Trade Organization, International Trade Center, and United Nations Conference on Trade and Development.

Millennium Development Goal 8 focuses on the multidimensional nature of development and the need for wealthy countries and developing countries to work together to create an environment in which rapid, sustainable development is possible. It recognizes that development challenges differ for large and small countries and for those that are landlocked or isolated by large expanses of ocean and that building and sustaining partnership are ongoing processes that do not stop on a given date or when a specific target is reached. Increased aid flows and debt relief for the poorest, highly indebted countries are only part of what is required. In parallel, Millennium Development Goal 8 underscores the need to reduce barriers to trade, to support infrastructure development, and to share the benefits of new communications technology.

In 2013 members of the Organisation for Economic Co-operation and Development's (OECD) Development Assistance Committee (DAC) provided $135 billion in official development assistance (ODA), an increase of 6.1 percent in real terms over 2012. After falling through much of the 1990s, ODA grew steadily from $71 billion in 1997 to $134 billion in 2010. The financial crisis that began in 2008 forced many governments to implement austerity measures and trim aid budgets, and ODA fell in 2011 and 2012. The rebound in 2013 resulted from several members stepping up spending on foreign aid, despite continued budget pressure, and from an expansion of the DAC by five new member countries: the Czech Republic, Iceland, Poland, the Slovak Republic, and Slovenia (figure 8a).

Collectively OECD members, mostly high-income economies but also some upper middle-income economies such as Mexico and Turkey, spend almost 2.5 times as much on support to domestic agricultural producers as they do on ODA. In 2013 the OECD estimate of total support to agriculture was $344 billion, 62 percent of which went to EU and US producers (figure 8b).

Many rich countries are committed to opening their markets to exports from developing countries, and pledges to facilitate trade and reform border procedures were reiterated at the December 2013 World Trade Organization Ministerial Meeting in Bali. The share of goods (excluding arms) admitted duty free by OECD economies continues to rise, albeit it moderately. However, arcane rules of origin and phytosanitary standards prevent many developing

 Front   User guide World view People   Environment

countries from qualifying for duty-free access and, in turn, inhibit development of export-oriented industries (figure 8c).

Since 2000, developing countries have seen much improvement in their external debt servicing capacity thanks to increased export earnings, improved debt management, debt restructuring, and—more recently—attractive borrowing conditions in international capital markets. The poorest, most indebted countries have also benefitted from extensive debt relief: 35 of the 39 countries eligible for the Heavily Indebted Poor Country Initiative and the Multilateral Debt Relief Initiative have completed the process. The debt service–to-export ratio averaged 11 percent in 2013, half its 2000 level, but with wide disparity across regions (figure 8d). Going forward the ratio is likely to be on an upward trajectory in light of the fragile global outlook, soft commodity prices, and projected 20 percent rise in developing countries' external debt service over the next two to three years, following the 33 percent increase in their combined external debt stock since 2010.

Telecommunications is an essential tool for development, and new technologies are creating opportunities everywhere. The growth of fixed-line phone systems has peaked in high-income economies and will never reach the same level of use in developing countries. Mobile cellular subscriptions topped 6.7 billion in 2013 worldwide, and early estimates show close to 7 billion for 2014. High-income economies had 121 subscriptions per 100 people in 2013—more than one per person—and upper middle-income economies have reached 100 subscriptions per 100 people. Lower middle-income economies had 85, and low-income economies had 55 (figure 8e).

Mobile phones are one of several ways to access the Internet. In 2000 Internet use was spreading rapidly in high-income economies but was barely under way in developing country regions. Now developing countries are beginning to catch up. Since 2000, Internet users per 100 people in developing economies has grown 27 percent a year. For instance, the percentage of the population with access to the Internet has doubled in South Asia since 2010, reaching 14 percent in 2013. Like telephones, Internet use is strongly correlated with income. The low-income economies of South Asia and Sub-Saharan Africa lag behind, accounting for 50 percent of the more than 4 billion people who are not yet using the Internet (figure 8f).

Debt service burdens beginning to rise 8d

Total debt service (% of exports of goods, services, and income)

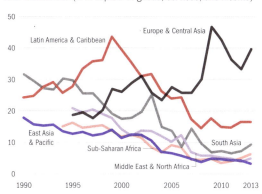

Source: World Development Indicators database.

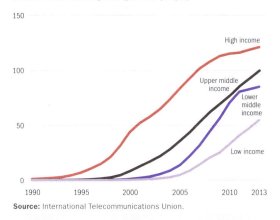

Mobile phone access growing rapidly 8e

Mobile cellular subscriptions (per 100 people)

Source: International Telecommunications Union.

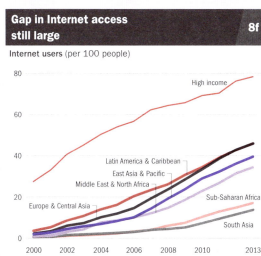

Gap in Internet access still large 8f

Internet users (per 100 people)

Source: International Telecommunications Union.

Millennium Development Goals

Goals and targets from the Millennium Declaration | **Indicators for monitoring progress**

Goal 1 — Eradicate extreme poverty and hunger

Target 1.A Halve, between 1990 and 2015, the proportion of people whose income is less than $1 a day	1.1 Proportion of population below $1 purchasing power parity (PPP) a day[a] 1.2 Poverty gap ratio [incidence × depth of poverty] 1.3 Share of poorest quintile in national consumption
Target 1.B Achieve full and productive employment and decent work for all, including women and young people	1.4 Growth rate of GDP per person employed 1.5 Employment to population ratio 1.6 Proportion of employed people living below $1 (PPP) a day 1.7 Proportion of own-account and contributing family workers in total employment
Target 1.C Halve, between 1990 and 2015, the proportion of people who suffer from hunger	1.8 Prevalence of underweight children under five years of age 1.9 Proportion of population below minimum level of dietary energy consumption

Goal 2 — Achieve universal primary education

Target 2.A Ensure that by 2015 children everywhere, boys and girls alike, will be able to complete a full course of primary schooling	2.1 Net enrollment ratio in primary education 2.2 Proportion of pupils starting grade 1 who reach last grade of primary education 2.3 Literacy rate of 15- to 24-year-olds, women and men

Goal 3 — Promote gender equality and empower women

Target 3.A Eliminate gender disparity in primary and secondary education, preferably by 2005, and in all levels of education no later than 2015	3.1 Ratios of girls to boys in primary, secondary, and tertiary education 3.2 Share of women in wage employment in the nonagricultural sector 3.3 Proportion of seats held by women in national parliament

Goal 4 — Reduce child mortality

Target 4.A Reduce by two-thirds, between 1990 and 2015, the under-five mortality rate	4.1 Under-five mortality rate 4.2 Infant mortality rate 4.3 Proportion of one-year-old children immunized against measles

Goal 5 — Improve maternal health

Target 5.A Reduce by three-quarters, between 1990 and 2015, the maternal mortality ratio	5.1 Maternal mortality ratio 5.2 Proportion of births attended by skilled health personnel
Target 5.B Achieve by 2015 universal access to reproductive health	5.3 Contraceptive prevalence rate 5.4 Adolescent birth rate 5.5 Antenatal care coverage (at least one visit and at least four visits) 5.6 Unmet need for family planning

Goal 6 — Combat HIV/AIDS, malaria, and other diseases

Target 6.A Have halted by 2015 and begun to reverse the spread of HIV/AIDS	6.1 HIV prevalence among population ages 15–24 years 6.2 Condom use at last high-risk sex 6.3 Proportion of population ages 15–24 years with comprehensive, correct knowledge of HIV/AIDS 6.4 Ratio of school attendance of orphans to school attendance of nonorphans ages 10–14 years
Target 6.B Achieve by 2010 universal access to treatment for HIV/AIDS for all those who need it	6.5 Proportion of population with advanced HIV infection with access to antiretroviral drugs
Target 6.C Have halted by 2015 and begun to reverse the incidence of malaria and other major diseases	6.6 Incidence and death rates associated with malaria 6.7 Proportion of children under age five sleeping under insecticide-treated bednets 6.8 Proportion of children under age five with fever who are treated with appropriate antimalarial drugs 6.9 Incidence, prevalence, and death rates associated with tuberculosis 6.10 Proportion of tuberculosis cases detected and cured under directly observed treatment short course

Note: The Millennium Development Goals and targets come from the Millennium Declaration, signed by 189 countries, including 147 heads of state and government, in September 2000 (www.un.org/millennium/declaration/ares552e.htm) as updated by the 60th UN General Assembly in September 2005. The revised Millennium Development Goal (MDG) monitoring framework shown here, including new targets and indicators, was presented to the 62nd General Assembly, with new numbering as recommended by the Inter-agency and Expert Group on MDG Indicators at its 12th meeting on November 14, 2007. The goals and targets are interrelated and should be seen as a whole. They represent a partnership between the developed countries and the developing countries "to create an environment—at the national and global levels alike—which is conducive to development and the elimination of poverty." All indicators should be disaggregated by sex and urban-rural location as far as possible.

Goals and targets from the Millennium Declaration   Indicators for monitoring progress

Goal 7	**Ensure environmental sustainability**		

Target 7.A	Integrate the principles of sustainable development into country policies and programs and reverse the loss of environmental resources	7.1 7.2 7.3	Proportion of land area covered by forest Carbon dioxide emissions, total, per capita and per $1 GDP (PPP) Consumption of ozone-depleting substances
Target 7.B	Reduce biodiversity loss, achieving, by 2010, a significant reduction in the rate of loss	7.4 7.5 7.6 7.7	Proportion of fish stocks within safe biological limits Proportion of total water resources used Proportion of terrestrial and marine areas protected Proportion of species threatened with extinction
Target 7.C	Halve by 2015 the proportion of people without sustainable access to safe drinking water and basic sanitation	7.8 7.9	Proportion of population using an improved drinking water source Proportion of population using an improved sanitation facility
Target 7.D	Achieve by 2020 a significant improvement in the lives of at least 100 million slum dwellers	7.10	Proportion of urban population living in slums[b]

Goal 8	**Develop a global partnership for development**		

Some of the indicators listed below are monitored separately for the least developed countries (LDCs), Africa, landlocked developing countries, and small island developing states.

Target 8.A	Develop further an open, rule-based, predictable, nondiscriminatory trading and financial system (Includes a commitment to good governance, development, and poverty reduction—both nationally and internationally.)		**Official development assistance (ODA)** 8.1 Net ODA, total and to the least developed countries, as percentage of OECD/DAC donors' gross national income 8.2 Proportion of total bilateral, sector-allocable ODA of OECD/DAC donors to basic social services (basic education, primary health care, nutrition, safe water, and sanitation)
Target 8.B	Address the special needs of the least developed countries (Includes tariff and quota-free access for the least developed countries' exports; enhanced program of debt relief for heavily indebted poor countries (HIPC) and cancellation of official bilateral debt; and more generous ODA for countries committed to poverty reduction.)		8.3 Proportion of bilateral official development assistance of OECD/DAC donors that is untied 8.4 ODA received in landlocked developing countries as a proportion of their gross national incomes 8.5 ODA received in small island developing states as a proportion of their gross national incomes
Target 8.C	Address the special needs of landlocked developing countries and small island developing states (through the Programme of Action for the Sustainable Development of Small Island Developing States and the outcome of the 22nd special session of the General Assembly)		**Market access** 8.6 Proportion of total developed country imports (by value and excluding arms) from developing countries and least developed countries, admitted free of duty 8.7 Average tariffs imposed by developed countries on agricultural products and textiles and clothing from developing countries 8.8 Agricultural support estimate for OECD countries as a percentage of their GDP 8.9 Proportion of ODA provided to help build trade capacity
Target 8.D	Deal comprehensively with the debt problems of developing countries through national and international measures in order to make debt sustainable in the long term		**Debt sustainability** 8.10 Total number of countries that have reached their HIPC decision points and number that have reached their HIPC completion points (cumulative) 8.11 Debt relief committed under HIPC Initiative and Multilateral Debt Relief Initiative (MDRI) 8.12 Debt service as a percentage of exports of goods and services
Target 8.E	In cooperation with pharmaceutical companies, provide access to affordable essential drugs in developing countries	8.13	Proportion of population with access to affordable essential drugs on a sustainable basis
Target 8.F	In cooperation with the private sector, make available the benefits of new technologies, especially information and communications	8.14 8.15 8.16	Fixed-line telephones per 100 population Mobile cellular subscribers per 100 population Internet users per 100 population

a. Where available, indicators based on national poverty lines should be used for monitoring country poverty trends.

b. The proportion of people living in slums is measured by a proxy, represented by the urban population living in households with at least one of these characteristics: lack of access to improved water supply, lack of access to improved sanitation, overcrowding (three or more people per room), and dwellings made of nondurable material.

The poverty headcount ratio at $1.25 a day is the share of the population living on less than $1.25 a day in 2005 purchasing power parity (PPP) terms. It is also referred as extreme poverty. The PPP 2005 $1.25 a day poverty line is the average poverty line of the 15 poorest countries in the world, estimated from household surveys conducted by national statistical offices or by private agencies under the supervision of government or international agencies. Income and consumption data used for estimating poverty are also collected from household surveys. The latest comprehensive update is the 2011 estimates, which draw on more than 2 million randomly sampled households, representing 85 percent of the population in developing countries. It covers 128 developing countries (as defined in 1990). This map shows the country-level poverty estimates for generating the 2011 regional and global poverty numbers.

Poverty

**SHARE OF POPULATION LIVING ON
LESS THAN $1.25 A DAY, 2011 (%)**

■	50.0 or more
■	25.0–49.9
■	10.0–24.9
■	2.0–9.9
□	Less than 2.0
■	No data

Greenland
(Den)

Canada

United States

Bermuda
(UK)

Mexico

The Bahamas
Cuba
Turks and Caicos Is. (UK)
Jamaica
Belize
Haiti
Guatemala
Honduras
El Salvador
Nicaragua
Costa Rica
Panama
R.B. de
Venezuela
Guyana
Suriname
French Guiana (Fr)
Colombia

Ecuador

Kiribati

Peru
Brazil

Bolivia

Samoa
American
Samoa (US)
French
Polynesia (Fr)
Paraguay

Fiji
Tonga

Chile

Argentina
Uruguay

Caribbean inset

Dominican
Republic
Puerto
Rico, US
Anguilla (UK)
St. Maarten (Neth)
St. Martin (Fr)
Antigua and
Barbuda
U.S. Virgin
Islands (US)
Guadeloupe (Fr)
St. Kitts
and Nevis
Dominica
Martinique (Fr)
Curaçao
(Neth)
St. Lucia
Barbados
St. Vincent and
the Grenadines
Grenada
Trinidad and
Tobago
R.B. de Venezuela

IBRD 41450

Developing countries as a whole met the Millennium
Development Goal target of halving extreme poverty rates five years ahead of the 2015 deadline.

The share of people living on less than $1.25 a day in
developing countries fell from 43.6 percent in 1990 to 17.0 percent in 2011.

Between 1990 and 2011 the number of people living on
less than $1.25 a day in the world fell from 1.9 billion to 1 billion, and it is forecast to be halved by 2015 from its 1990 level.

In 2011 nearly 60 percent of the world's 1 billion
extremely poor people lived in just five countries: India, Nigeria, China, Bangladesh, and the Democratic Republic of the Congo.

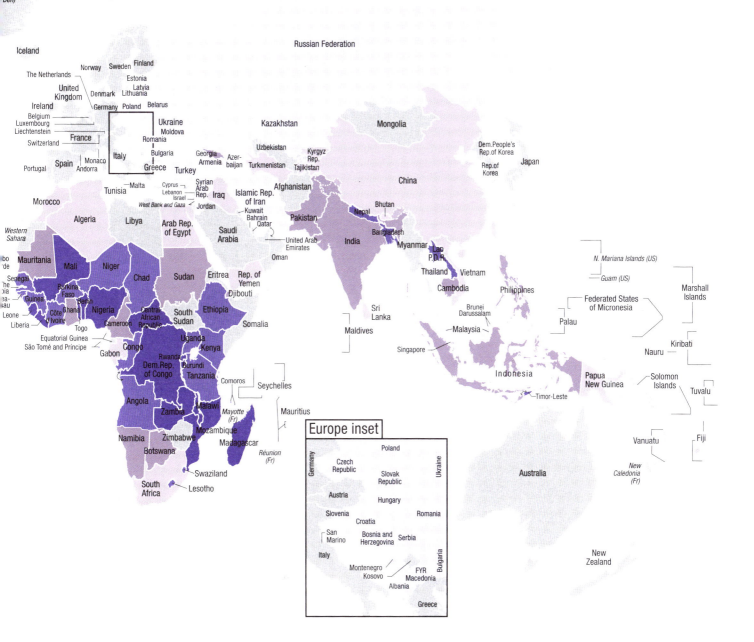

1 World view

	Population	Surface area	Population density	Urban population	Gross national income				Gross domestic product	
					Atlas method		Purchasing power parity			
	millions	thousand sq. km	people per sq. km	% of total population	$ billions	Per capita $	$ billions	Per capita $	% growth	Per capita % growth
	2013	2013	2013	2013	2013	2013	2013	2013	2012–13	2012–13
Afghanistan	30.6	652.9	47	26	21.0	690	59.9[a]	1,960[a]	1.9	−0.5
Albania	2.9	28.8	106	55	13.1	4,510	28.8	9,950	1.4	1.5
Algeria	39.2	2,381.7	17	70	208.8	5,330	512.5	13,070	2.8	0.9
American Samoa	0.1	0.2	276	87	..	..[b]	..	..	..	..
Andorra	0.1	0.5	169	86	..	..[c]	..	..	..	..
Angola	21.5	1,246.7	17	42	110.9	5,170	150.2	7,000	6.8	3.6
Antigua and Barbuda	0.1	0.4	205	25	1.2	13,050	1.8	20,490	−0.1	−1.1
Argentina	41.4	2,780.4	15	91	..[d]	..[b,d]	..[d]	..[d]	2.9[e]	..[d]
Armenia	3.0	29.7	105	63	11.3	3,800	24.3	8,180	3.5	3.2
Aruba	0.1	0.2	572	42	..	..[c]	..	..	..	..
Australia	23.1	7,741.2	3	89	1,512.6	65,400	974.1	42,110	2.5	0.7
Austria	8.5	83.9	103	66	427.3	50,390	381.9	45,040	0.2	−0.4
Azerbaijan	9.4	86.6	114	54	69.2	7,350	152.4	16,180	5.8	4.4
Bahamas, The	0.4	13.9	38	83	8.1	21,570	8.6	22,700	0.7	−0.8
Bahrain	1.3	0.8	1,753	89	26.0	19,700	47.8	36,290	5.3	4.2
Bangladesh	156.6	148.5	1,203	33	158.8	1,010	498.8	3,190	6.0	4.7
Barbados	0.3	0.4	662	32	4.3	15,080	4.3	15,090	0.0	−0.5
Belarus	9.5	207.6	47	76	63.7	6,730	160.5	16,950	0.9	0.9
Belgium	11.2	30.5	369	98	518.2	46,340	460.2	41,160	0.3	−0.2
Belize	0.3	23.0	15	44	1.5	4,510	2.6	7,870	1.5	−0.9
Benin	10.3	114.8	92	43	8.2	790	18.4	1,780	5.6	2.8
Bermuda	0.1	0.1	1,301	100	6.8	104,610	4.3	66,430	−4.9	−5.2
Bhutan	0.8	38.4	20	37	1.8	2,330	5.2	6,920	2.0	0.4
Bolivia	10.7	1,098.6	10	68	27.2	2,550	61.3	5,750	6.8	5.0
Bosnia and Herzegovina	3.8	51.2	75	39	18.3	4,780	37.0	9,660	2.5	2.6
Botswana	2.0	581.7	4	57	15.7	7,770	31.6	15,640	5.8	4.9
Brazil	200.4	8,515.8	24	85	2,342.6	11,690	2,956.0	14,750	2.5	1.6
Brunei Darussalam	0.4	5.8	79	77	..	..[c]	..	..	−1.8	−3.1
Bulgaria	7.3	111.0	67	73	53.5	7,360	110.5	15,210	1.1	1.6
Burkina Faso	16.9	274.2	62	28	12.7	750	28.5	1,680	6.6	3.7
Burundi	10.2	27.8	396	11	2.6	260	7.8	770	4.6	1.4
Cabo Verde	0.5	4.0	124	64	1.8	3,620	3.1	6,210	0.5	−0.4
Cambodia	15.1	181.0	86	20	14.4	950	43.8	2,890	7.4	5.5
Cameroon	22.3	475.4	47	53	28.6	1,290	61.7	2,770	5.6	2.9
Canada	35.2	9,984.7	4	81	1,835.4	52,210	1,480.8	42,120	2.0	0.9
Cayman Islands	0.1	0.3	244	100	..	..[c]	..	..	..	..
Central African Republic	4.6	623.0	7	40	1.5	320	2.8	600	−36.0	−37.3
Chad	12.8	1,284.0	10	22	13.2	1,030	25.7	2,010	4.0	0.9
Channel Islands	0.2	0.2	853	31	..	..[c]	..	..	..	..
Chile	17.6	756.1	24	89	268.3	15,230	371.1	21,060	4.1	3.2
China	1,357.4	9,562.9	145	53	8,905.3	6,560	16,084.5	11,850	7.7	7.1
Hong Kong SAR, China	7.2	1.1	6,845	100	276.1	38,420	390.1	54,270	2.9	2.5
Macao SAR, China	0.6	0.0[f]	18,942	100	35.7	64,050	62.5	112,230	11.9	10.0
Colombia	48.3	1,141.7	44	76	366.6	7,590	577.8	11,960	4.7	3.3
Comoros	0.7	1.9	395	28	0.6	840	1.1	1,490	3.5	1.0
Congo, Dem. Rep.	67.5	2,344.9	30	41	29.1	430	49.9	740	8.5	5.6
Congo, Rep.	4.4	342.0	13	65	11.5	2,590	20.5	4,600	3.4	0.9

 Front | User guide | World view | People | Environment

	Population	Surface area	Population density	Urban population	Gross national income				Gross domestic product	
					Atlas method		Purchasing power parity			
	millions	thousand sq. km	people per sq. km	% of total population	$ billions	Per capita $	$ billions	Per capita $	% growth	Per capita % growth
	2013	2013	2013	2013	2013	2013	2013	2013	2012–13	2012–13
Costa Rica	4.9	51.1	95	75	46.5	9,550	66.1	13,570	3.5	2.1
Côte d'Ivoire	20.3	322.5	64	53	29.5	1,450	62.7	3,090	8.7	6.2
Croatia	4.3	56.6	76	58	57.1	13,420	88.6	20,810	–0.9	–0.7
Cuba	11.3	109.9	106	77	66.4	5,890	208.9	18,520	2.7	2.8
Curaçao	0.2	0.4	346	90	..	..[c]	..	..	..	..
Cyprus	1.1	9.3	124	67	21.9[g]	25,210[g]	24.0[g]	27,630[g]	–5.4[g]	–5.8[g]
Czech Republic	10.5	78.9	136	73	199.4	18,970	283.6	26,970	–0.7	–0.7
Denmark	5.6	43.1	132	87	346.3	61,670	254.3	45,300	–0.5	–0.9
Djibouti	0.9	23.2	38	77	..	..[h]	..	..	5.0	3.4
Dominica	0.1	0.8	96	69	0.5	6,930	0.7	10,060	–0.9	–1.4
Dominican Republic	10.4	48.7	215	77	60.0	5,770	121.0	11,630	4.6	3.3
Ecuador	15.7	256.4	63	63	90.6	5,760	168.8	10,720	4.6	3.0
Egypt, Arab Rep.	82.1	1,001.5	82	43	257.4	3,140	885.1	10,790	2.1	0.4
El Salvador	6.3	21.0	306	66	23.6	3,720	47.5	7,490	1.7	1.0
Equatorial Guinea	0.8	28.1	27	40	10.8	14,320	17.6	23,270	–4.8	–7.4
Eritrea	6.3	117.6	63	22	3.1	490	7.5[a]	1,180[a]	1.3	–1.9
Estonia	1.3	45.2	31	68	23.4	17,780	32.8	24,920	1.6	2.0
Ethiopia	94.1	1,104.3	94	19	44.5	470	129.6	1,380	10.5	7.7
Faeroe Islands	0.0[i]	1.4	35	42	..	..[c]	..	..	..	..
Fiji	0.9	18.3	48	53	3.9	4,370	6.7	7,590	3.5	2.7
Finland	5.4	338.4	18	84	265.5	48,820	216.8	39,860	–1.2	–1.7
France	65.9	549.1	120	79	2,869.8	43,520	2,517.8	38,180	0.3	–0.2
French Polynesia	0.3	4.0	76	56	..	..[c]	..	..	..	..
Gabon	1.7	267.7	7	87	17.8	10,650	28.8	17,230	5.9	3.4
Gambia, The	1.8	11.3	183	58	0.9	500	3.0	1,610	4.8	1.5
Georgia	4.5[j]	69.7	78[j]	53	16.0[j]	3,560[j]	31.5[j]	7,020[j]	3.3[j]	3.4[j]
Germany	80.7	357.2	231	75	3,810.6	47,250	3,630.5	45,010	0.1	–0.2
Ghana	25.9	238.5	114	53	45.8	1,770	101.0	3,900	7.6	5.4
Greece	11.0	132.0	86	77	250.3	22,690	283.0	25,660	–3.3	–2.7
Greenland	0.1	410.5[k]	0[l]	86	..	..[c]	..	..	..	..
Grenada	0.1	0.3	311	36	0.8	7,490	1.2	11,230	2.4	2.0
Guam	0.2	0.5	306	94	..	..[c]	..	..	..	..
Guatemala	15.5	108.9	144	51	51.6	3,340	110.3	7,130	3.7	1.1
Guinea	11.7	245.9	48	36	5.4	460	13.6	1,160	2.3	–0.3
Guinea-Bissau	1.7	36.1	61	48	1.0	590	2.4	1,410	0.3	–2.1
Guyana	0.8	215.0	4	28	3.0	3,750	5.3[a]	6,610[a]	5.2	4.7
Haiti	10.3	27.8	374	56	8.4	810	17.7	1,720	4.3	2.8
Honduras	8.1	112.5	72	54	17.7	2,180	34.6	4,270	2.6	0.5
Hungary	9.9	93.0	109	70	131.2	13,260[m]	224.2	22,660	1.5	1.8
Iceland	0.3	103.0	3	94	15.0	46,290	13.3	41,090	3.5	2.5
India	1,252.1	3,287.3	421	32	1,961.6	1,570	6,700.1	5,350	6.9	5.6
Indonesia	249.9	1,910.9	138	52	895.0	3,580	2,315.1	9,270	5.8	4.5
Iran, Islamic Rep.	77.4	1,745.2	48	72	447.5	5,780	1,208.6	15,610	–5.8	–7.0
Iraq	33.4	435.2	77	69	224.6	6,720	499.0	14,930	4.2	1.6
Ireland	4.6	70.3	67	63	198.1	43,090	178.7	38,870	0.2	–0.1
Isle of Man	0.1	0.6	151	52	..	..[c]	..	..	..	..
Israel	8.1	22.1	372	92	273.5	33,930	256.2	31,780	3.2	1.3

1 World view

	Population	Surface area	Population density	Urban population	Gross national income				Gross domestic product	
					Atlas method		Purchasing power parity			
	millions 2013	thousand sq. km 2013	people per sq. km 2013	% of total population 2013	$ billions 2013	Per capita $ 2013	$ billions 2013	Per capita $ 2013	% growth 2012–13	Per capita % growth 2012–13
Italy	60.2	301.3	205	69	2,145.3	35,620	2,121.5	35,220	–1.9	–3.1
Jamaica	2.7	11.0	251	54	14.2	5,220	23.0	8,490	1.3	1.0
Japan	127.3	378.0	349	92	5,899.9	46,330	4,782.2	37,550	1.6	1.8
Jordan	6.5	89.3	73	83	32.0	4,950	75.3	11,660	2.8	0.6
Kazakhstan	17.0	2,724.9	6	53	196.8	11,550	352.3	20,680	6.0	4.5
Kenya	44.4	580.4	78	25	51.6	1,160[n]	123.3	2,780	5.7	2.9
Kiribati	0.1	0.8	126	44	0.3	2,620	0.3[a]	2,780[a]	3.0	1.4
Korea, Dem. People's Rep.	24.9	120.5	207	61	..	..[o]	..	..	..	..
Korea, Rep.	50.2	100.2	516	82	1,301.6	25,920	1,675.2	33,360	3.0	2.5
Kosovo	1.8	10.9	168	..	7.2	3,940	16.6[a]	9,090[a]	3.0	2.0
Kuwait	3.4	17.8	189	98	*141.0*	*45,130*	265.0	84,800	*8.3*	*4.1*
Kyrgyz Republic	5.7	199.9	30	35	6.9	1,210	17.6	3,080	10.5	8.4
Lao PDR	6.8	236.8	29	36	9.8	1,450	30.8	4,550	8.5	6.5
Latvia	2.0	64.5	32	67	30.8	15,290	45.3	22,510	4.1	5.2
Lebanon	4.5	10.5	437	88	44.1	9,870	77.7[a]	17,400[a]	0.9	–0.1
Lesotho	2.1	30.4	68	26	3.1	1,500	6.5	3,160	5.5	4.3
Liberia	4.3	111.4	45	49	1.7	410	3.4	790	11.3	8.6
Libya	6.2	1,759.5	4	78	..	..[b]	..	..	–10.9	–11.6
Liechtenstein	0.0[i]	0.2	231	14	..	..[c]	..	..	..	..
Lithuania	3.0	65.3	47	67	44.1	14,900	72.6	24,530	3.3	4.3
Luxembourg	0.5	2.6	210	90	38.0	69,880	31.4	57,830	2.0	–0.3
Macedonia, FYR	2.1	25.7	84	57	10.3	4,870	24.3	11,520	3.1	3.0
Madagascar	22.9	587.3	39	34	10.2	440	31.4	1,370	2.4	–0.4
Malawi	16.4	118.5	174	16	4.4	270	12.3	750	5.0	2.0
Malaysia	29.7	330.8	90	73	309.9	10,430	669.5	22,530	4.7	3.1
Maldives	0.3	0.3	1,150	43	1.9	5,600	3.4	9,900	3.7	1.7
Mali	15.3	1,240.2	13	38	10.2	670	23.6	1,540	2.1	–0.8
Malta	0.4	0.3	1,323	95	8.9	20,980	11.4	27,020	2.9	1.9
Marshall Islands	0.1	0.2	292	72	0.2	4,310	0.2[a]	4,630[a]	3.0	2.8
Mauritania	3.9	1,030.7	4	59	4.1	1,060	11.1	2,850	6.7	4.1
Mauritius	1.3	2.0	620	40	12.0	9,570	22.3	17,730	3.2	3.0
Mexico	122.3	1,964.4	63	79	1,216.1	9,940	1,960.0	16,020	1.1	–0.2
Micronesia, Fed. Sts.	0.1	0.7	148	22	0.3	3,280	0.4[a]	3,680[a]	–4.0	–4.1
Moldova	3.6[p]	33.9	124[p]	45	8.8[p]	2,470[p]	18.5[p]	5,180[p]	8.9[p]	8.9[p]
Monaco	0.0[i]	0.0[f]	18,916	100	..	..[c]	..	..	..	..
Mongolia	2.8	1,564.1	2	70	10.7	3,770	25.0	8,810	11.7	10.1
Montenegro	0.6	13.8	46	64	4.5	7,250	9.0	14,410	3.3	3.3
Morocco	33.0	446.6	74	59	101.6[q]	3,020[q]	235.0[q]	7,000[q]	4.4[q]	2.8[q]
Mozambique	25.8	799.4	33	32	15.8	610	28.5	1,100	7.4	4.8
Myanmar	53.3	676.6	82	33	..	..[o]	..	..	..	..
Namibia	2.3	824.3	3	45	13.5	5,870	21.9	9,490	5.1	3.1
Nepal	27.8	147.2	194	18	20.3	730	62.9	2,260	3.8	2.6
Netherlands	16.8	41.5	498	89	858.0	51,060	777.4	46,260	–0.7	–1.0
New Caledonia	0.3	18.6	14	69	..	..[c]	..	..	..	..
New Zealand	4.4	267.7	17	86	*157.6*	*35,760*	*136.5*	*30,970*	2.5	1.7
Nicaragua	6.1	130.4	51	58	10.9	1,790	27.4	4,510	4.6	3.1
Niger	17.8	1,267.0	14	18	7.1	400	15.9	890	4.1	0.2

	Population	Surface area	Population density	Urban population	Gross national income				Gross domestic product	
					Atlas method		Purchasing power parity			
	millions	thousand sq. km	people per sq. km	% of total population	$ billions	Per capita $	$ billions	Per capita $	% growth	Per capita % growth
	2013	2013	2013	2013	2013	2013	2013	2013	2012–13	2012–13
Nigeria	173.6	923.8	191	46	469.7	2,710	930.2	5,360	5.4	2.5
Northern Mariana Islands	0.1	0.5	117	89	..	..c	..	..	..	..
Norway	5.1	385.2	14	80	521.7	102,700	332.5	65,450	0.6	−0.6
Oman	3.6	309.5	12	77	83.4	25,150	174.9	52,780	5.8	−3.5
Pakistan	182.1	796.1	236	38	247.0	1,360	881.4	4,840	4.4	2.7
Palau	0.0j	0.5	45	86	0.2	10,970	0.3a	14,540a	−0.3	−1.1
Panama	3.9	75.4	52	66	41.3	10,700	74.6	19,300	8.4	6.6
Papua New Guinea	7.3	462.8	16	13	14.8	2,020	18.4a	2,510a	5.5	3.3
Paraguay	6.8	406.8	17	59	27.3	4,010	52.2	7,670	14.2	12.3
Peru	30.4	1,285.2	24	78	190.5	6,270	338.9	11,160	5.8	4.4
Philippines	98.4	300.0	330	45	321.8	3,270	771.3	7,840	7.2	5.3
Poland	38.5	312.7	126	61	510.0	13,240	879.2	22,830	1.7	1.7
Portugal	10.5	92.2	114	62	222.4	21,270	284.4	27,190	−1.4	−0.8
Puerto Rico	3.6	8.9	408	94	69.4	19,210	86.2a	23,840a	−0.6	0.4
Qatar	2.2	11.6	187	99	188.2	86,790	278.8	128,530	6.3	−0.2
Romania	20.0	238.4	87	54	180.8	9,050	367.5	18,390	3.5	3.9
Russian Federation	143.5	17,098.2	9	74	1,987.7	13,850	3,484.5	24,280	1.3	1.1
Rwanda	11.8	26.3	477	27	7.4	630	17.1	1,450	4.7	1.9
Samoa	0.2	2.8	67	19	0.8	3,970	1.1a	5,560a	−1.1	−1.9
San Marino	0.0j	0.1	524	94	..	..c	..	..	..	..
São Tomé and Príncipe	0.2	1.0	201	64	0.3	1,470	0.6	2,950	4.0	1.4
Saudi Arabia	28.8	2,149.7f	13	83	757.1	26,260	1,546.5	53,640	4.0	1.9
Senegal	14.1	196.7	73	43	14.8	1,050	31.3	2,210	2.8	−0.2
Serbia	7.2	88.4	82	55	43.3	6,050	89.4	12,480	2.6	3.1
Seychelles	0.1	0.5	194	53	1.2	13,210j	2.1	23,730	5.3	4.2
Sierra Leone	6.1	72.3	84	39	4.1	660	10.3	1,690	5.5	3.6
Singapore	5.4	0.7	7,713	100	291.8	54,040	415.0	76,860	3.9	2.2
Sint Maarten	0.0j	0.0f	1,167	100	..	..c	..	..	..	..
Slovak Republic	5.4	49.0	113	54	96.4	17,810	140.6	25,970	1.4	1.3
Slovenia	2.1	20.3	102	50	47.8	23,220	59.0	28,650	−1.0	−1.1
Solomon Islands	0.6	28.9	20	21	0.9	1,600	1.0a	1,810a	3.0	0.8
Somalia	10.5	637.7	17	39	..	..o	..	..	..	..
South Africa	53.2	1,219.1	44	64	393.8	7,410	666.0	12,530	2.2	0.6
South Sudan	11.3	644.3	..	18	10.8	950s	21.0a	1,860a	13.1	8.5
Spain	46.6	505.6	93	79	1,395.9	29,940	1,532.1	32,870	−1.2	−0.9
Sri Lanka	20.5	65.6	327	18	65.0	3,170	194.1	9,470	7.3	6.4
St. Kitts and Nevis	0.1	0.3	208	32	0.8	13,890	1.1	20,990	4.2	3.0
St. Lucia	0.2	0.6	299	18	1.3	7,060	1.9	10,290	−0.4	−1.2
St. Martin	0.0j	0.1	575	..	..	..c	..	..	..	..
St. Vincent & the Grenadines	0.1	0.4	280	50	0.7	6,460	1.1	10,440	1.7	1.7
Sudan	38.0	1,879.4	21t	33	58.8	1,550	122.7	3,230	−6.0	−7.9
Suriname	0.5	163.8	3	66	5.1	9,370	8.6	15,960	2.9	2.0
Swaziland	1.2	17.4	73	21	3.7	2,990	7.6	6,060	2.8	1.3
Sweden	9.6	447.4	24	86	592.4	61,710	443.3	46,170	1.5	0.6
Switzerland	8.1	41.3	205	74	733.4	90,680	482.1	59,610	1.9	0.8
Syrian Arab Republic	22.8	185.2	124	57	..	..h	..	..	..	..
Tajikistan	8.2	142.6	59	27	8.1	990	20.5	2,500	7.4	4.8

	Population	Surface area	Population density	Urban population	Gross national income				Gross domestic product	
					Atlas method		Purchasing power parity			
	millions	thousand sq. km	people per sq. km	% of total population	$ billions	Per capita $	$ billions	Per capita $	% growth	Per capita % growth
	2013	**2013**	**2013**	**2013**	**2013**	**2013**	**2013**	**2013**	**2012–13**	**2012–13**
Tanzania	49.3	947.3	56	30	41.0u	860u	116.3u	2,430u	7.3u	3.8u
Thailand	67.0	513.1	131	48	357.7	5,340	899.7	13,430	1.8	1.4
Timor-Leste	1.2	14.9	79	31	*4.5*	*3,940*	*8.8*a	*7,670*a	*7.8*	*5.2*
Togo	6.8	56.8	125	39	3.6	530	8.1	1,180	5.1	2.4
Tonga	0.1	0.8	146	24	0.5	4,490	0.6a	5,450a	0.5	0.1
Trinidad and Tobago	1.3	5.1	261	9	21.1	15,760	35.2	26,220	1.6	1.3
Tunisia	10.9	163.6	70	66	45.8	4,200	115.5	10,610	2.5	1.5
Turkey	74.9	783.6	97	72	821.7	10,970	1,391.4	18,570	4.1	2.8
Turkmenistan	5.2	488.1	11	49	36.1	6,880	67.7a	12,920a	10.2	8.8
Turks and Caicos Islands	0.0i	1.0	35	91	..	..c	..	..	..	..
Tuvalu	0.0i	0.0f	329	58	0.1	5,840	0.1a	5,260a	1.3	1.1
Uganda	37.6	241.6	188	15	22.5	600	61.2	1,630	3.3	−0.1
Ukraine	45.5	603.6	79	69	179.9	3,960	407.8	8,970	1.9	2.1
United Arab Emirates	9.3	83.6	112	85	*353.1*	*38,360*	*551.3*	*59,890*	5.2	*1.2*
United Kingdom	64.1	243.6	265	82	2,671.7	41,680	2,433.9	37,970	1.7	1.1
United States	316.1	9,831.5	35	81	16,903.0	53,470	16,992.4	53,750	2.2	1.5
Uruguay	3.4	176.2	19	95	51.7	15,180	64.5	18,940	4.4	4.0
Uzbekistan	30.2	447.4	71	36	56.9	1,880	159.9a	5,290a	8.0	6.3
Vanuatu	0.3	12.2	21	26	0.8	3,130	0.7a	2,870a	2.0	−0.3
Venezuela, RB	30.4	912.1	34	89	381.6	12,550	544.2	17,900	1.3	−0.2
Vietnam	89.7	331.0	289	32	156.4	1,740	455.0	5,070	5.4	4.3
Virgin Islands (U.S.)	0.1	0.4	299	95	..	..c	..	..	..	..
West Bank and Gaza	4.2	6.0	693	75	*12.4*	*3,070*	*21.4*	*5,300*	−4.4	−7.2
Yemen, Rep.	24.4	528.0	46	33	32.6	1,330	93.3	3,820	4.2	1.8
Zambia	14.5	752.6	20	40	26.3	1,810	55.4	3,810	6.7	3.3
Zimbabwe	14.1	390.8	37	33	12.2	860	24.0	1,690	4.5	1.3
World	**7,125.1 s**	**134,324.7 s**	**55 w**	**53 w**	**76,119.3 t**	**10,683 w**	**102,197.6 t**	**14,343 w**	**2.3 w**	**1.1 w**
Low income	848.7	15,359.5	57	30	617.7	728	1,662.6	1,959	5.6	3.3
Middle income	4,970.0	65,026.4	78	50	23,628.9	4,754	47,504.2	9,558	4.9	3.8
Lower middle income	2,561.1	21,590.5	123	39	5,312.2	2,074	15,280.5	5,966	5.8	4.3
Upper middle income	2,408.9	43,436.0	56	62	18,316.9	7,604	32,292.8	13,405	4.7	3.9
Low & middle income	5,818.7	80,385.9	74	47	24,252.8	4,168	49,134.9	8,444	5.0	3.6
East Asia & Pacific	2,005.8	16,270.8	126	51	11,104.7	5,536	21,519.5	10,729	7.1	6.4
Europe & Central Asia	272.4	6,478.6	43	60	1,937.5	7,114	3,711.8	13,628	3.7	3.0
Latin America & Carib.	588.0	19,461.7	31	79	5,610.9	9,542	8,340.8	14,185	2.5	1.3
Middle East & N. Africa	345.4	8,775.4	40	60	..	..	..	..	−0.5	−2.2
South Asia	1,670.8	5,136.2	350	32	2,477.5	1,483	8,405.8	5,031	6.6	5.2
Sub-Saharan Africa	936.3	24,263.1	40	37	1,578.8	1,686	3,103.1	3,314	4.1	1.4
High income	1,306.4	53,938.8	25	80	52,009.9	39,812	53,285.4	40,788	1.4	0.9
Euro area	337.3	2,758.5	126	75	13,272.8	39,350	12,801.4	37,953	−0.5	−0.8

a. Based on regression; others are extrapolated from the 2011 International Comparison Program benchmark estimates. b. Estimated to be upper middle income ($4,126–$12,745). c. Estimated to be high income ($12,746 or more). d. Data series will be calculated once ongoing revisions to official statistics reported by the National Statistics and Censuses Institute of Argentina have been finalized. e. Data for Argentina are officially reported by the National Statistics and Censuses Institute of Argentina. The International Monetary Fund has, however, issued a declaration of censure and called on Argentina to adopt remedial measures to address the quality of official GDP and consumer price index data. Alternative data sources have shown significantly lower real growth and higher inflation than the official data since 2008. In this context, the World Bank is also using alternative data sources and estimates for the surveillance of macroeconomic developments in Argentina. f. Greater than 0 but less than 50. g. Data are for the area controlled by the government of Cyprus. h. Estimated to be lower middle income ($1,046–$4,125). i. Greater than 0 but less than 50,000. j. Excludes Abkhazia and South Ossetia. k. Refers to area free from ice. l. Greater than 0 but less than 0.5. m. Included in the aggregates for upper middle-income economies based on earlier data. n. Included in the aggregates for low-income economies based on earlier data. o. Estimated to be low income ($1,045 or less). p. Excludes Transnistria. q. Includes Former Spanish Sahara. r. Provisional estimate. s. Included in the aggregates for lower middle-income economies based on earlier data. t. Includes South Sudan. u. Covers mainland Tanzania only.

About the data

Population, land area, income (as measured by gross national income, GNI), and output (as measured by gross domestic product, GDP) are basic measures of the size of an economy. They also provide a broad indication of actual and potential resources and are therefore used throughout *World Development Indicators* to normalize other indicators.

Population

Population estimates are usually based on national population censuses. Estimates for the years before and after the census are interpolations or extrapolations based on demographic models. Errors and undercounting occur even in high-income countries; in developing countries errors may be substantial because of limits in the transport, communications, and other resources required to conduct and analyze a full census.

The quality and reliability of official demographic data are also affected by public trust in the government, government commitment to full and accurate enumeration, confidentiality and protection against misuse of census data, and census agencies' independence from political influence. Moreover, comparability of population indicators is limited by differences in the concepts, definitions, collection procedures, and estimation methods used by national statistical agencies and other organizations that collect the data.

More countries conducted a census in the 2010 census round (2005–14) than in previous rounds. As of December 2014 (the end of the 2010 census round), about 93 percent of the estimated world population has been enumerated in a census. The currentness of a census and the availability of complementary data from surveys or registration systems are important indicators of demographic data quality. See *Primary data documentation* for the most recent census or survey year and for the completeness of registration.

Current population estimates for developing countries that lack recent census data and pre- and post-census estimates for countries with census data are provided by the United Nations Population Division and other agencies. The cohort component method—a standard method for estimating and projecting population—requires fertility, mortality, and net migration data, often collected from sample surveys, which can be small or limited in coverage. Population estimates are from demographic modeling and so are susceptible to biases and errors from shortcomings in the model and in the data. Because the five-year age group is the cohort unit and five-year period data are used, interpolations to obtain annual data or single age structure may not reflect actual events or age composition.

Surface area

Surface area includes inland bodies of water and some coastal waterways and thus differs from land area, which excludes bodies of water, and from gross area, which may include offshore territorial waters. It is particularly important for understanding an economy's agricultural capacity and the environmental effects of human activity. Innovations in satellite mapping and computer databases have resulted in more precise measurements of land and water areas.

Urban population

There is no consistent and universally accepted standard for distinguishing urban from rural areas, in part because of the wide variety of situations across countries. Most countries use an urban classification related to the size or characteristics of settlements. Some define urban areas based on the presence of certain infrastructure and services. And other countries designate urban areas based on administrative arrangements. Because the estimates in the table are based on national definitions of what constitutes a city or metropolitan area, cross-country comparisons should be made with caution.

Size of the economy

GNI measures total domestic and foreign value added claimed by residents. GNI comprises GDP plus net receipts of primary income (compensation of employees and property income) from nonresident sources. GDP is the sum of gross value added by all resident producers in the economy plus any product taxes (less subsidies) not included in the valuation of output. GNI is calculated without deducting for depreciation of fabricated assets or for depletion and degradation of natural resources. Value added is the net output of an industry after adding up all outputs and subtracting intermediate inputs. The World Bank uses GNI per capita in U.S. dollars to classify countries for analytical purposes and to determine borrowing eligibility. For definitions of the income groups in *World Development Indicators,* see *User guide.*

When calculating GNI in U.S. dollars from GNI reported in national currencies, the World Bank follows the *World Bank Atlas* conversion method, using a three-year average of exchange rates to smooth the effects of transitory fluctuations in exchange rates. (For further discussion of the *World Bank Atlas* method, see *Statistical methods*.)

Because exchange rates do not always reflect differences in price levels between countries, the table also converts GNI and GNI per capita estimates into international dollars using purchasing power parity (PPP) rates. PPP rates provide a standard measure allowing comparison of real levels of expenditure between countries, just as conventional price indexes allow comparison of real values over time.

PPP rates are calculated by simultaneously comparing the prices of similar goods and services among a large number of countries. In the most recent round of price surveys by the International Comparison Program (ICP) in 2011, 177 countries and territories fully participated and 22 partially participated. PPP rates for 47 high- and upper middle-income countries are from Eurostat and the Organisation for Economic Co-operation and Development (OECD); PPP estimates incorporate new price data collected since 2011. For the remaining 2011 ICP economies PPP rates are extrapolated from the 2011 ICP benchmark results, which account for relative price changes between each economy and the United States. For countries that did not participate in the 2011 ICP round, PPP rates are imputed using a statistical model. More information on the results of the 2011 ICP is available at http://icp.worldbank.org.

Growth rates of GDP and GDP per capita are calculated using constant price data in local currency. Constant price U.S. dollar series are used to calculate regional and income group growth rates. Growth rates in the table are annual averages (see *Statistical methods*).

Definitions

• **Population** is based on the de facto definition of population, which counts all residents regardless of legal status or citizenship—except for refugees not permanently settled in the country of asylum, who are generally considered part of the population of their country of origin. The values shown are midyear estimates. • **Surface area** is a country's total area, including areas under inland bodies of water and some coastal waterways. • **Population density** is midyear population divided by land area. • **Urban population** is the midyear population of areas defined as urban in each country and obtained by the United Nations Population Division. • **Gross national income,** *Atlas* **method,** is the sum of value added by all resident producers plus any product taxes (less subsidies) not included in the valuation of output plus net receipts of primary income (compensation of employees and property income) from abroad. Data are in current U.S. dollars converted using the *World Bank Atlas* method (see *Statistical methods*). • **Gross national income, purchasing power parity,** is GNI converted to international dollars using PPP rates. An international dollar has the same purchasing power over GNI that a U.S. dollar has in the United States. • **Gross national income per capita** is GNI divided by midyear population. • **Gross domestic product** is the sum of value added by all resident producers plus any product taxes (less subsidies) not included in the valuation of output. Growth is calculated from constant price GDP data in local currency. • **Gross domestic product per capita** is GDP divided by midyear population.

Data sources

The World Bank's population estimates are compiled and produced by its Development Data Group in consultation with its Health Global Practice, operational staff, and country offices. The United Nations Population Division (2013) is a source of the demographic data for more than half the countries, most of them developing countries. Other important sources are census reports and other statistical publications from national statistical offices, Eurostat's Population database, the United Nations Statistics Division's *Population and Vital Statistics Report,* and the U.S. Bureau of the Census's International Data Base.

Data on surface and land area are from the Food and Agriculture Organization, which gathers these data from national agencies through annual questionnaires and by analyzing the results of national agricultural censuses.

Data on urban population shares are from United Nations Population Division (2014).

GNI, GNI per capita, GDP growth, and GDP per capita growth are estimated by World Bank staff based on national accounts data collected by World Bank staff during economic missions or reported by national statistical offices to other international organizations such as the OECD. PPP conversion factors are estimates by Eurostat/OECD and by World Bank staff based on data collected by the ICP.

References

Eurostat. n.d. *Population database.* [http://ec.europa.eu/eurostat/]. Luxembourg.

FAO (Food and Agriculture Organization), IFAD (International Fund for Agricultural Development), and WFP (World Food Programme). 2014. *The State of Food Insecurity in the World 2014: Strengthening the Enabling Environment for Food Security and Nutrition.* Rome. [www.fao.org/3/a-i4030e.pdf].

OECD (Organisation for Economic Co-operation and Development). n.d. OECD.StatExtracts database. [http://stats.oecd.org/]. Paris.

UNAIDS (Joint United Nations Programme on HIV/AIDS). 2014. *The Gap Report.* [www.unaids.org/en/resources/campaigns/2014/2014gapreport/gapreport/]. Geneva.

UNESCO (United Nations Educational, Scientific and Cultural Organization). 2004. *Education for All Global Monitoring Report 2003/4: Gender and Education for All—The Leap to Equality.* Paris.

UNFPA (United Nations Population Fund) and Guttmacher Institute. 2014. *Adding It Up 2014: The Costs and Benefits of Investing in Sexual and Reproductive Health.* [www.unfpa.org/sites/default/files/pub-pdf/Adding%20It%20Up-Final-11.18.14.pdf]. New York.

UNICEF (United Nations Children's Fund). 2014. *Committing to Child Survival: A Promise Renewed—Progress Report 2014.* [http://files.unicef.org/publications/files/APR_2014_web_15Sept14.pdf]. New York.

UNICEF (United Nations Children's Fund), WHO (World Health Organization), and World Bank. 2014. *2013 Joint Child Malnutrition Estimates—Levels and Trends.* New York: UNICEF. [www.who.int/nutgrowthdb/estimates2013/].

United Nations. 2014. *A World That Counts: Mobilising the Data Revolution for Sustainable Development.* New York. [www.undatarevolution.org/wp-content/uploads/2014/12/A-World-That-Counts2.pdf].

United Nations Population Division. 2013. *World Population Prospects: The 2012 Revision.* [http://esa.un.org/unpd/wpp/Documentation/publications.htm]. New York.

United Nations Statistics Division. Various years. *Population and Vital Statistics Report.* New York.

———. 2014. *World Urbanization Prospects: The 2014 Revision.* [http://esa.un.org/unpd/wup/]. New York.

WHO (World Health Organization). 2014a. *Global Tuberculosis Report 2014.* [http://who.int/tb/publications/global_report/]. Geneva.

———. 2014b. "Maternal Mortality." Fact sheet 348. [www.who.int/mediacentre/factsheets/fs348/]. Geneva.

———. 2014c. *World Malaria Report 2014.* [www.who.int/malaria/publications/world_malaria_report_2014/]. Geneva.

World Bank. 2015. *Global Monitoring Report 2014/2015: Ending Poverty and Sharing Prosperity.* Washington, DC.

Online tables and indicators

To access the World Development Indicators online tables, use the URL http://wdi.worldbank.org/table/ and the table number (for example, http://wdi.worldbank.org/table/1.1). To view a specific indicator online, use the URL http://data.worldbank.org/indicator/ and the indicator code (for example, http://data.worldbank.org /indicator/SP.POP.TOTL).

1.1 Size of the economy

Population ♀♂	SP.POP.TOTL
Surface area	AG.SRF.TOTL.K2
Population density	EN.POP.DNST
Gross national income, *Atlas* method	NY.GNP.ATLS.CD
Gross national income per capita, *Atlas* method	NY.GNP.PCAP.CD
Purchasing power parity gross national income	NY.GNP.MKTP.PP.CD
Purchasing power parity gross national income, Per capita	NY.GNP.PCAP.PP.CD
Gross domestic product	NY.GDP.MKTP.KD.ZG
Gross domestic product, Per capita	NY.GDP.PCAP.KD.ZG

1.2 Millennium Development Goals: eradicating poverty and saving lives

Share of poorest quintile in national consumption or income	SI.DST.FRST.20
Vulnerable employment ♀♂	SL.EMP.VULN.ZS
Prevalence of malnutrition, Underweight ♀♂	SH.STA.MALN.ZS
Primary completion rate ♀♂	SE.PRM.CMPT.ZS
Ratio of girls to boys enrollments in primary and secondary education ♀♂	SE.ENR.PRSC.FM.ZS
Under-five mortality rate ♀♂	SH.DYN.MORT

1.3 Millennium Development Goals: protecting our common environment

Maternal mortality ratio, Modeled estimate	SH.STA.MMRT
Contraceptive prevalence rate	SP.DYN.CONU.ZS
Prevalence of HIV	SH.DYN.AIDS.ZS
Incidence of tuberculosis	SH.TBS.INCD

Carbon dioxide emissions per capita	EN.ATM.CO2E.PC
Nationally protected terrestrial and marine areas	ER.PTD.TOTL.ZS
Access to improved sanitation facilities	SH.STA.ACSN
Internet users	IT.NET.USER.PZ

1.4 Millennium Development Goals: overcoming obstacles

This table provides data on net official development assistance by donor, least developed countries' access to high-income markets, and the Debt Initiative for Heavily Indebted Poor Countries. ..[a]

1.5 Women in development

Female population ♀♂	SP.POP.TOTL.FE.ZS
Life expectancy at birth, Male ♀♂	SP.DYN.LE00.MA.IN
Life expectancy at birth, Female ♀♂	SP.DYN.LE00.FE.IN
Pregnant women receiving prenatal care	SH.STA.ANVC.ZS
Teenage mothers	SP.MTR.1519.ZS
Women in wage employment in nonagricultural sector	SL.EMP.INSV.FE.ZS
Unpaid family workers, Male ♀♂	SL.FAM.WORK.MA.ZS
Unpaid family workers, Female ♀♂	SL.FAM.WORK.FE.ZS
Female part-time employment ♀♂	SL.TLF.PART.TL.FE.ZS
Female legislators, senior officials, and managers	SG.GEN.LSOM.ZS
Women in parliaments	SG.GEN.PARL.ZS

♀♂ Data disaggregated by sex are available in the World Development Indicators database.
a. Available online only as part of the table, not as an individual indicator.

Poverty rates

	International poverty line in local currency		Population below international poverty lines[a]									
	$1.25 a day 2005	$2 a day 2005	Reference year[b]	Population below $1.25 a day %	Poverty gap at $1.25 a day %	Population below $2 a day %	Poverty gap at $2 a day %	Reference year[b]	Population below $1.25 a day %	Poverty gap at $1.25 a day %	Population below $2 a day %	Poverty gap at $2 a day %
Albania	75.5	120.8	2008[c]	<2	<0.5	<2	<0.5	2012[c]	<2	<0.5	3.0	0.6
Algeria	48.4[d]	77.5[d]	1988	7.1	1.1	23.7	6.4	1995	6.4	1.3	22.8	6.2
Angola	88.1	141.0		..	..	..	..	2009	43.4	16.5	67.4	31.5
Argentina	1.7	2.7	2010[e,f]	<2	0.9	4.0	1.6	2011[e,f]	<2	0.8	2.9	1.3
Armenia	245.2	392.4	2011[c]	2.5	<0.5	17.6	3.5	2012[c]	<2	<0.5	15.5	3.1
Azerbaijan	2,170.9	3,473.5	2005[c]	<2	<0.5	<2	<0.5	2008[c]	<2	<0.5	2.4	0.5
Bangladesh	31.9	51.0	2005	50.5	14.2	80.3	34.3	2010	43.3	11.2	76.5	30.4
Belarus	949.5	1,519.2	2010[c]	<2	<0.5	<2	<0.5	2011[c]	<2	<0.5	<2	<0.5
Belize	1.8[d]	2.9[d]	1998[f]	11.3	4.8	26.4	10.3	1999[f]	12.2	5.5	22.0	9.9
Benin	344.0	550.4	2003	47.3	15.7	75.3	33.5	2011	51.6	18.8	74.3	35.9
Bhutan	23.1	36.9	2007	10.2	1.8	29.8	8.5	2012	2.4	<0.5	15.2	3.3
Bolivia	3.2	5.1	2011[f]	7.0	3.1	12.0	5.5	2012[f]	8.0	4.2	12.7	6.5
Bosnia and Herzegovina	1.1	1.7	2004[c]	<2	<0.5	<2	<0.5	2007[c]	<2	<0.5	<2	<0.5
Botswana	4.2	6.8	2003[c]	24.4	8.5	41.6	17.9	2009[c]	13.4	4.0	27.8	10.2
Brazil	2.0	3.1	2011[f]	4.5	2.5	8.2	3.9	2012[f]	3.8	2.1	6.8	3.3
Bulgaria	0.9	1.5	2010[f]	<2	0.6	3.3	1.2	2011[f]	<2	0.8	3.9	1.6
Burkina Faso	303.0	484.8	2003	48.9	18.3	72.5	34.7	2009	44.5	14.6	72.4	31.6
Burundi	558.8	894.1	1998	86.4	47.3	95.4	64.1	2006	81.3	36.4	93.5	56.1
Cabo Verde	97.7	156.3	2002	21.0	6.1	40.9	15.2	2007	13.7	3.2	34.7	11.1
Cambodia	2,019.1	3,230.6	2010	11.3	1.7	40.9	10.6	2011	10.1	1.4	41.3	10.3
Cameroon	368.1	589.0	2001	24.9	6.7	50.7	18.5	2007	27.6	7.2	53.2	20.0
Central African Republic	384.3	614.9	2003	62.4	28.3	81.9	45.3	2008	62.8	31.3	80.1	46.8
Chad	409.5	655.1	2002	61.9	25.6	83.3	43.9	2011	36.5	14.2	60.5	27.3
Chile	484.2	774.7	2009[f]	<2	0.7	2.6	1.1	2011[f]	<2	<0.5	<2	0.8
China	5.1[g]	8.2[g]	2010[h]	9.2	2.0	23.2	7.3	2011[h]	6.3	1.3	18.6	5.5
Colombia	1,489.7	2,383.5	2011[f]	5.0	2.0	11.3	4.3	2012[f]	5.6	2.3	12.0	4.7
Comoros	368.0	588.8		..	..	..	..	2004	46.1	20.8	65.0	34.2
Congo, Dem. Rep.	395.3	632.5		..	..	..	..	2005	87.7	52.8	95.2	67.6
Congo, Rep.	469.5	751.1	2005	54.1	22.8	74.4	38.8	2011	32.8	11.5	57.3	24.2
Costa Rica	348.7[d]	557.9[d]	2011[f]	<2	0.6	3.2	1.2	2012[f]	<2	0.6	3.1	1.2
Côte d'Ivoire	5.6	8.9	2004[c]	<2	<0.5	<2	<0.5	2008[c]	<2	<0.5	<2	<0.5
Croatia	19.0	30.4	2010[f]	<2	<0.5	<2	<0.5	2011[f]	<2	<0.5	<2	<0.5
Czech Republic	407.3	651.6	2002	29.7	9.1	56.9	22.0	2008	35.0	12.7	59.1	25.9
Djibouti	134.8	215.6		..	..	..	..	2002	18.8	5.3	41.2	14.6
Dominican Republic	25.5[d]	40.8[d]	2011[f]	2.5	0.6	8.5	2.4	2012[f]	2.3	0.6	8.8	2.4
Ecuador	0.6	1.0	2011[f]	4.0	1.9	9.0	3.6	2012[f]	4.0	1.8	8.4	3.4
Egypt, Arab Rep.	2.5	4.0	2004	2.3	<0.5	20.1	3.8	2008	<2	<0.5	15.4	2.8
El Salvador	6.0[d]	9.6[d]	2011[f]	2.8	0.6	10.3	2.7	2012[f]	2.5	0.6	8.8	2.4
Estonia	11.0	17.7	2010[f]	<2	1.0	<2	1.0	2011[f]	<2	1.2	<2	1.2
Ethiopia	3.4	5.5	2005	39.0	9.6	77.6	28.9	2010	36.8	10.4	72.2	27.6
Fiji	1.9	3.1	2002	29.2	11.3	48.7	21.8	2008	5.9	1.1	22.9	6.0
Gabon	554.7	887.5		..	..	..	..	2005	6.1	1.3	20.9	5.8
Gambia, The	12.9	20.7	1998	65.6	33.8	81.2	49.1	2003	33.6	11.7	55.9	24.4
Georgia	1.0	1.6	2011[c]	16.1	5.6	33.5	12.8	2012[c]	14.1	4.5	31.3	11.4
Ghana	5,594.8	8,951.6	1998	39.1	14.4	63.3	28.5	2005	28.6	9.9	51.8	21.3
Guatemala	5.7[d]	9.1[d]	2006[f]	13.5	4.7	26.0	10.4	2011[f]	13.7	4.8	29.8	11.2
Guinea	1,849.5	2,959.1	2007	39.3	13.0	65.9	28.3	2012	40.9	12.7	72.7	29.8

 Front User guide World view People | Environment

	International poverty line in local currency		Population below international poverty lines[a]									
	$1.25 a day	$2 a day	Reference year[b]	Population below $1.25 a day %	Poverty gap at $1.25 a day %	Population below $2 a day %	Poverty gap at $2 a day %	Reference year[b]	Population below $1.25 a day %	Poverty gap at $1.25 a day %	Population below $2 a day %	Poverty gap at $2 a day %
	2005	2005										
Guinea-Bissau	355.3	568.6	1993	65.3	29.0	84.6	46.8	2002	48.9	16.6	78.0	34.9
Guyana	131.5[d]	210.3[d]	1992[i]	6.9	1.5	17.1	5.4	1998[i]	8.7	2.8	18.0	6.7
Haiti	24.2[d]	38.7[d]	..	..	..	..	..	2001[f]	61.7	32.3	77.5	46.7
Honduras	12.1[d]	19.3[d]	2010[f]	13.4	4.8	26.3	10.5	2011[f]	16.5	7.2	29.2	13.2
Hungary	171.9	275.0	2010[f]	<2	<0.5	<2	<0.5	2011[f]	<2	<0.5	<2	<0.5
India	19.5[j]	31.2[j]	2009[h]	32.7	7.5	68.8	24.5	2011[h]	23.6	4.8	59.2	19.0
Indonesia	5,241.0[j]	8,385.7[j]	2010[h]	18.0	3.3	46.3	14.3	2011[h]	16.2	2.7	43.3	13.0
Iran, Islamic Rep.	3,393.5	5,429.6	1998	<2	<0.5	8.3	1.8	2005	<2	<0.5	8.0	1.8
Iraq	799.8	1,279.7	2007[c]	3.4	0.6	22.4	4.7	2012[c]	3.9	0.6	21.2	4.7
Jamaica	54.2[d]	86.7[d]	2002	<2	<0.5	8.5	1.5	2004	<2	<0.5	5.9	0.9
Jordan	0.6	1.0	2008	<2	<0.5	2.0	<0.5	2010	<2	<0.5	<2	<0.5
Kazakhstan	81.2	129.9	2008[c]	<2	<0.5	<2	<0.5	2010[c]	<2	<0.5	<2	<0.5
Kenya	40.9	65.4	1997	31.8	9.8	56.2	22.9	2005	43.4	16.9	67.2	31.8
Kyrgyz Republic	16.2	26.0	2010[c]	6.0	1.4	21.1	5.8	2011[c]	5.1	1.2	21.1	5.3
Lao PDR	4,677.0	7,483.2	2007	35.1	9.2	68.3	25.7	2012	30.3	7.7	62.0	22.4
Latvia	0.4	0.7	2010[f]	<2	1.3	2.9	1.6	2011[f]	<2	1.0	2.0	1.2
Lesotho	4.3	6.9	2002	55.2	28.0	73.7	42.0	2010	56.2	29.2	73.4	42.9
Liberia	0.6	1.0	..	..	..	..	..	2007	83.8	40.9	94.9	59.6
Lithuania	2.1	3.3	2010[f]	<2	1.3	2.5	1.5	2011[f]	<2	0.8	<2	0.9
Macedonia, FYR	29.5	47.2	2006	<2	<0.5	4.6	1.1	2008	<2	<0.5	4.2	0.7
Madagascar	945.5	1,512.8	2005	82.4	40.4	93.1	58.6	2010	87.7	48.6	95.1	64.9
Malawi	71.2	113.8	2004	75.0	33.2	90.8	52.6	2010	72.2	34.3	88.1	52.1
Malaysia	2.6	4.2	2007[i]	<2	<0.5	2.9	<0.5	2009[i]	<2	<0.5	2.3	<0.5
Maldives	12.2	19.5	1998	25.6	13.1	37.0	20.0	2004	<2	<0.5	12.2	2.5
Mali	362.1	579.4	2006	51.4	18.8	77.1	36.5	2010	50.6	16.5	78.8	35.3
Mauritania	157.1	251.3	2004	25.4	7.0	52.6	19.2	2008	23.4	6.8	47.7	17.7
Mauritius	22.2	35.5	2006	<2	<0.5	<2	<0.5	2012	<2	<0.5	<2	<0.5
Mexico	9.6	15.3	2010[f]	4.0	1.8	8.3	3.4	2012[f]	3.3	1.4	7.5	2.9
Micronesia, Fed. Sts.	0.8[d]	1.3[d]	..	..	..	..	..	2000[e]	31.2	16.3	44.7	24.5
Moldova	6.0	9.7	2010[c]	<2	<0.5	4.0	0.7	2011[c]	<2	<0.5	2.8	<0.5
Montenegro	0.6	1.0	2010[c]	<2	<0.5	<2	<0.5	2011[c]	<2	<0.5	<2	<0.5
Morocco	6.9	11.0	2001	6.3	0.9	24.4	6.3	2007	2.6	0.6	14.2	3.2
Mozambique	14,532.1	23,251.4	2002	74.7	35.4	90.0	53.6	2009	60.7	25.8	82.5	43.7
Namibia	6.3	10.1	2004[i]	31.9	9.5	51.1	21.8	2009[i]	23.5	5.7	43.2	16.4
Nepal	33.1	52.9	2003	53.1	18.4	77.3	36.6	2010	23.7	5.2	56.0	18.4
Nicaragua	9.1[d]	14.6[d]	2005[f]	12.1	4.2	28.3	10.2	2009[f]	8.5	2.9	20.8	7.2
Niger	334.2	534.7	2007	42.1	11.8	74.1	29.9	2011	40.8	10.4	76.1	29.3
Nigeria	98.2	157.2	2004	61.8	26.9	83.3	44.7	2010	62.0	27.5	82.2	44.8
Pakistan	25.9	41.4	2007	17.2	2.6	55.8	15.7	2010	12.7	1.9	50.7	13.3
Panama	0.8[d]	1.2[d]	2011[f]	3.6	1.1	8.4	3.0	2012[f]	4.0	1.3	8.9	3.2
Papua New Guinea	2.1[d]	3.4[d]	..	..	..	..	..	1996	35.8	12.3	57.4	25.5
Paraguay	2,659.7	4,255.6	2011[f]	4.4	1.7	11.0	4.0	2012[f]	3.0	1.0	7.7	2.6
Peru	2.1	3.3	2011[f]	3.0	0.8	8.7	2.6	2012[f]	2.9	0.8	8.0	2.5
Philippines	30.2	48.4	2009	18.1	3.6	41.1	13.6	2012	19.0	4.0	41.7	14.1
Poland	2.7	4.3	2010[c]	<2	<0.5	<2	<0.5	2011[c]	<2	<0.5	<2	<0.5
Romania	2.1	3.4	2010[f]	3.0	1.3	7.7	2.8	2011[f]	4.0	1.8	8.8	3.5
Russian Federation	16.7	26.8	2008[c]	<2	<0.5	<2	<0.5	2009[c]	<2	<0.5	<2	<0.5

Poverty rates

	International poverty line in local currency		Population below international poverty lines[a]									
	$1.25 a day 2005	$2 a day 2005	Reference year[b]	Population below $1.25 a day %	Poverty gap at $1.25 a day %	Population below $2 a day %	Poverty gap at $2 a day %	Reference year[b]	Population below $1.25 a day %	Poverty gap at $1.25 a day %	Population below $2 a day %	Poverty gap at $2 a day %
Rwanda	295.9	473.5	2006	72.0	34.7	87.4	52.1	2011	63.0	26.5	82.3	44.5
São Tomé and Príncipe	7,953.9	12,726.3	2000	28.2	7.9	54.2	20.6	2010	43.5	13.9	73.1	31.2
Senegal	372.8	596.5	2005	33.5	10.8	60.4	24.7	2011	34.1	11.1	60.3	25.0
Serbia	42.9	68.6	2009[c]	<2	<0.5	<2	<0.5	2010[c]	<2	<0.5	<2	<0.5
Seychelles	5.6[d]	9.0[d]	1999	<2	<0.5	<2	<0.5	2006	<2	<0.5	<2	<0.5
Sierra Leone	1,745.3	2,792.4	2003	59.4	22.7	82.0	41.4	2011	56.6	19.2	82.5	39.0
Slovak Republic	23.5	37.7	2010[f]	<2	<0.5	<2	<0.5	2011[f]	<2	<0.5	<2	<0.5
Slovenia	198.2	317.2	2010[f]	<2	<0.5	<2	<0.5	2011[f]	<2	<0.5	<2	<0.5
South Africa	5.7	9.1	2009	13.7	2.3	31.2	10.1	2011	9.4	1.2	26.2	7.7
Sri Lanka	50.0	80.1	2006	7.0	1.0	29.1	7.4	2009	4.1	0.7	23.9	5.4
St. Lucia	2.4[d]	3.8[d]		..	..	..	..	1995[i]	21.0	7.2	40.6	15.6
Sudan	154.4	247.0		..	..	..	..	2009	19.8	5.5	44.1	15.4
Suriname	2.3[d]	3.7[d]		..	..	..	..	1999[i]	15.5	5.9	27.2	11.7
Swaziland	4.7	7.5	2000	43.0	14.9	64.1	29.8	2009	39.3	15.2	59.1	28.3
Syrian Arab Republic	30.8	49.3		..	..	..	..	2004	<2	<0.5	16.9	3.3
Tajikistan	1.2	1.9	2007[c]	12.2	4.4	36.9	11.5	2009[c]	6.5	1.3	27.4	6.7
Tanzania	603.1	964.9	2007	67.9	28.1	87.9	47.5	2012	43.5	13.0	73.0	30.6
Thailand	21.8	34.9	2008[c]	<2	<0.5	4.6	0.7	2010[c]	<2	<0.5	3.5	0.6
Timor-Leste	0.6[d]	1.0[d]		..	..	..	..	2007	34.9	8.1	71.1	25.7
Togo	352.8	564.5	2006	53.2	20.3	75.3	37.3	2011	52.5	22.5	72.8	38.0
Trinidad and Tobago	5.8[d]	9.2[d]	1988[i]	<2	<0.5	8.6	1.9	1992[i]	4.2	1.1	13.5	3.9
Tunisia	0.9	1.4	2005	<2	<0.5	7.6	1.7	2010	<2	<0.5	4.5	1.0
Turkey	1.3	2.0	2010[c]	<2	<0.5	3.1	0.7	2011[c]	<2	<0.5	2.6	<0.5
Turkmenistan	5,961.1[d]	9,537.7[d]		..	..	..	..	1998	24.8	7.0	49.7	18.4
Uganda	930.8	1,489.2	2009	37.9	12.2	64.7	27.3	2012	37.8	12.0	62.9	26.8
Ukraine	2.1	3.4	2009	<2	<0.5	<2	<0.5	2010[c]	<2	<0.5	<2	<0.5
Uruguay	19.1	30.6	2011[f]	<2	<0.5	<2	<0.5	2012[f]	<2	<0.5	<2	<0.5
Venezuela, RB	1,563.9	2,502.2	2005[f]	13.2	8.0	20.9	11.3	2006[f]	6.6	3.7	12.9	5.9
Vietnam	7,399.9	11,839.8	2010	3.9	0.8	16.8	4.2	2012	2.4	0.6	12.5	2.9
West Bank and Gaza	2.7[d]	4.3[d]	2007[c]	<2	<0.5	3.5	0.7	2009[c]	<2	<0.5	<2	<0.5
Yemen, Rep.	113.8	182.1	1998	10.5	2.4	32.1	9.4	2005	9.8	1.9	37.3	9.9
Zambia	3,537.9	5,660.7	2006	68.5	37.0	82.6	51.8	2010	74.3	41.8	86.6	56.6

a. Based on nominal per capita consumption averages and distributions estimated parametrically from grouped household survey data, unless otherwise noted. b. Refers to the period of reference of a survey. For surveys in which the period of reference covers multiple years, it is the year with the majority of the survey respondents. For surveys in which the period of reference is half in one year and half in another, it is the first year. c. Estimated nonparametrically from nominal consumption per capita distributions based on unit-record household survey data. d. Based on purchasing power parity (PPP) dollars imputed using regression. e. Covers urban areas only. f. Estimated nonparametrically from nominal income per capita distributions based on unit-record household survey data. g. PPP conversion factor based on urban prices. h. Population-weighted average of urban and rural estimates. i. Based on per capita income averages and distribution data estimated parametrically from grouped household survey data. j. Based on benchmark national PPP estimate rescaled to account for cost-of-living differences in urban and rural areas.

 Front User guide World view People   Environment

Trends in poverty indicators by region, 1990–2015

Region	1990	1993	1996	1999	2002	2005	2008	2011	2015 forecast	Trend, 1990–2011
Share of population living on less than 2005 PPP $1.25 a day (%)										
East Asia & Pacific	57.0	51.7	38.3	35.9	27.3	16.7	13.7	7.9	4.1	
Europe & Central Asia	1.5	2.9	4.3	3.8	2.1	1.3	0.5	0.5	0.3	
Latin America & Caribbean	12.2	11.9	10.5	11.0	10.2	7.3	5.4	4.6	4.3	
Middle East & North Africa	5.8	5.3	4.8	4.8	3.8	3.0	2.1	1.7	2.0	
South Asia	54.1	52.1	48.6	45.0	44.1	39.3	34.1	24.5	18.1	
Sub-Saharan Africa	56.6	60.9	59.7	59.3	57.1	52.8	49.7	46.8	40.9	
Developing countries	43.4	41.6	35.9	34.2	30.6	24.8	21.9	17.0	13.4	
World	36.4	35.1	30.4	29.1	26.1	21.1	18.6	14.5	11.5	
People living on less than 2005 PPP $1.25 a day (millions)										
East Asia & Pacific	939	887	682	661	518	324	272	161	86	
Europe & Central Asia	7	13	20	18	10	6	2	2	1	
Latin America & Caribbean	53	55	51	55	54	40	31	28	27	
Middle East & North Africa	13	13	12	13	11	9	7	6	7	
South Asia	620	636	630	617	638	596	540	399	311	
Sub-Saharan Africa	290	338	359	385	400	398	403	415	403	
Developing countries	1,923	1,942	1,754	1,751	1,631	1,374	1,255	1,011	836	
World	1,923	1,942	1,754	1,751	1,631	1,374	1,255	1,011	836	
Regional distribution of people living on less than $1.25 a day (% of total population living on less than $1.25 a day)										
East Asia & Pacific	48.8	45.7	38.9	37.7	31.8	23.6	21.7	15.9	10.3	
Europe & Central Asia	0.4	0.7	1.1	1.0	0.6	0.4	0.2	0.2	0.2	
Latin America & Caribbean	2.8	2.8	2.9	3.1	3.3	2.9	2.5	2.8	3.2	
Middle East & North Africa	0.7	0.7	0.7	0.7	0.7	0.7	0.6	0.6	0.9	
South Asia	32.2	32.7	35.9	35.2	39.1	43.4	43.0	39.5	37.2	
Sub-Saharan Africa	15.1	17.4	20.5	22.0	24.5	29.0	32.1	41.0	48.3	
Survey coverage (% of total population represented by surveys conducted within five years of the reference year)										
East Asia & Pacific	92.4	93.3	93.7	93.4	93.5	93.2	93.6	92.9	..	
Europe & Central Asia	81.5	87.3	97.1	93.9	96.3	94.7	89.9	89.0	..	
Latin America & Caribbean	94.9	91.8	95.9	97.7	97.5	95.9	94.5	99.1	..	
Middle East & North Africa	76.8	65.3	81.7	70.0	21.5	85.7	46.7	15.7	..	
South Asia	96.5	98.2	98.1	20.1	98.0	98.0	97.9	98.2	..	
Sub-Saharan Africa	46.0	68.8	68.0	53.1	65.7	82.7	81.7	67.5	..	
Developing countries	86.4	89.4	91.6	68.2	87.8	93.0	90.2	86.5	..	

Source: World Bank PovcalNet (http://iresearch.worldbank.org/PovcalNet/).

Poverty rates

About the data

The World Bank produced its first global poverty estimates for developing countries for *World Development Report 1990: Poverty* (World Bank 1990) using household survey data for 22 countries (Ravallion, Datt, and van de Walle 1991). Since then there has been considerable expansion in the number of countries that field household income and expenditure surveys. The World Bank's Development Research Group maintains a database that is updated regularly as new survey data become available (and thus may contain more recent data or revisions that are not incorporated into the table) and conducts a major reassessment of progress against poverty about every three years. The most recent comprehensive reassessment was completed in October 2014, when the 2011 extreme poverty estimates for developing country regions, developing countries as a whole (that is, countries classified as low or middle income in 1990), and the world were released. The revised and updated poverty data are also available in the World Development Indicators online tables and database.

As in previous rounds, the new poverty estimates combine purchasing power parity (PPP) exchange rates for household consumption from the 2005 International Comparison Program with income and consumption data from primary household surveys. The 2015 projections use the newly released 2011 estimates as the baseline and assumes that mean household income or consumption will grow in line with the aggregate economic projections reported in *Global Economic Prospects 2014* (World Bank 2014) and that inequality within countries will remain unchanged. Estimates of the number of people living in extreme poverty use population projections in the World Bank's HealthStats database (http://datatopics.worldbank.org/hnp).

PovcalNet (http://iresearch.worldbank.org/PovcalNet) is an interactive computational tool that allows users to replicate these internationally comparable $1.25 and $2 a day poverty estimates for countries, developing country regions, and the developing world as a whole and to compute poverty measures for custom country groupings and for different poverty lines. The Poverty and Equity Data portal (http://povertydata.worldbank.org/poverty/home) provides access to the database and user-friendly dashboards with graphs and interactive maps that visualize trends in key poverty and inequality indicators for different regions and countries. The country dashboards display trends in poverty measures based on the national poverty lines (see online table 2.7) alongside the internationally comparable estimates in the table produced from and consistent with PovcalNet.

Data availability

The World Bank's internationally comparable poverty monitoring database draws on income or detailed consumption data from more than 1,000 household surveys across 128 developing countries and 21 high-income countries (as defined in 1990). For high-income countries, estimates are available for inequality and income distribution only. The 2011 estimates use more than million randomly sampled households, representing 85 percent of the population in developing countries. Despite progress in the last decade, the challenges of measuring poverty remain. The timeliness, frequency, accessibility, quality, and comparability of household surveys need to increase substantially, particularly in the poorest countries. The availability and quality of poverty monitoring data remain low in small states, fragile situations, and low-income countries and even in some middle-income countries.

The low frequency and lack of comparability of the data available in some countries create uncertainty over the magnitude of poverty reduction. The table on trends in poverty indicators reports the percentage of the regional and global population represented by household survey samples collected during the reference year or during the two preceding or two subsequent years (in other words, within a five-year window centered on the reference year). Data coverage in Sub-Saharan Africa and the Middle East and North Africa remains low and variable. The need to improve household survey programs for monitoring poverty is clearly urgent. But institutional, political, and financial obstacles continue to limit data collection, analysis, and public access.

Data quality

Besides the frequency and timeliness of survey data, other data quality issues arise in measuring household living standards. The surveys ask detailed questions on sources of income and how it was spent, which must be carefully recorded by trained personnel. Income is generally more difficult to measure accurately, and consumption comes closer to the notion of living standards. Moreover, income can vary over time even if living standards do not. But consumption data are not always available: the latest estimates reported here use consumption for about two-thirds of countries.

However, even similar surveys may not be strictly comparable because of differences in timing, sampling frames, or the quality and training of enumerators. Comparisons of countries at different levels of development also pose a potential problem because of differences in the relative importance of the consumption of nonmarket goods. The local market value of all consumption in kind (including own production, particularly important in underdeveloped rural economies) should be included in total consumption expenditure, but in practice are often not. Most survey data now include valuations for consumption or income from own production, but valuation methods vary.

The statistics reported here are based on consumption data or, when unavailable, on income data. Analysis of some 20 countries for which both consumption and income data were available from the same surveys found income to yield a higher mean than consumption but also higher inequality. When poverty measures based on consumption and income were compared, the two effects roughly cancelled each other out: there was no significant statistical difference.

Invariably some sampled households do not participate in surveys because they refuse to do so or because nobody is at home during the interview visit. This is referred to as "unit nonresponse" and is distinct from "item nonresponse," which occurs when some of the sampled respondents participate but refuse to answer certain questions, such as those pertaining to income or consumption. To the extent that survey nonresponse is random, there is no concern regarding biases in survey-based inferences; the sample will still be representative of

 Front User guide World view People Environment

the population. However, households with different income might not be equally likely to respond. Richer households may be less likely to participate because of the high opportunity cost of their time or concerns because of privacy concerns. It is conceivable that the poorest can likewise be underrepresented; some are homeless or nomadic and hard to reach in standard household survey designs, and some may be physically or socially isolated and thus less likely to be interviewed. This can bias both poverty and inequality measurement if not corrected for (Korinek, Mistiaen, and Ravallion 2007).

International poverty lines

International comparisons of poverty estimates entail both conceptual and practical problems. Countries have different definitions of poverty, and consistent comparisons across countries can be difficult. National poverty lines tend to have higher purchasing power in rich countries, where more generous standards are used, than in poor countries. Poverty measures based on an international poverty line attempt to hold the real value of the poverty line constant across countries, as is done when making comparisons over time. Since *World Development Report 1990* the World Bank has aimed to apply a common standard in measuring extreme poverty, anchored to what *poverty* means in the world's poorest countries. The welfare of people living in different countries can be measured on a common scale by adjusting for differences in the purchasing power of currencies. The commonly used $1 a day standard, measured in 1985 international prices and adjusted to local currency using PPPs, was chosen for *World Development Report 1990* because it was typical of the poverty lines in low-income countries at the time.

Early editions of *World Development Indicators* used PPPs from the Penn World Tables to convert values in local currency to equivalent purchasing power measured in U.S dollars. Later editions used 1993 consumption PPP estimates produced by the World Bank. International poverty lines were revised following the release of PPPs compiled in the 2005 round of the International Comparison Program, along with data from an expanded set of household income and expenditure surveys. The current extreme poverty line is set at $1.25 a day in 2005 PPP terms, which represents the mean of the poverty lines found in the poorest 15 countries ranked by per capita consumption (Ravallion, Chen, and Sangraula 2009). This poverty line maintains the same standard for extreme poverty—the poverty line typical of the poorest countries in the world—but updates it using the latest information on the cost of living in developing countries. The international poverty line will be updated again later this year using the PPP estimates from the 2011 round of the International Comparison Program.

PPP exchange rates are used to estimate global poverty because they take into account the local prices of goods and services not traded internationally. But PPP rates were designed for comparing aggregates from national accounts, not for making international poverty comparisons. As a result, there is no certainty that an international poverty line measures the same degree of need or deprivation across countries. So-called poverty PPPs, designed to compare the consumption of the poorest people in the world, might provide a better basis for comparison of poverty across countries. Work on these measures is ongoing.

Definitions

• **International poverty line in local currency** is the international poverty lines of $1.25 and $2.00 a day in 2005 prices, converted to local currency using the PPP conversion factors estimated by the International Comparison Program. • **Reference year** is the period of reference of a survey. For surveys in which the period of reference covers multiple years, it is the year with the majority of the survey respondents. For surveys in which the period of reference is half in one year and half in another, it is the first year. • **Population below $1.25 a day** and **population below $2 a day** are the percentages of the population living on less than $1.25 a day and $2 a day at 2005 international prices. As a result of revisions in PPP exchange rates, consumer price indexes, or welfare aggregates, poverty rates for individual countries cannot be compared with poverty rates reported in earlier editions. The PovcalNet online database and tool (http://iresearch.worldbank.org/PovcalNet) always contain the most recent full time series of comparable country data. • **Poverty gap** is the mean shortfall from the poverty line (counting the nonpoor as having zero shortfall), expressed as a percentage of the poverty line. This measure reflects the depth of poverty as well as its incidence.

Data sources

The poverty measures are prepared by the World Bank's Development Research Group. The international poverty lines are based on nationally representative primary household surveys conducted by national statistical offices or by private agencies under the supervision of government or international agencies and obtained from government statistical offices and World Bank Group country departments. For details on data sources and methods used in deriving the World Bank's latest estimates, see http://iresearch.worldbank.org/povcalnet.

References

Chen, Shaohua, and Martin Ravallion. 2011. "The Developing World Is Poorer Than We Thought, But No Less Successful in the Fight Against Poverty." *Quarterly Journal of Economics* 125(4): 1577–1625.

Korinek, Anton, Johan A. Mistiaen, and Martin Ravallion. 2007. "An Econometric Method of Correcting for Unit Nonresponse Bias in Surveys." *Journal of Econometrics* 136: 213–35.

Ravallion, Martin, Guarav Datt, and Dominique van de Walle. 1991. "Quantifying Absolute Poverty in the Developing World." *Review of Income and Wealth* 37(4): 345–61.

Ravallion, Martin, Shaohua Chen, and Prem Sangraula. 2009. "Dollar a Day Revisited." *World Bank Economic Review* 23(2): 163–84.

World Bank. 1990. *World Development Report 1990: Poverty.* Washington, DC.

———. 2014. *Global Economic Prospects: Coping with Policy Normalization in High-income Countries.* Volume 8, January 14. Washington, DC.

Shared prosperity

	Period		Annualized growth of survey mean income or consumption per capita		Survey mean income or consumption per capita			
			%		2005 PPP $ a day			
			Bottom 40% of the population	Total population	Bottom 40% of the population		Total population	
	Baseline year	Most recent year			Baseline	Most recent	Baseline	Most recent
Albania	2008	2012	−1.2	−1.3	3.5	3.3	6.3	6.0
Argentina	2006	2011	6.5	3.4	4.0	5.4	13.0	15.3
Armenia	2006	2011	0.5	0.0	2.0	2.0	3.8	3.8
Bangladesh	2005	2010	1.8	1.4	0.8	0.9	1.6	1.7
Belarus	2006	2011	9.1	8.1	6.3	9.8	11.3	16.7
Bhutan	2007	2012	6.5	6.4	1.6	2.2	3.7	5.1
Bolivia	2006	2011	12.8	4.0	1.6	2.9	7.3	8.9
Botswana	2003	2009	5.3	2.1	1.1	1.6	6.4	7.4
Brazil	2006	2011	5.8	3.6	2.6	3.5	10.7	12.7
Bulgaria	2007	2011	1.4	0.5	4.9	5.2	10.7	10.8
Cambodia	2007	2011	9.2	3.0	1.1	1.5	2.5	2.8
Chile	2006	2011	3.9	2.8	4.4	5.4	14.7	16.9
China	2005	2010	7.2	7.9	1.3	1.9	3.6	5.3
Colombia	2008	2011	8.8	5.6	2.1	2.7	8.8	10.4
Congo, Rep.	2005	2011	7.3	4.3	0.6	0.9	1.8	2.3
Costa Rica	2004	2009	5.5	6.3	3.2	4.2	10.6	14.4
Czech Republic	2006	2011	1.8	1.8	12.2	13.4	20.5	22.4
Dominican Republic	2006	2011	2.3	−0.6	2.6	2.9	8.8	8.6
Ecuador	2006	2011	4.4	0.5	2.5	3.1	8.8	9.0
El Salvador	2006	2011	1.1	−0.6	2.5	2.7	7.1	6.9
Estonia	2005	2010	4.1	3.7	7.1	8.7	14.3	17.1
Ethiopia	2005	2010	−0.4	1.4	1.0	0.9	1.7	1.8
Georgia	2007	2012	0.7	1.5	1.4	1.5	3.5	3.8
Guatemala	2006	2011	−1.9	−4.6	1.7	1.5	6.5	5.2
Honduras	2006	2011	4.1	2.2	1.2	1.4	5.6	6.2
Hungary	2006	2011	−0.5	−0.2	8.3	8.0	14.7	14.6
India	2004	2011	3.3	3.8	0.9	1.2	1.8	2.3
Iraq	2007	2012	0.3	1.0	1.9	1.9	3.3	3.5
Jordan	2006	2010	2.8	2.6	3.2	3.6	6.4	7.1
Kazakhstan	2006	2010	6.2	5.4	3.2	4.0	5.7	7.1
Kyrgyz Republic	2006	2011	5.8	2.5	1.4	1.9	3.4	3.8
Lao PDR	2007	2012	1.4	2.0	1.0	1.0	2.0	2.2
Latvia	2006	2011	0.4	0.4	6.3	6.4	13.7	14.0
Lithuania	2006	2011	1.1	0.7	6.9	7.3	14.2	14.7
Madagascar	2005	2010	−4.5	−3.5	0.4	0.3	0.9	0.8
Malawi	2004	2010	−1.5	1.8	0.5	0.5	1.1	1.2
Mali	2006	2010	2.3	−1.5	0.7	0.8	1.6	1.5
Mauritius	2007	2012	0.0	0.0	3.9	3.9	8.1	8.2
Mexico	2006	2010	0.4	−0.3	3.6	3.6	10.8	10.6
Moldova	2006	2011	5.7	2.9	2.6	3.4	5.4	6.3
Montenegro	2006	2011	2.5	2.8	4.5	5.1	8.3	9.6
Mozambique	2002	2009	3.8	3.7	0.4	0.6	1.2	1.5
Namibia	2004	2009	3.4	1.9	1.0	1.2	4.8	5.4
Nepal	2003	2010	7.3	3.7	0.7	1.2	1.8	2.3
Nicaragua	2005	2009	4.8	1.0	1.6	1.9	5.3	5.5
Nigeria	2004	2010	−0.3	0.8	0.5	0.5	1.3	1.4
Pakistan	2005	2010	3.0	1.8	1.2	1.4	2.2	2.4

	Period		Annualized growth of survey mean income or consumption per capita		Survey mean income or consumption per capita			
			%		2005 PPP $ a day			
			Bottom 40% of the population	Total population	Bottom 40% of the population		Total population	
	Baseline year	Most recent year			Baseline	Most recent	Baseline	Most recent
Panama	2008	2011	5.4	4.3	3.2	3.8	12.0	13.6
Paraguay	2006	2011	7.5	7.3	2.1	3.0	7.8	11.1
Peru	2006	2011	8.0	6.1	2.3	3.3	7.4	10.0
Philippines	2006	2012	1.4	0.7	1.2	1.3	3.3	3.4
Poland	2006	2011	3.3	2.8	5.3	6.2	10.7	12.3
Romania	2006	2011	5.8	4.3	3.0	4.0	5.6	7.0
Russian Federation	2004	2009	9.6	8.2	4.0	6.2	9.9	14.6
Rwanda	2006	2011	4.6	3.4	0.5	0.6	1.5	1.7
Senegal	2006	2011	−0.2	0.3	0.9	0.9	2.2	2.2
Serbia	2007	2010	−1.7	−1.3	5.7	5.4	10.4	10.0
Slovak Republic	2006	2011	8.4	9.3	8.9	13.4	14.8	23.1
Slovenia	2006	2011	1.5	1.6	17.1	18.4	27.9	30.2
South Africa	2006	2011	4.3	3.6	1.4	1.8	8.7	10.5
Sri Lanka	2006	2009	3.0	−0.4	1.7	1.9	3.9	3.9
Tajikistan	2004	2009	6.1	4.9	1.2	1.6	2.5	3.1
Tanzania	2007	2012	9.8	9.1	0.5	0.9	1.2	1.8
Thailand	2006	2010	4.3	2.2	2.7	3.2	6.9	7.5
Togo	2006	2011	−2.1	1.0	0.7	0.6	1.7	1.8
Tunisia	2005	2010	3.5	2.6	2.9	3.4	6.6	7.5
Turkey	2006	2011	5.4	5.1	3.6	4.6	8.8	11.3
Uganda	2005	2012	3.5	4.4	0.7	0.9	1.7	2.3
Ukraine	2005	2010	5.2	3.1	5.0	6.5	9.0	10.5
Uruguay	2006	2011	8.4	6.1	3.9	5.9	12.0	16.1
Vietnam	2004	2010	6.2	7.8	1.4	2.0	3.3	5.1
West Bank and Gaza	2004	2009	2.3	2.3	4.4	4.9	9.0	10.0

Shared prosperity

The World Bank Group released the Global Database of Shared Prosperity in October 2014, a year and half after announcing its new twin goals of ending extreme poverty and promoting shared prosperity around the world. It contains data for monitoring the goal of promoting shared prosperity that have been published in the World Development Indicators online tables and database and are now featured in this edition of *World Development Indicators*.

Promoting shared prosperity is defined as fostering income growth of the bottom 40 percent of the welfare distribution in every country and is measured by calculating the annualized growth of mean per capita real income or consumption of the bottom 40 percent. The choice of the bottom 40 percent as the target population is one of practical compromise. The bottom 40 percent differs across countries depending on the welfare distribution, and it can change over time within a country. Because boosting shared prosperity is a country-specific goal, there is no numerical target defined globally. And at the country level the shared prosperity goal is unbounded.

Improvements in shared prosperity require both a growing economy and a consideration for equity. Shared prosperity explicitly recognizes that while growth is necessary for improving economic welfare in a society, progress is measured by how those gains are shared with its poorest members. It also recognizes that for prosperity to be truly shared in a society, it is not sufficient to raise everyone above an absolute minimum standard of living. Rather, for a society that seeks to become more inclusive, the goal is to ensure that economic progress increases prosperity among the poorer members of society over time.

The decision to measure shared prosperity based on income or consumption was not taken to ignore the many other dimensions of welfare. It is motivated by the need for an indicator that is easy to understand, communicate, and measure—though measurement challenges exist. Indeed, shared prosperity comprises many dimensions of well-being of the less well-off, and when analyzing shared prosperity in the context of a country, it is important to consider a wide range of indicators of welfare.

To generate measures of shared prosperity that are reasonably comparable across countries, the World Bank Group has a standardized approach for choosing time periods, data sources, and other relevant parameters. The Global Database of Shared Prosperity is the result of these efforts. Its purpose is to allow for cross-country comparison and benchmarking, but users should consider alternative choices for surveys and time periods when cross-country comparison is not the primary consideration.

The indicators from the database in this edition of *World Development Indicators* are survey mean per capita real income or consumption of the bottom 40 percent, survey mean per capita real income or consumption of the total population, annualized growth of survey mean per capita real income or consumption of the bottom 40 percent, and annualized growth of survey mean per capita real income or consumption of the total population. Related information, such

as survey years defining the growth period and the type of welfare aggregate used to calculate the growth rates, are provided in the footnotes.

The World Bank Group is committed to updating the shared prosperity indicators every year. Given that new household surveys are not available every year for most countries, updated estimates will be reported only for a subset of countries each year.

Calculation of growth rates

Growth rates are calculated as annualized average growth rates over a roughly five-year period. Since many countries do not conduct surveys on a precise five-year schedule, the following rules guide selection of the survey years used to calculate the growth rates: the final year of the growth period (T_1) is the most recent year of a survey but no earlier than 2009, and the initial year (T_0) is as close to $T_1 - 5$ as possible, within a two-year band. Thus the gap between initial and final survey years ranges from three to seven years. If two surveys are equidistant from $T_1 - 5$, other things being equal, the more recent survey year is selected as T_0. The comparability of welfare aggregates (income or consumption) for the years chosen for T_0 and T_1 is assessed for every country. If comparability across the two surveys is a major concern, the selection criteria are re-applied to select the next best survey year.

Once two surveys are selected for a country, the annualized growth of mean per capita real income or consumption is computed by first estimating the mean per capita real income or consumption of the bottom 40 percent of the welfare distribution in years T_0 and T_1 and then computing the annual average growth rate between those years using a compound growth formula. Growth of mean per capita real income or consumption of the total population is computed in the same way using data for the total population.

Data availability

This edition of World Development Indicators includes estimates of shared prosperity for 72 developing countries. While all countries are encouraged to estimate the annualized growth of mean per capita real income or consumption of the bottom 40 percent, the Global Database of Shared Prosperity includes only a subset of countries that meet certain criteria. The first important consideration is comparability across time and across countries. Household surveys are infrequent in most countries and are rarely aligned across countries in terms of timing. Consequently, comparisons across countries or over time should be made with a high degree of caution.

The second consideration is the coverage of countries, with data that are as recent as possible. Since shared prosperity must be estimated and used at the country level, there are good reasons for obtaining a wide coverage of countries, regardless of the size of their population. Moreover, for policy purposes it is important to have indicators for the most recent period possible for each country. The selection of survey years and countries needs to be made consistently and transparently, achieving a balance among matching

About the data

the time period as closely as possible across all countries, including the most recent data, and ensuring the widest possible coverage of countries, across regions and income levels. In practice, this means that time periods will not match perfectly across countries. This is a compromise: While it introduces a degree of incomparability, it also creates a database that includes a larger set of countries than would be possible otherwise.

Data quality

Like poverty rate estimates, estimates of annualized growth of mean per capita real income or consumption of the bottom 40 percent are based on income or consumption data collected in household surveys, and the same quality issues apply. See the discussion in the *Poverty rates* section.

Definitions

• **Period** is the period of reference of a survey. For surveys in which the period of reference covers multiple years, it is the year with the majority of the survey respondents. For surveys in which the period of reference is half in one year and half in another, it is the first year.
• **Annualized growth of survey mean per capita real income or consumption** is the annualized growth in mean per capita real income consumption from household surveys over a roughly five-year period. It is calculated for the bottom 40 percent of a country's population and for the total population of a country. • **Survey mean per capita real consumption or income** is the mean income or consumption per capita from household surveys used in calculating the welfare growth rate, expressed in purchasing power parity (PPP)–adjusted dollars per day at 2005 prices. It is calculated for the bottom 40 percent of a country's population and for the total population of a country.

Data sources

The Global Database of Shared Prosperity was prepared by the Global Poverty Working Group, which comprises poverty measurement specialists of different departments of the World Bank Group. The database's primary source of data is the World Bank Group's PovcalNet database, an interactive computational tool that allows users to replicate the World Bank Group's official poverty estimates measured at international poverty lines ($1.25 or $2 per day per capita). The datasets included in PovcalNet are provided and reviewed by the members of the Global Poverty Working Group. The choice of consumption or income to measure shared prosperity for a country is consistent with the welfare aggregate used to estimate extreme poverty rates in PovcalNet, unless there are strong arguments for using a different welfare aggregate. The practice adopted by the World Bank Group for estimating global and regional poverty rates is, in principle, to use per capita consumption expenditure as the welfare measure wherever available and to use income as the welfare measure for countries for which consumption data are unavailable. However, in some cases data on consumption may be available but are outdated or not shared with the World Bank Group for recent survey years. In these cases, if data on income are available, income is used for estimating shared prosperity.

References

Ambar, Narayan, Jaime Saavedra-Chanduvi, and Sailesh Tiwari. 2013. "Shared Prosperity: Links to Growth, Inequality and Inequality of Opportunity." Policy Research Working Paper 6649. World Bank, Washington, DC.

World Bank. 2014a. "A Measured Approach to Ending Poverty and Boosting Shared Prosperity: Concepts, Data, and the Twin Goals." Washington, DC.

———. 2014b. Global Database of Shared Prosperity. [http://www.worldbank.org/en/topic/poverty/brief/global-database-of-shared-prosperity]. Washington, DC.

———. Various years. PovcalNet. [http://iresearch.worldbank.org/PovcalNet/]. Washington, DC.

PEOPLE

The *People* section presents indicators of education, health, jobs, social protection, and gender, complementing other important indicators of human development presented in *World view,* such as population, poverty, and shared prosperity. Together, they provide a multidimensional portrait of societal progress.

Many of these indicators are also used for monitoring the Millennium Development Goals. Over the last 15 years data for estimating these indicators have been collected and compiled through the efforts of national authorities and various international development agencies, including the World Bank, working together in the Inter-agency and Expert Group organized by the United Nations Statistics Division and in several thematic interagency groups.

These groups have made international development statistics more readily available and consistent, over time and between countries. For example, estimates of child mortality used to vary by data source and by methodology, making their interpretation for global monitoring purposes difficult. The United Nations Inter-agency Group for Child Mortality Estimation, established in 2004, has addressed this issue by compiling all available data, assessing data quality, and fitting an appropriate statistical model to generate a smooth trend curve. This effort has produced harmonized and good quality estimates of neonatal, infant, and under-five mortality rates that span more than 50 years. Similar interagency efforts have also been made to improve maternal mortality estimates. In gender statistics, the World Bank is contributing to the work to obtain better estimates of female asset ownership and entrepreneurship, and a minimum set of gender indicators has been endorsed by the United Nations Statistics Commission to help focus national efforts to produce, compile, and disseminate relevant data.

People includes indicators disaggregated by socioeconomic and demographic variables, such as sex, age, and wealth. This year, some indicators such as malnutrition and poverty are available disaggregated by subnational location at http://data.worldbank.org/data-catalog/sub-national-poverty-data. These data provide important perspectives on disparities within countries, and *World Development Indicators* will continue to expand coverage in this direction, wherever data sources permit.

An important new addition this year is an indicator for monitoring the World Bank Group's new goal of promoting shared prosperity. This is detailed further in *World view* and available at www.worldbank.org/en/topic/poverty/brief/global-database-of-shared-prosperity. Other new indicators include the share of the youth population that is not in education, employment, or training and the share of students who obtained the lowest levels of proficiency on the Organisation for Economic Co-operation and Development's Program for International Student Assessment scores in mathematics, reading, and science, which serves to improve coverage of the outcomes of education systems.

Highlights

Pupil–teacher ratios in primary education are improving very slowly

Pupil–teacher ratio, primary education

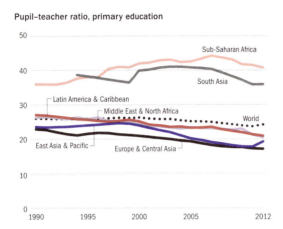

While substantial progress has been made in achieving universal primary education, pupil–teacher ratios, an important indicator of the quality of education, have shown only slight improvement, declining from a global average of 26 in 1990 to 24 in 2012. In Sub-Saharan Africa the average pupil–teacher ratio rose from 36 in 1990 to 41 in 2012, indicating that the increase in the number of teachers is not keeping pace with the increase in primary enrollment. South Asia's average pupil–teacher ratio (36) also remains far above the world average. However, there has been a steady improvement in both regions in recent years. Although East Asia and Pacific has reduced its pupil–teacher ratio remarkably since 2000, there was an increasing trend in 2012, due mainly to an increase in the ratio in China.

Source: United Nations Educational, Scientific and Cultural Organization Institute for Statistics and online table 2.10.

The adolescent fertility rate declines as more women attend secondary education

Adolescent fertility rate (births per 1,000 women ages 15–19)

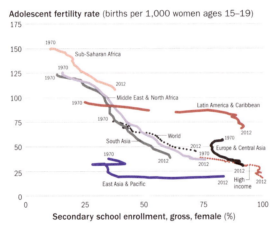

Secondary school enrollment, gross, female (%)

Teenage women are less likely to become mothers when they attend secondary school. Globally, the adolescent fertility rate declined from 77 per 1,000 women ages 15–19 in 1970 to 45 in 2012, while female secondary school enrollment increased from 35 percent to 72 percent. The relationship between the two tends to be similar across regions, except for Latin America and the Caribbean and East Asia and Pacific, where the correlation is much weaker. Both the Middle East and North Africa and South Asia saw large drops in adolescent fertility rates as secondary education has expanded. The rates in the Middle East and North Africa and South Asia in 2012 are similar to those in high-income countries in 1970. Sub-Saharan Africa has the highest adolescent fertility rate and the lowest female secondary gross enrollment ratio.

Source: United Nations Population Division, United Nations Educational, Scientific and Cultural Organization Institute for Statistics, and online tables 2.11 and 2.17.

Growth in many countries between 2006 and 2011 seems to be inclusive

Annualized growth of mean per capita income or consumption of the bottom 40 percent of the population (%)

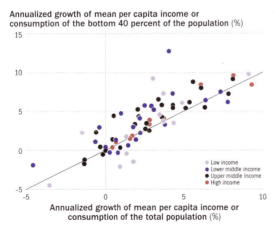

Annualized growth of mean per capita income or consumption of the total population (%)

Many countries have seen growth in income or consumption among the bottom 40 percent of the population in their welfare distribution between 2006 and 2011. The bottom 40 percent fared better in middle- and high-income countries than in low-income countries. The median annualized growth of mean per capita income or consumption of the bottom 40 percent was 3.9 percent in middle- and high-income countries, 0.4 percentage point higher than in low-income countries. Furthermore, growth was more inclusive in richer countries. In particular, the annualized growth of mean per capita income or consumption was faster for the bottom 40 percent than for the total population in 7 of 9 high-income countries (78 percent), 20 of 26 upper middle-income countries (77 percent), 16 of 22 lower middle-income countries (73 percent), and 8 of 13 low-income countries (62 percent).

Source: World Bank Global Database of Shared Prosperity and online table 2.9.2.

Large rich-poor gap in contraceptive use in Sub-Saharan Africa

The contraceptive prevalence rate is an important indicator of the success of family planning programs. While most regions have attained a contraceptive prevalence rate of more than 50 percent (80 percent in East Asia and Pacific and 64 percent in the Middle East and North Africa), Sub-Saharan Africa's rate remains at less than 25 percent, with a wide gap between the rich and the poor. Nine of the ten countries with the widest rich-poor gap are in Sub-Saharan Africa. In Cameroon and Nigeria the contraceptive prevalence rate is less than 3 percent among women in the poorest quintile and over 36 percent among women in the richest quintile. Contraceptive use among women in poor families is low in nearly all countries across Sub-Saharan Africa.

Contraceptive prevalence rate among countries with the widest rich-poor gaps, most recent year available during 2008–14 (%)

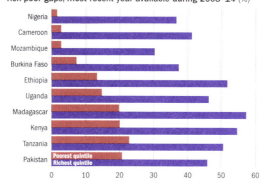

Source: United Nations Children's Fund, household surveys (including Demographic and Health Surveys and Multiple Indicator Cluster Surveys), and online table 2.22.3.

Labor force participation is lowest in the Middle East and North Africa

Labor force participation rates—the proportion of the population ages 15 and older that engages actively in the labor market, by either working or looking for work—are higher in East Asia and Pacific and Sub-Saharan Africa than in other regions. In contrast, in the Middle East and North Africa less than 50 percent of the working-age population is in the labor force, lower than in any other region. This is driven largely by low female participation. A low labor force participation rate typically results from a host of obstacles that prevent people from entering the labor market. The region has a large number of unemployed people, and high unemployment rates could be another reason that discourages people from seeking work. Only 41 percent of the working-age population in the Middle East and North Africa is employed.

Labor force status, 2013 (% of population ages 15 and older)
■ Employed ■ Unemployed ■ Not in the labor force

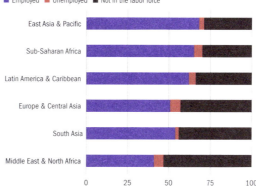

Source: International Labour Organization' Key Indicators of the Labour Market, 8th edition, database and online tables 2.2, 2.4, and 2.5.

Women occupy few top management positions in developing countries

Women's participation in economic activities, particularly in business leadership roles as the top managers in firms, highlights their economic empowerment and advancement. Globally the share of firms with female top managers is low, at about 20 percent. The highest share is in East Asia and Pacific (almost 30 percent); the lowest is in the Middle East and North Africa (less than 5 percent) and South Asia (almost 9 percent). These statistics do not fully describe women-led firms, which tend to be smaller than male-led firms and concentrated in such areas as retail businesses (Amin and Islam 2014). These statistics are based on World Bank Enterprise Surveys, which collect data from registered firms with five or more employees and thus exclude small informal firms, which are believed to be important for women.

Share of firms with a female top manager (%)

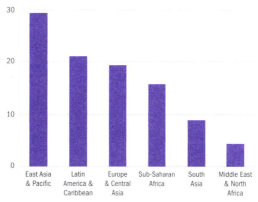

Source: World Bank Enterprise Surveys and online table 5.2.

The under-five mortality rate is the probability of dying between birth and exactly 5 years of age, expressed per 1,000 live births. It is a key indicator of child well-being, including health and nutrition status. Also, it is among the indicators most frequently used to compare socioeconomic development across countries. The world has made substantial progress, reducing the rate from 183 deaths per 1,000 live births in 1960 to 90 deaths in 1990 to 46 deaths in 2013. Despite this progress, 6.3 million children still died before their fifth birthday in 2013—roughly 17,000 a day—mostly from preventable causes and treatable diseases. The number of child deaths has been falling in every region, but the reduction is slowest in Sub-Saharan Africa. In 2013 around 44 percent of under-five deaths occurred during the first 28 days of life—the neonatal period—which is the most vulnerable time for a child.

Child mortality

UNDER-FIVE MORTALITY RATE
PER 1,000 LIVE BIRTHS, 2013

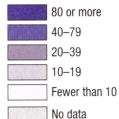

- 80 or more
- 40–79
- 20–39
- 10–19
- Fewer than 10
- No data

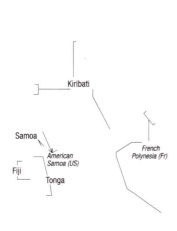

Caribbean inset

IBRD 41451

 Front | User guide | World view | People | Environment

Twelve countries have an under-five mortality rate above
100 deaths per 1,000 live births: Angola, Sierra Leone, Chad, Somalia, Central African Republic, Guinea-Bissau, Mali, the Democratic Republic of the Congo, Nigeria, Niger, Guinea, and Côte d'Ivoire.

The highest under-five mortality rates are in Sub-Saharan
Africa (92 deaths per 1,000 live births) and South Asia (57), compared with 20 in East Asia and Pacific, 23 in Europe and Central Asia, 18 in Latin America and the Caribbean, 26 in the Middle East and North Africa, and 6 in high-income countries.

About half of under-five deaths worldwide occur in only
five countries: India, Nigeria, Pakistan, the Democratic Republic of the Congo, and China.

On average, 1 in 11 children born in Sub-Saharan Africa
dies before age 5.

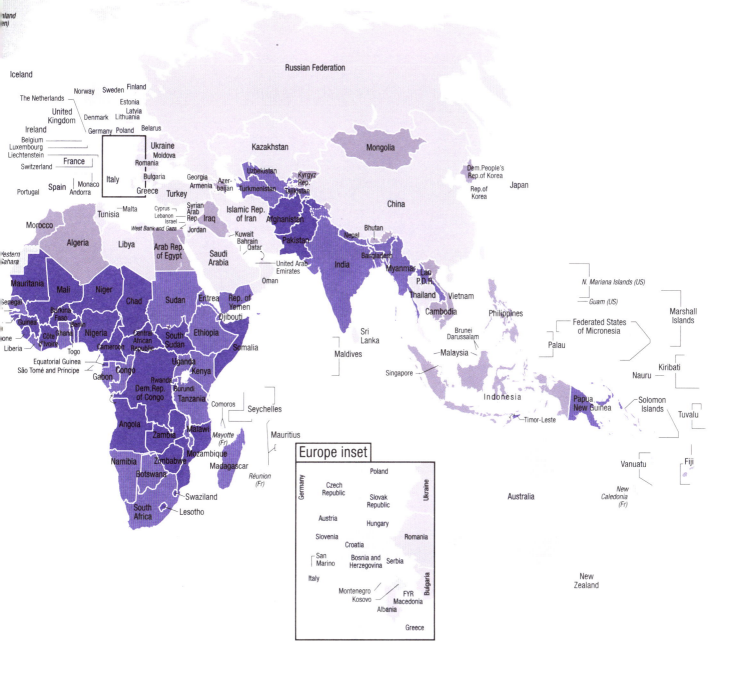

2 People

	Prevalence of child malnutrition, underweight % of children under age 5 2007–13ᵃ	Under-five mortality rate per 1,000 live births 2013	Maternal mortality ratio Modeled estimate per 100,000 live births 2013	Adolescent fertility rate births per 1,000 women ages 15–19 2013	Prevalence of HIV % of population ages 15–49 2013	Primary completion rate % of relevant age group 2009–13ᵃ	Youth literacy rate % of population ages 15–24 2005–13ᵃ	Labor force participation rate Modeled ILO estimate % of population ages 15 and older 2013	Vulnerable employment Unpaid family workers and own-account workers % of total employment 2009–13ᵃ	Unemployment Modeled ILO estimate % of total labor force 2013	Female legislators, senior officials, and managers % of total 2009–13ᵃ
Afghanistan	..	97	400	83	<0.1	..	47	48	..	8	..
Albania	6.3	15	21	14	<0.1	..	99	55	58	16	22
Algeria	..	25	89	10	0.1	100	92	44	27	10	11
American Samoa	..	..	..	..	..	..	..	..	..	..	..
Andorra	..	3	..	..	..	..	..	..	..	..	..
Angola	15.6	167	460	167	2.4	54	73	70	..	7	..
Antigua and Barbuda	..	9	..	48	..	100	..	..	..	..	..
Argentina	..	13	69	54	..	110	99	61	19	8	..
Armenia	5.3	16	29	27	0.2	..	100	63	30	16	..
Aruba	..	..	..	25	..	95	99	..	..	..	43
Australia	0.2	4	6	11	0.2	..	..	65	..	6	..
Austria	..	4	4	3	..	97	..	61	9	5	27
Azerbaijan	..	34	26	39	0.2	92	100	66	56	6	..
Bahamas, The	..	13	37	28	3.2	93	..	74	..	14	52
Bahrain	..	6	22	14	..	..	98	70	2	7	..
Bangladesh	31.9	41	170	79	<0.1	75	80	71	..	4	5
Barbados	3.5	14	52	48	0.9	104	..	71	..	12	48
Belarus	..	5	1	20	0.5	100	100	56	2	6	46
Belgium	..	4	6	6	..	90	..	53	11	8	30
Belize	6.2	17	45	70	1.5	109	..	66	..	15	..
Benin	..	85	340	88	1.1	76	42	73	..	1	..
Bermuda	..	..	..	..	..	88	..	..	..	..	44
Bhutan	12.8	36	120	40	0.1	98	74	73	53	2	17
Bolivia	4.5	39	200	71	0.3	89	99	73	55	3	35
Bosnia and Herzegovina	1.5	7	8	15	..	..	100	45	25	28	..
Botswana	11.2	47	170	43	21.9	95	96	77	13	18	39
Brazil	2.2	14	69	70	0.6	..	99	70	25	6	..
Brunei Darussalam	..	10	27	23	..	98	100	64	..	4	..
Bulgaria	..	12	5	34	..	98	98	53	8	13	37
Burkina Faso	26.2	98	400	112	0.9	63	39	83	..	3	..
Burundi	29.1	83	740	30	1.0	70	89	83	..	7	..
Cabo Verde	..	26	53	69	0.5	95	98	68	..	7	..
Cambodia	29.0	38	170	44	0.7	97	87	83	64	0	..
Cameroon	15.1	95	590	113	4.3	73	81	70	76	4	..
Canada	..	5	11	14	..	..	..	66	..	7	..
Cayman Islands	..	..	..	..	..	..	99	..	..	..	..
Central African Republic	23.5	139	880	97	3.8	45	36	79	..	8	..
Chad	30.3	148	980	147	2.5	39	49	72	..	7	..
Channel Islands	..	..	..	8	..	..	..	..	..	..	..
Chile	0.5	8	22	55	0.3	97	99	62	..	6	..
China	3.4	13	32	9	..	..	100	71	..	5	..
Hong Kong SAR, China	..	..	..	3	..	96	..	59	7	3	32
Macao SAR, China	..	..	..	4	..	..	100	72	4	2	32
Colombia	3.4	17	83	68	0.5	113	98	67	49	11	53
Comoros	16.9	78	350	50	..	74	86	58	..	7	..
Congo, Dem. Rep.	23.4	119	730	134	1.1	73	66	72	..	8	..
Congo, Rep.	11.8	49	410	125	2.5	73	81	71	..	7	..

 Front User guide World view People | Environment

	Prevalence of child malnutrition, underweight % of children under age 5 2007–13[a]	Under-five mortality rate per 1,000 live births 2013	Maternal mortality ratio Modeled estimate per 100,000 live births 2013	Adolescent fertility rate births per 1,000 women ages 15–19 2013	Prevalence of HIV % of population ages 15–49 2013	Primary completion rate % of relevant age group 2009–13[a]	Youth literacy rate % of population ages 15–24 2005–13[a]	Labor force participation rate Modeled ILO estimate % of population ages 15 and older 2013	Vulnerable employment Unpaid family workers and own-account workers % of total employment 2009–13[a]	Unemployment Modeled ILO estimate % of total labor force 2013	Female legislators, senior officials, and managers % of total 2009–13[a]
Costa Rica	1.1	10	38	60	0.2	90	99	63	20	8	35
Côte d'Ivoire	15.7	100	720	126	2.7	60	48	67	..	4	..
Croatia	..	5	13	13	..	93	100	51	14	18	25
Cuba	..	6	80	43	0.2	93	100	57	..	3	..
Curaçao	..	..	..	27	..	..	..	..	..	..	..
Cyprus	..	4	10	5	<0.1	100	100	64	14	16	14
Czech Republic	..	4	5	5	<0.1	102	..	60	15	7	26
Denmark	..	4	5	5	0.2	99	..	63	6	7	28
Djibouti	29.8	70	230	18	0.9	61[b]	..	52	..	..	..
Dominica	..	11	..	..	..	103	..	..	..	..	..
Dominican Republic	4.0	28	100	98	0.7	90	97	65	37	15	37
Ecuador	6.4	23	87	76	0.4	111	99	69	51	4	40
Egypt, Arab Rep.	6.8	22	45	42	<0.1	107	89	49	26	13	7
El Salvador	6.6	16	69	75	0.5	101	97	62	38	6	37
Equatorial Guinea	5.6	96	290	111	..	55	98	87	..	8	..
Eritrea	38.8	50	380	63	0.6	..	91	85	..	7	..
Estonia	..	3	11	16	1.3	96	100	62	5	9	36
Ethiopia	25.2[b]	64	420	76	1.2	..	55	84	..	6	22
Faeroe Islands	..	..	..	..	..	..	..	..	..	..	..
Fiji	..	24	59	42	0.1	104	..	55	..	8	..
Finland	..	3	4	9	..	99	..	60	9	8	32
France	..	4	12	6	..	..	..	56	7	10	39
French Polynesia	..	..	..	38	..	..	..	56	..	..	..
Gabon	6.5	56	240	99	3.9	..	89	61	..	20	..
Gambia, The	17.4	74	430	114	1.2	71	69	77	..	7	..
Georgia	1.1	13	41	46	0.3	109	100	65	61	14	..
Germany	..	4	7	3	0.2	98	..	60	7	5	30
Ghana	13.4	78	380	57	1.3	97[b]	86	69	77	5	..
Greece	..	4	5	11	..	101	99	53	30	27	23
Greenland	..	..	..	..	..	..	..	..	..	..	..
Grenada	..	12	23	34	..	112	..	..	..	..	..
Guam	..	..	..	50	..	..	..	63	..	..	..
Guatemala	13.0	31	140	95	0.6	86	94	68	..	3	..
Guinea	16.3	101	650	127	1.7	61	31	72	..	2	..
Guinea-Bissau	18.1	124	560	97	3.7	64	74	73	..	7	..
Guyana	11.1	37	250	87	1.4	85	93	61	..	11	..
Haiti	11.6	73	380	41	2.0	..	72	66	..	7	..
Honduras	7.1	22	120	82	0.5	93	95	63	53	4	..
Hungary	..	6	14	12	..	99	99	52	6	10	40
Iceland	..	2	4	11	..	97	..	74	8	6	40
India	..	53	190	32	0.3	96	81	54	81	4	14
Indonesia	19.9	29	190	48	0.5	105	99	68	33	6	23
Iran, Islamic Rep.	..	17	23	31	0.1	104	98	45	..	13	..
Iraq	8.5	34	67	68	..	..	82	42	..	16	..
Ireland	..	4	9	8	..	..	..	61	13	13	33
Isle of Man	..	..	..	..	..	..	..	..	..	..	..
Israel	..	4	2	7	..	106	100	63	..	6	..

	Prevalence of child malnutrition, underweight % of children under age 5 2007–13[a]	Under-five mortality rate per 1,000 live births 2013	Maternal mortality ratio Modeled estimate per 100,000 live births 2013	Adolescent fertility rate births per 1,000 women ages 15–19 2013	Prevalence of HIV % of population ages 15–49 2013	Primary completion rate % of relevant age group 2009–13[a]	Youth literacy rate % of population ages 15–24 2005–13[a]	Labor force participation rate Modeled ILO estimate % of population ages 15 and older 2013	Vulnerable employment Unpaid family workers and own-account workers % of total employment 2009–13[a]	Unemployment Modeled ILO estimate % of total labor force 2013	Female legislators, senior officials, and managers % of total 2009–13[a]
Italy	..	4	4	4	0.3	99	100	49	18	12	25
Jamaica	3.2	17	80	69	1.8	86	96	63	38	15	..
Japan	..	3	6	5	..	102	..	59	..	4	..
Jordan	3.0	19	50	26	..	93	99	42	10	13	..
Kazakhstan	3.7	16	26	29	..	102	100	73	29	5	..
Kenya	16.4	71	400	92	6.0	..	82	67	..	9	..
Kiribati	14.9	58	130	16	..	..	..	..	..	..	36
Korea, Dem. People's Rep.	15.2	27	87	1	..	..	100	78	..	5	..
Korea, Rep.	0.6	4	27	2	..	111	..	61	..	3	..
Kosovo	..	..	..	..	..	..	..	..	17	..	15
Kuwait	2.2	10	14	14	..	..	99	68	2	3	..
Kyrgyz Republic	2.8[b]	24	75	28	0.2	98	100	68	..	8	..
Lao PDR	26.5	71	220	64	0.2	101	84	78	..	1	..
Latvia	..	8	13	13	..	103	100	61	7	11	45
Lebanon	..	9	16	12	..	89	99	48	..	7	..
Lesotho	13.5	98	490	86	22.9	74	83	66	..	25	..
Liberia	15.3	71	640	114	1.1	59[b]	49	62	79	4	..
Libya	5.6	15	15	2	..	..	100	53	..	20	..
Liechtenstein	..	..	..	..	..	102	..	..	..	..	..
Lithuania	..	5	11	10	..	98	100	61	10	12	38
Luxembourg	..	2	11	8	..	85	..	58	6	6	24
Macedonia, FYR	1.3	7	7	18	<0.1	94	99	55	23	29	28
Madagascar	..	56	440	121	0.4	68	65	89	88	4	25
Malawi	16.7[b]	68	510	143	10.3	75	72	83	..	8	..
Malaysia	..	9	29	6	0.4	..	98	59	22	3	25
Maldives	17.8	10	31	4	<0.1	110	99	67	..	12	..
Mali	..	123	550	174	0.9	59	47	66	..	8	..
Malta	..	6	9	18	..	88	98	52	9	7	23
Marshall Islands	..	38	..	..	..	100	..	..	..	..	..
Mauritania	19.5	90	320	72	..	71	56	54	..	31	..
Mauritius	..	14	73	31	1.1	102	98	59	17	8	..
Mexico	2.8	15	49	62	0.2	99	99	62	..	5	..
Micronesia, Fed. Sts.	..	36	96	17	..	..	..	..	..	..	..
Moldova	2.2	15	21	29	0.6	93	100	41	31	5	44
Monaco	..	4	..	..	..	..	..	..	..	..	..
Mongolia	1.6	32	68	18	<0.1	..	98	63	51	5	..
Montenegro	1.0	5	7	15	..	101	99	50	..	20	30
Morocco	3.1	30	120	35	0.2	101[b]	82	51	51	9	..
Mozambique	15.6	87	480	133	10.8	49	67	84	..	8	..
Myanmar	22.6	51	200	11	0.6	95	96	79	..	3	..
Namibia	13.2	50	130	52	14.3	85	87	59	8	17	43
Nepal	29.1	40	190	72	0.2	102[b]	82	83	..	3	..
Netherlands	..	4	6	6	..	..	..	64	12	7	30
New Caledonia	..	..	..	21	..	..	100	57	..	..	..
New Zealand	..	6	8	24	..	..	..	68	..	6	..
Nicaragua	..	24	100	99	0.2	80	87	63	47	7	..
Niger	37.9	104	630	205	0.4	49	24	65	..	5	..

 Front   User guide   World view   People   Environment

	Prevalence of child malnutrition, underweight % of children under age 5 2007–13[a]	Under-five mortality rate per 1,000 live births 2013	Maternal mortality ratio Modeled estimate per 100,000 live births 2013	Adolescent fertility rate births per 1,000 women ages 15–19 2013	Prevalence of HIV % of population ages 15–49 2013	Primary completion rate % of relevant age group 2009–13[a]	Youth literacy rate % of population ages 15–24 2005–13[a]	Labor force participation rate Modeled ILO estimate % of population ages 15 and older 2013	Vulnerable employment Unpaid family workers and own-account workers % of total employment 2009–13[a]	Unemployment Modeled ILO estimate % of total labor force 2013	Female legislators, senior officials, and managers % of total 2009–13[a]
Nigeria	31.0	117	560	118	3.2	76	66	56	..	8	..
Northern Mariana Islands	..	..	..	..	..	..	..	..	..	..	..
Norway	..	3	4	7	..	99	..	65	5	4	31
Oman	8.6	11	11	10	..	104	98	65	..	8	..
Pakistan	31.6	86	170	27	<0.1	73	71	54	..	5	..
Palau	..	18	..	..	..	83[b]	100	..	..	..	..
Panama	3.9	18	85	77	0.7	96[b]	98	66	29	4	46
Papua New Guinea	27.9	61	220	61	0.7	78	71	72	..	2	..
Paraguay	..	22	110	66	0.4	86	99	70	43	5	32
Peru	3.5	17	89	50	0.4	93	99	76	46	4	30
Philippines	20.2	30	120	46	..	91	98	65	40	7	..
Poland	..	5	3	12	..	95	100	57	18	10	38
Portugal	..	4	8	12	..	..	99	60	17	17	33
Puerto Rico	..	..	20	47	..	..	99	43	..	14	..
Qatar	..	8	6	9	..	..	99	87	0	1	12
Romania	..	12	33	31	0.1	94	99	57	31	7	31
Russian Federation	..	10	24	26	..	97	100	64	..	6	..
Rwanda	11.7	52	320	32	2.9	59	77	86	..	1	..
Samoa	..	18	58	28	..	102	100	42	38	..	36
San Marino	..	3	..	..	..	93	..	..	..	..	..
São Tomé and Príncipe	14.4	51	210	63	0.6	104	80	61	..	..	24
Saudi Arabia	..	16	16	10	..	108	99	55	..	6	7
Senegal	16.8	55	320	92	0.5	61[b]	66	77	58	10	..
Serbia	1.8[b]	7	16	17	<0.1	99	99	52	29	22	33
Seychelles	..	14	..	56	..	..	99	..	..	..	..
Sierra Leone	18.1	161	1,100	98	1.6	71	63	67	..	3	..
Singapore	..	3	6	6	..	..	100	68	9	3	34
Sint Maarten	..	..	..	..	..	..	..	..	..	..	..
Slovak Republic	..	7	7	15	..	95	..	60	12	14	31
Slovenia	..	3	7	1	..	101	100	58	14	10	38
Solomon Islands	11.5	30	130	64	..	86	..	66	..	4	..
Somalia	..	146	850	107	0.5	..	..	56	..	7	..
South Africa	8.7	44	140	49	19.1	..	99	52	10	25	31
South Sudan	27.6	99	730	72	2.2	37	..	..	..	..	..
Spain	..	4	4	10	0.4	102	100	59	13	27	30
Sri Lanka	26.3	10	29	17	<0.1	97	98	55	43	4	28
St. Kitts and Nevis	..	10	..	..	..	90	..	..	..	..	..
St. Lucia	2.8	15	34	55	..	..	..	69	..	..	..
St. Martin	..	..	..	..	..	..	..	..	..	..	..
St. Vincent & the Grenadines	..	19	45	54	..	107	..	67	..	..	..
Sudan	..	77	360	80	0.2	57	88	54	..	15	..
Suriname	5.8	23	130	34	0.9	85	98	55	..	8	36
Swaziland	5.8	80	310	69	27.4	78	94	57	..	23	..
Sweden	..	3	4	6	..	102	..	64	7	8	35
Switzerland	..	4	6	2	0.4	97	..	68	9	4	33
Syrian Arab Republic	10.1	15	49	41	..	64	96	44	33	11	9
Tajikistan	13.3	48	44	41	0.3	98[b]	100	68	47	11	..

2 People

	Prevalence of child malnutrition, underweight % of children under age 5 2007–13[a]	Under-five mortality rate per 1,000 live births 2013	Maternal mortality ratio Modeled estimate per 100,000 live births 2013	Adolescent fertility rate births per 1,000 women ages 15–19 2013	Prevalence of HIV % of population ages 15–49 2013	Primary completion rate % of relevant age group 2009–13[a]	Youth literacy rate % of population ages 15–24 2005–13[a]	Labor force participation rate Modeled ILO estimate % of population ages 15 and older 2013	Vulnerable employment Unpaid family workers and own-account workers % of total employment 2009–13[a]	Unemployment Modeled ILO estimate % of total labor force 2013	Female legislators, senior officials, and managers % of total 2009–13[a]
Tanzania	13.6	52	410	121	5.0	76	75	89	74	4	..
Thailand	9.2	13	26	40	1.1	..	97	72	56	1	25
Timor-Leste	45.3	55	270	50	..	71	80	38	70	4	10
Togo	16.5	85	450	89	2.3	81	80	81	..	7	..
Tonga	..	12	120	17	..	100	99	64	..	..	..
Trinidad and Tobago	..	21	84	34	1.7	95	100	64	..	6	..
Tunisia	2.3	15	46	4	<0.1	98	97	48	29	13	..
Turkey	1.9	19	20	29	..	101	99	49	31	10	10
Turkmenistan	..	55	61	17	..	..	100	62	..	11	..
Turks and Caicos Islands	..	..	..	..	..	..	..	..	..	..	..
Tuvalu	1.6	29	..	..	..	80	..	..	..	..	..
Uganda	14.1	66	360	122	7.4	54	87	78	..	4	..
Ukraine	..	10	23	25	0.8	110	100	59	18	8	38
United Arab Emirates	..	8	8	27	..	111	95	80	1	4	..
United Kingdom	..	5	8	26	0.3	..	..	62	12	8	34
United States	0.5	7	28	30	..	..	..	63	..	7	..
Uruguay	4.5	11	14	58	0.7	104	99	66	22	7	44
Uzbekistan	..	43	36	37	0.2	92	100	62	..	11	..
Vanuatu	11.7	17	86	44	..	84	95	71	70	..	29
Venezuela, RB	2.9	15	110	82	0.6	96	99	65	30	8	..
Vietnam	12.0	24	49	29	0.4	97	97	78	63	2	..
Virgin Islands (U.S.)	..	..	..	48	..	..	..	63	..	..	..
West Bank and Gaza	1.4[b]	22	47	45	..	93	99	41	26	23	..
Yemen, Rep.	35.5	51	270	46	<0.1	70	87	49	30	17	5
Zambia	14.9	87	280	122	12.5	84	64	79	..	13	..
Zimbabwe	11.2[b]	89	470	58	15.0	92	91	87	..	5	..
World	**15.0 w**	**46 w**	**210 w**	**45 w**	**0.8 w**	**92 w**	**89 w**	**63 w**	**.. w**	**6 w**	
Low income	21.4	76	440	92	2.3	71	72	76	..	5	
Middle income	15.8	43	170	40	..	96	91	63	..	6	
Lower middle income	24.4	59	240	46	0.7	92	83	58	68	5	
Upper middle income	2.7	20	57	32	..	102	99	67	..	6	
Low & middle income	17.0	50	230	49	1.2	91	88	64	..	6	
East Asia & Pacific	5.2	20	75	20	..	105	99	71	..	5	
Europe & Central Asia	1.6	23	28	29	..	99	99	57	28	10	
Latin America & Carib.	2.8	18	87	68	0.5	95	98	67	32	6	
Middle East & N. Africa	6.0	26	78	37	0.1	95	91	47	..	13	
South Asia	32.5	57	190	38	0.3	91	79	56	80	4	
Sub-Saharan Africa	21.0	92	510	106	4.5	70	70	70	..	8	
High income	0.9	6	17	18	..	99	..	61	..	8	
Euro area	..	4	7	6	..	98	100	57	11	12	

a. Data are for the most recent year available. b. Data are for 2014.

 Front User guide World view People Environment

About the data

Though not included in the table due to space limitations, many indicators in this section are available disaggregated by sex, place of residence, wealth, and age in the World Development Indicators database.

Child malnutrition

Good nutrition is the cornerstone for survival, health, and development. Well-nourished children perform better in school, grow into healthy adults, and in turn give their children a better start in life. Well-nourished women face fewer risks during pregnancy and childbirth, and their children set off on firmer developmental paths, both physically and mentally. Undernourished children have lower resistance to infection and are more likely to die from common childhood ailments such as diarrheal diseases and respiratory infections. Frequent illness saps the nutritional status of those who survive, locking them into a vicious cycle of recurring sickness and faltering growth.

The proportion of underweight children is the most common child malnutrition indicator. Being even mildly underweight increases the risk of death and inhibits cognitive development in children. And it perpetuates the problem across generations, as malnourished women are more likely to have low-birthweight babies. Estimates of prevalence of underweight children are from the World Health Organization's (WHO) Global Database on Child Growth and Malnutrition, a standardized compilation of child growth and malnutrition data from national nutritional surveys. To better monitor global child malnutrition, the United Nations Children's Fund (UNICEF), the WHO, and the World Bank have jointly produced estimates for 2013 and trends since 1990 for regions, income groups, and the world, using a harmonized database and aggregation method.

Under-five mortality

Mortality rates for children and others are important indicators of health status. When data on the incidence and prevalence of diseases are unavailable, mortality rates may be used to identify vulnerable populations. And they are among the indicators most frequently used to compare socioeconomic development across countries.

The main sources of mortality data are vital registration systems and direct or indirect estimates based on sample surveys or censuses. A complete vital registration system—covering at least 90 percent of vital events in the population—is the best source of age-specific mortality data. But complete vital registration systems are fairly uncommon in developing countries. Thus estimates must be obtained from sample surveys or derived by applying indirect estimation techniques to registration, census, or survey data (see *Primary data documentation*). Survey data are subject to recall error.

To make estimates comparable and to ensure consistency across estimates by different agencies, the UN Inter-agency Group for Child Mortality Estimation, which comprises UNICEF, the WHO, the United Nations Population Division, the World Bank, and other universities and research institutes, has developed and adopted a statistical method that uses all available information to reconcile differences.

Trend lines are obtained by fitting a country-specific regression model of mortality rates against their reference dates. (For further discussion of childhood mortality estimates, see UN Inter-agency Group for Child Mortality Estimation [2014]; for detailed background data and for a graphic presentation, see www.childmortality.org).

Maternal mortality

Measurements of maternal mortality are subject to many types of errors. In countries with incomplete vital registration systems, deaths of women of reproductive age or their pregnancy status may not be reported, or the cause of death may not be known. Even in high-income countries with reliable vital registration systems, misclassification of maternal deaths has been found to lead to serious underestimation. Surveys and censuses can be used to measure maternal mortality by asking respondents about survivorship of sisters. But these estimates are retrospective, referring to a period approximately five years before the survey, and may be affected by recall error. Further, they reflect pregnancy-related deaths (deaths while pregnant or within 42 days of pregnancy termination, irrespective of the cause of death) and need to be adjusted to conform to the strict definition of maternal death.

Maternal mortality ratios in the table are modeled estimates based on work by the WHO, UNICEF, the United Nations Population Fund (UNFPA), the World Bank, and the United Nations Population Division and include country-level time series data. For countries without complete registration data but with other types of data and for countries with no data, maternal mortality is estimated with a multilevel regression model using available national maternal mortality data and socioeconomic information, including fertility, birth attendants, and gross domestic product. The methodology differs from that used for previous estimates, so data presented here should not be compared across editions (WHO and others 2014).

Adolescent fertility

Reproductive health is a state of physical and mental well-being in relation to the reproductive system and its functions and processes. Means of achieving reproductive health include education and services during pregnancy and childbirth, safe and effective contraception, and prevention and treatment of sexually transmitted diseases. Complications of pregnancy and childbirth are the leading cause of death and disability among women of reproductive age in developing countries.

Adolescent pregnancies are high risk for both mother and child. They are more likely to result in premature delivery, low birthweight, delivery complications, and death. Many adolescent pregnancies are unintended, but young girls may continue their pregnancies, giving up opportunities for education and employment, or seek unsafe abortions. Estimates of adolescent fertility rates are based on vital registration systems or, in their absence, censuses or sample surveys and are generally considered reliable measures of fertility in the recent past. Where no empirical information on age-specific fertility rates is available, a model is used to estimate the share of births to adolescents. For countries without vital registration systems fertility rates are generally based on extrapolations from trends observed in censuses or surveys from earlier years.

Prevalence of HIV

HIV prevalence rates reflect the rate of HIV infection in each country's population. Low national prevalence rates can be misleading, however. They often disguise epidemics that are initially concentrated in certain localities or population groups and threaten to spill over into the wider population. In many developing countries most new infections occur in young adults, with young women especially vulnerable.

Data on HIV prevalence are from the Joint United Nations Programme on HIV/AIDS. Changes in procedures and assumptions for estimating the data and better coordination with countries have resulted in improved estimates. The models, which are routinely updated, track the course of HIV epidemics and their impacts, making full use of information on HIV prevalence trends from surveillance data as well as survey data. The models take into account reduced infectivity among people receiving antiretroviral therapy (which is having a larger impact on HIV prevalence and allowing HIV-positive people to live longer) and allow for changes in urbanization over time in generalized epidemics (important because prevalence is higher in urban areas and because many countries have seen rapid urbanization over the past two decades). The estimates include plausibility bounds, available at http://data.worldbank.org, which reflect the certainty associated with each of the estimates.

Primary completion

Many governments publish statistics that indicate how their education systems are working and developing—statistics on enrollment, graduates, financial and human resources, and efficiency indicators such as repetition rates, pupil–teacher ratios, and cohort progression. Primary completion, measured by the gross intake ratio to last grade of primary education, is a core indicator of an education system's performance. It reflects an education system's coverage and the educational attainment of students. It is a key measure of progress toward the Millennium Development Goals and the Education for All initiative.

The indicator reflects the primary cycle, which typically lasts six years (with a range of four to seven years), as defined by the International Standard Classification of Education (ISCED2011). It is a proxy that should be taken as an upper estimate of the actual primary completion rate, since data limitations preclude adjusting for students who drop out during the final year of primary education.

There are many reasons why the primary completion rate may exceed 100 percent. The numerator may include late entrants and overage children who have repeated one or more grades of primary education as well as children who entered school early, while the denominator is the number of children at the entrance age for the last grade of primary education.

Youth literacy

The youth literacy rate for ages 15–24 is a standard measure of recent progress in student achievement. It reflects the accumulated outcomes of primary and secondary education by indicating the proportion of the population that has acquired basic literacy and numeracy skills over the previous 10 years or so.

Conventional literacy statistics that divide the population into two groups—literate and illiterate—are widely available and useful for tracking global progress toward universal literacy. In practice, however, literacy is difficult to measure. Estimating literacy rates requires census or survey measurements under controlled conditions. Many countries report the number of literate or illiterate people from self-reported data. Some use educational attainment data as a proxy but apply different lengths of school attendance or levels of completion. And there is a trend among recent national and international surveys toward using a direct reading test of literacy skills. Because definitions and methods of data collection differ across countries, data should be used cautiously. Generally, literacy encompasses numeracy, the ability to make simple arithmetic calculations.

Data on youth literacy are compiled by the United Nations Educational, Scientific and Cultural Organization (UNESCO) Institute for Statistics based on national censuses and household surveys during 1975–2012 and, for countries without recent literacy data, using the Global Age-Specific Literacy Projection Model. For detailed information, see www.uis.unesco.org.

Labor force participation

The labor force is the supply of labor available for producing goods and services in an economy. It includes people who are currently employed, people who are unemployed but seeking work, and first-time job-seekers. Not everyone who works is included, however. Unpaid workers, family workers, and students are often omitted, and some countries do not count members of the armed forces. Labor force size tends to vary during the year as seasonal workers enter and leave.

Data on the labor force are compiled by the International Labour Organization (ILO) from labor force surveys, censuses, and establishment censuses and surveys and from administrative records such as employment exchange registers and unemployment insurance schemes. Labor force surveys are the most comprehensive source for internationally comparable labor force data. Labor force data from population censuses are often based on a limited number of questions on the economic characteristics of individuals, with little scope to probe. Establishment censuses and surveys provide data on the employed population only, not unemployed workers, workers in small establishments, or workers in the informal sector (ILO, *Key Indicators of the Labour Market 2001–2002*).

Besides the data sources, there are other important factors that affect data comparability, such as census or survey reference period, definition of working age, and geographic coverage. For

country-level information on source, reference period, or definition, consult the footnotes in the World Development Indicators database or the ILO's Key Indicators of the Labour Market, 8th edition, database.

The labor force participation rates in the table are modeled estimates from the ILO's Key Indicators of the Labour Market, 8th edition, database. These harmonized estimates use strict data selection criteria and enhanced methods to ensure comparability across countries and over time to avoid the inconsistencies mentioned above. Estimates are based mainly on labor force surveys, with other sources (population censuses and nationally reported estimates) used only when no survey data are available. National estimates of labor force participation rates are available in the World Development Indicators online database. Because other employment data are mostly national estimates, caution should be used when comparing the modeled labor force participation rate and other employment data.

Vulnerable employment

The proportion of unpaid family workers and own-account workers in total employment is derived from information on status in employment. Each group faces different economic risks, and unpaid family workers and own-account workers are the most vulnerable—and therefore the most likely to fall into poverty. They are the least likely to have formal work arrangements, are the least likely to have social protection and safety nets to guard against economic shocks, and are often incapable of generating enough savings to offset these shocks. A high proportion of unpaid family workers in a country indicates weak development, little job growth, and often a large rural economy.

Data on vulnerable employment are drawn from labor force and general household sample surveys, censuses, and official estimates. Besides the limitation mentioned for calculating labor force participation rates, there are other reasons to limit comparability. For example, information provided by the Organisation for Economic Co-operation and Development relates only to civilian employment, which can result in an underestimation of "employees" and "workers not classified by status," especially in countries with large armed forces. While the categories of unpaid family workers and own-account workers would not be affected, their relative shares would be.

Unemployment

The ILO defines the unemployed as members of the economically active population who are without work but available for and seeking work, including people who have lost their jobs or who have voluntarily left work. Some unemployment is unavoidable. At any time some workers are temporarily unemployed—between jobs as employers look for the right workers and workers search for better jobs. Such unemployment, often called frictional unemployment, results from the normal operation of labor markets.

Changes in unemployment over time may reflect changes in the demand for and supply of labor, but they may also reflect changes in reporting practices. In countries without unemployment or welfare benefits people eke out a living in vulnerable employment. In countries with well-developed safety nets workers can afford to wait for suitable or desirable jobs. But high and sustained unemployment indicates serious inefficiencies in resource allocation.

The criteria for people considered to be seeking work, and the treatment of people temporarily laid off or seeking work for the first time, vary across countries. In many developing countries it is especially difficult to measure employment and unemployment in agriculture. The timing of a survey can maximize the effects of seasonal unemployment in agriculture. And informal sector employment is difficult to quantify where informal activities are not tracked.

Data on unemployment are drawn from labor force surveys and general household surveys, censuses, and official estimates. Administrative records, such as social insurance statistics and employment office statistics, are not included because of their limitations in coverage.

Women tend to be excluded from the unemployment count for various reasons. Women suffer more from discrimination and from structural, social, and cultural barriers that impede them from seeking work. Also, women are often responsible for the care of children and the elderly and for household affairs. They may not be available for work during the short reference period, as they need to make arrangements before starting work. Further, women are considered to be employed when they are working part-time or in temporary jobs, despite the instability of these jobs or their active search for more secure employment.

The unemployment rates in the table are modeled estimates from the ILO's Key Indicators of the Labour Market, 8th edition, database. National estimates of unemployment are available in the World Development Indicators online database.

Female legislators, senior officials, and managers

Despite much progress in recent decades, gender inequalities remain pervasive in many dimensions of life. While gender inequalities exist throughout the world, they are most prevalent in developing countries. Inequalities in the allocation of education, health care, nutrition, and political voice matter because of their strong association with well-being, productivity, and economic growth. These patterns of inequality begin at an early age, with boys usually receiving a larger share of education and health spending than girls, for example. The share of women in high-skilled occupations such as legislators, senior officials, and managers indicates women's status and role in the labor force and society at large. Women are vastly underrepresented in decisionmaking positions in government, although there is some evidence of recent improvement.

Data on female legislators, senior officials, and managers are based on the employment by occupation estimates, classified according to the International Standard Classification of

2 People

Occupations 1988. Data are drawn mostly from labor force surveys, supplemented in limited cases with other household surveys, population censuses, and official estimates. Countries could apply different practice whether or where the armed forces are included. Armed forces constitute a separate major group, but in some countries they are included in the most closely matching civilian occupation or in nonclassifiable workers. For country-level information on classification, source, reference period, or definition, consult the footnotes in the World Development Indicators database or the ILO's Key Indicators of the Labour Market, 8th edition, database.

Definitions

• **Prevalence of child malnutrition, underweight,** is the percentage of children under age 5 whose weight for age is more than two standard deviations below the median for the international reference population ages 0–59 months. Data are based on the WHO child growth standards released in 2006. • **Under-five mortality rate** is the probability of a child born in a specific year dying before reaching age 5, if subject to the age-specific mortality rates of that year. The probability is expressed as a rate per 1,000 live births. • **Maternal mortality ratio, modeled estimate,** is the number of women who die from pregnancy-related causes while pregnant or within 42 days of pregnancy termination, per 100,000 live births. • **Adolescent fertility rate** is the number of births per 1,000 women ages 15–19. • **Prevalence of HIV** is the percentage of people who are infected with HIV in the relevant age group. • **Primary completion rate,** or gross intake ratio to the last grade of primary education, is the number of new entrants (enrollments minus repeaters) in the last grade of primary education, regardless of age, divided by the population at the entrance age for the last grade of primary education. Data limitations preclude adjusting for students who drop out during the final year of primary education. • **Youth literacy rate** is the percentage of people ages 15–24 who can both read and write with understanding a short simple statement about their everyday life. • **Labor force participation rate** is the proportion of the population ages 15 and older that engages actively in the labor market, by either working or looking for work during a reference period. Data are modeled ILO estimates. • **Vulnerable employment** is unpaid family workers and own-account workers as a percentage of total employment. • **Unemployment** is the share of the labor force without work but available for and seeking employment. Definitions of labor force and unemployment may differ by country. Data are modeled ILO estimates. • **Female legislators, senior officials, and managers** are the percentage of legislators, senior officials, and managers (International Standard Classification of Occupations–88 category 1) who are female.

Data sources

Data on child malnutrition prevalence are from the WHO's Global Database on Child Growth and Malnutrition (www.who.int/nutgrowthdb). Data on under-five mortality rates are from the UN Inter-agency Group for Child Mortality Estimation (www.childmortality.org) and are based mainly on household surveys, censuses, and vital registration data. Modeled estimates of maternal mortality ratios are from the UN Maternal Mortality Estimation Inter-agency Group (www.who.int/reproductivehealth/publications/monitoring/maternal-mortality-2013/). Data on adolescent fertility rates are from United Nations Population Division (2013), with annual data linearly interpolated by the World Bank's Development Data Group. Data on HIV prevalence are from UNAIDS (2014). Data on primary completion rates and youth literacy rates are from the UNESCO Institute for Statistics (www.uis.unesco.org). Data on labor force participation rates, vulnerable employment, unemployment, and female legislators, senior officials, and managers are from the ILO's Key Indicators of the Labour Market, 8th edition, database.

References

Amin, Mohammad, and Asif Islam. 2014. "Are There More Female Managers in the Retail Sector? Evidence from Survey Data in Developing Countries." Policy Research Working Paper 6843. World Bank, Washington, DC.

ILO (International Labour Organization). Various years. *Key Indicators of the Labour Market.* Geneva: International Labour Office.

UNAIDS (Joint United Nations Programme on HIV/AIDS). 2014. *The Gap Report.* [www.unaids.org/en/resources/campaigns/2014/2014gapreport/gapreport/]. Geneva.

UNICEF (United Nations Children's Fund), WHO (World Health Organization), and the World Bank. 2014. *2013 Joint Child Malnutrition Estimates - Levels and Trends.* New York: UNICEF. [www.who.int/nutgrowthdb/estimates2013/].

UN Inter-agency Group for Child Mortality Estimation. 2014. *Levels and Trends in Child Mortality: Report 2014.* [www.unicef.org/media/files/Levels_and_Trends_in_Child_Mortality_2014.pdf]. New York.

United Nations Population Division. 2013. *World Population Prospects: The 2012 Revision.* [http://esa.un.org/unpd/wpp/Documentation/publications.htm]. New York: United Nations, Department of Economic and Social Affairs.

WHO (World Health Organization), UNICEF (United Nations Children's Fund), UNFPA (United Nations Population Fund), World Bank, and United Nations Population Division. 2014. *Trends in Maternal Mortality: 1990 to 2013.* [www.who.int/reproductivehealth/publications/monitoring/maternal-mortality-2013/]. Geneva: WHO.

World Bank. 2014. Global Database of Shared Prosperity. [http://www.worldbank.org/en/topic/poverty/brief/global-database-of-shared-prosperity]. Washington, DC.

Online tables and indicators

To access the World Development Indicators online tables, use the URL http://wdi.worldbank.org/table/ and the table number (for example, http://wdi.worldbank.org/table/2.1). To view a specific indicator online, use the URL http://data.worldbank.org/indicator/ and the indicator code (for example, http://data.worldbank.org /indicator/SP.POP.TOTL).

2.1 Population dynamics

Population ♀♂	SP.POP.TOTL
Population growth	SP.POP.GROW
Population ages 0–14 ♀♂	SP.POP.0014.TO.ZS
Population ages 15–64 ♀♂	SP.POP.1564.TO.ZS
Population ages 65+ ♀♂	SP.POP.65UP.TO.ZS
Dependency ratio, Young	SP.POP.DPND.YG
Dependency ratio, Old	SP.POP.DPND.OL
Crude death rate	SP.DYN.CDRT.IN
Crude birth rate	SP.DYN.CBRT.IN

2.2 Labor force structure

Labor force participation rate, Male ♀♂	SL.TLF.CACT.MA.ZS
Labor force participation rate, Female ♀♂	SL.TLF.CACT.FE.ZS
Labor force, Total ♀♂	SL.TLF.TOTL.IN
Labor force, Average annual growth	..[a,b]
Labor force, Female ♀♂	SL.TLF.TOTL.FE.ZS

2.3 Employment by sector

Agriculture, Male ♀♂	SL.AGR.EMPL.MA.ZS
Agriculture, Female ♀♂	SL.AGR.EMPL.FE.ZS
Industry, Male ♀♂	SL.IND.EMPL.MA.ZS
Industry, Female ♀♂	SL.IND.EMPL.FE.ZS
Services, Male ♀♂	SL.SRV.EMPL.MA.ZS
Services, Female ♀♂	SL.SRV.EMPL.FE.ZS

2.4 Decent work and productive employment

Employment to population ratio, Total ♀♂	SL.EMP.TOTL.SP.ZS
Employment to population ratio, Youth ♀♂	SL.EMP.1524.SP.ZS
Vulnerable employment, Male ♀♂	SL.EMP.VULN.MA.ZS
Vulnerable employment, Female ♀♂	SL.EMP.VULN.FE.ZS
GDP per person employed	SL.GDP.PCAP.EM.KD

2.5 Unemployment

Unemployment, Male ♀♂	SL.UEM.TOTL.MA.ZS
Unemployment, Female ♀♂	SL.UEM.TOTL.FE.ZS
Youth unemployment, Male ♀♂	SL.UEM.1524.MA.ZS
Youth unemployment, Female ♀♂	SL.UEM.1524.FE.ZS
Long-term unemployment, Total ♀♂	SL.UEM.LTRM.ZS
Long-term unemployment, Male ♀♂	SL.UEM.LTRM.MA.ZS
Long-term unemployment, Female ♀♂	SL.UEM.LTRM.FE.ZS
Unemployment by educational attainment, Primary ♀♂	SL.UEM.PRIM.ZS
Unemployment by educational attainment, Secondary ♀♂	SL.UEM.SECO.ZS
Unemployment by educational attainment, Tertiary ♀♂	SL.UEM.TERT.ZS

2.6 Children at work

Children in employment, Total ♀♂	SL.TLF.0714.ZS
Children in employment, Male ♀♂	SL.TLF.0714.MA.ZS
Children in employment, Female ♀♂	SL.TLF.0714.FE.ZS
Work only ♀♂	SL.TLF.0714.WK.ZS
Study and work ♀♂	SL.TLF.0714.SW.ZS
Employment in agriculture ♀♂	SL.AGR.0714.ZS
Employment in manufacturing ♀♂	SL.MNF.0714.ZS
Employment in services ♀♂	SL.SRV.0714.ZS
Self-employed ♀♂	SL.SLF.0714.ZS
Wage workers ♀♂	SL.WAG.0714.ZS
Unpaid family workers ♀♂	SL.FAM.0714.ZS

2.7 Poverty rates at national poverty lines

Poverty headcount ratio, Rural	SI.POV.RUHC
Poverty headcount ratio, Urban	SI.POV.URHC
Poverty headcount ratio, National	SI.POV.NAHC
Poverty gap, Rural	SI.POV.RUGP
Poverty gap, Urban	SI.POV.URGP
Poverty gap, National	SI.POV.NAGP

2.8 Poverty rates at international poverty lines

Population living below 2005 PPP $1.25 a day	SI.POV.DDAY
Poverty gap at 2005 PPP $1.25 a day	SI.POV.2DAY
Population living below 2005 PPP $2 a day	SI.POV.GAPS
Poverty gap at 2005 PPP $2 a day	SI.POV.GAP2

2.9 Distribution of income or consumption

Gini index	SI.POV.GINI
Share of consumption or income, Lowest 10% of population	SI.DST.FRST.10
Share of consumption or income, Lowest 20% of population	SI.DST.FRST.20
Share of consumption or income, Second 20% of population	SI.DST.02ND.20
Share of consumption or income, Third 20% of population	SI.DST.03RD.20
Share of consumption or income, Fourth 20% of population	SI.DST.04TH.20

Share of consumption or income, Highest 20% of population — SI.DST.05TH.20

Share of consumption or income, Highest 10% of population — SI.DST.10TH.10

2.9.2 Shared prosperity

Annualized growth in mean consumption or income per capita, bottom 40% — SI.SPR.PC40.ZG

Annualized growth in mean consumption or income per capita, total population — SI.SPR.PCAP.ZG

Mean consumption or income per capita, bottom 40% — SI.SPR.PC40

Mean consumption or income per capita, total population — SI.SPR.PCAP

2.10 Education inputs

Public expenditure per student, Primary — SE.XPD.PRIM.PC.ZS

Public expenditure per student, Secondary — SE.XPD.SECO.PC.ZS

Public expenditure per student, Tertiary — SE.XPD.TERT.PC.ZS

Public expenditure on education, % of GDP — SE.XPD.TOTL.GD.ZS

Public expenditure on education, % of total government expenditure — SE.XPD.TOTL.GB.ZS

Trained teachers in primary education ♀♂ — SE.PRM.TCAQ.ZS

Primary school pupil-teacher ratio — SE.PRM.ENRL.TC.ZS

2.11 Participation in education

Gross enrollment ratio, Preprimary ♀♂ — SE.PRE.ENRR

Gross enrollment ratio, Primary ♀♂ — SE.PRM.ENRR

Gross enrollment ratio, Secondary ♀♂ — SE.SEC.ENRR

Gross enrollment ratio, Tertiary ♀♂ — SE.TER.ENRR

Net enrollment rate, Primary ♀♂ — SE.PRM.NENR

Net enrollment rate, Secondary ♀♂ — SE.SEC.NENR

Adjusted net enrollment rate, Primary, Male ♀♂ — SE.PRM.TENR.MA

Adjusted net enrollment rate, Primary, Female ♀♂ — SE.PRM.TENR.FE

Primary school-age children out of school, Male ♀♂ — SE.PRM.UNER.MA

Primary school-age children out of school, Female ♀♂ — SE.PRM.UNER.FE

2.12 Education efficiency

Gross intake ratio in first grade of primary education, Male ♀♂ — SE.PRM.GINT.MA.ZS

Gross intake ratio in first grade of primary education, Female ♀♂ — SE.PRM.GINT.FE.ZS

Cohort survival rate, Reaching grade 5, Male ♀♂ — SE.PRM.PRS5.MA.ZS

Cohort survival rate, Reaching grade 5, Female ♀♂ — SE.PRM.PRS5.FE.ZS

Cohort survival rate, Reaching last grade of primary education, Male ♀♂ — SE.PRM.PRSL.MA.ZS

Cohort survival rate, Reaching last grade of primary education, Female ♀♂ — SE.PRM.PRSL.FE.ZS

Repeaters in primary education, Male ♀♂ — SE.PRM.REPT.MA.ZS

Repeaters in primary education, Female ♀♂ — SE.PRM.REPT.FE.ZS

Transition rate to secondary education, Male ♀♂ — SE.SEC.PROG.MA.ZS

Transition rate to secondary education, Female ♀♂ — SE.SEC.PROG.FE.ZS

2.13 Education completion and outcomes

Primary completion rate, Total ♀♂ — SE.PRM.CMPT.ZS

Primary completion rate, Male ♀♂ — SE.PRM.CMPT.MA.ZS

Primary completion rate, Female ♀♂ — SE.PRM.CMPT.FE.ZS

Youth literacy rate, Male ♀♂ — SE.ADT.1524.LT.MA.ZS

Youth literacy rate, Female ♀♂ — SE.ADT.1524.LT.FE.ZS

Adult literacy rate, Male ♀♂ — SE.ADT.LITR.MA.ZS

Adult literacy rate, Female ♀♂ — SE.ADT.LITR.FE.ZS

Students at lowest proficiency on PISA, Mathematics — ..b

Students at lowest proficiency on PISA, Reading — ..b

Students at lowest proficiency on PISA, Science — ..b

2.14 Education gaps by income, gender, and area

This table provides education survey data for the poorest and richest quintiles. — ..b

2.15 Health systems

Total health expenditure — SH.XPD.TOTL.ZS

Public health expenditure — SH.XPD.PUBL

Out-of-pocket health expenditure — SH.XPD.OOPC.TO.ZS

External resources for health — SH.XPD.EXTR.ZS

Health expenditure per capita, $ — SH.XPD.PCAP

Health expenditure per capita, PPP $ — SH.XPD.PCAP.PP.KD

Physicians — SH.MED.PHYS.ZS

Nurses and midwives — SH.MED.NUMW.P3

Community health workers — SH.MED.CMHW.P3

Hospital beds — SH.MED.BEDS.ZS

Completeness of birth registration — SP.REG.BRTH.ZS

2.16 Disease prevention coverage and quality

Access to an improved water source — SH.H2O.SAFE.ZS

Access to improved sanitation facilities — SH.STA.ACSN

Child immunization rate, Measles — SH.IMM.MEAS

Child immunization rate, DTP3 — SH.IMM.IDPT

Children with acute respiratory infection taken to health provider — SH.STA.ARIC.ZS

Children with diarrhea who received oral rehydration and continuous feeding — SH.STA.ORCF.ZS

Children sleeping under treated bed nets — SH.MLR.NETS.ZS

Children with fever receiving antimalarial drugs	SH.MLR.TRET.ZS
Tuberculosis treatment success rate	SH.TBS.CURE.ZS
Tuberculosis case detection rate	SH.TBS.DTEC.ZS

2.17 Reproductive health

Total fertility rate	SP.DYN.TFRT.IN
Adolescent fertility rate	SP.ADO.TFRT
Unmet need for contraception	SP.UWT.TFRT
Contraceptive prevalence rate	SP.DYN.CONU.ZS
Pregnant women receiving prenatal care	SH.STA.ANVC.ZS
Births attended by skilled health staff	SH.STA.BRTC.ZS
Maternal mortality ratio, National estimate	SH.STA.MMRT.NE
Maternal mortality ratio, Modeled estimate	SH.STA.MMRT
Lifetime risk of maternal mortality	SH.MMR.RISK

2.18 Nutrition and growth

Prevalence of undernourishment	SN.ITK.DEFC.ZS
Prevalence of underweight, Male ♀♂	SH.STA.MALN.MA.ZS
Prevalence of underweight, Female ♀♂	SH.STA.MALN.FE.ZS
Prevalence of stunting, Male ♀♂	SH.STA.STNT.MA.ZS
Prevalence of stunting, Female ♀♂	SH.STA.STNT.FE.ZS
Prevalence of wasting, Male ♀♂	SH.STA.WAST.MA.ZS
Prevalence of wasting, Female ♀♂	SH.STA.WAST.FE.ZS
Prevalence of severe wasting, Male ♀♂	SH.SVR.WAST.MA.ZS
Prevalence of severe wasting, Female ♀♂	SH.SVR.WAST.FE.ZS
Prevalence of overweight children, Male ♀♂	SH.STA.OWGH.MA.ZS
Prevalence of overweight children, Female ♀♂	SH.STA.OWGH.FE.ZS

2.19 Nutrition intake and supplements

Low-birthweight babies	SH.STA.BRTW.ZS
Exclusive breastfeeding	SH.STA.BFED.ZS
Consumption of iodized salt	SN.ITK.SALT.ZS
Vitamin A supplementation	SN.ITK.VITA.ZS
Prevalence of anemia among children under age 5	SH.ANM.CHLD.ZS
Prevalence of anemia among pregnant women	SH.PRG.ANEM

2.20 Health risk factors and future challenges

Prevalence of smoking, Male ♀♂	SH.PRV.SMOK.MA
Prevalence of smoking, Female ♀♂	SH.PRV.SMOK.FE
Incidence of tuberculosis	SH.TBS.INCD
Prevalence of diabetes	SH.STA.DIAB.ZS
Prevalence of HIV, Total	SH.DYN.AIDS.ZS
Women's share of population ages 15+ living with HIV ♀♂	SH.DYN.AIDS.FE.ZS
Prevalence of HIV, Youth male ♀♂	SH.HIV.1524.MA.ZS
Prevalence of HIV, Youth female ♀♂	SH.HIV.1524.FE.ZS
Antiretroviral therapy coverage	SH.HIV.ARTC.ZS
Death from communicable diseases and maternal, prenatal, and nutrition conditions	SH.DTH.COMM.ZS
Death from non-communicable diseases	SH.DTH.NCOM.ZS
Death from injuries	SH.DTH.INJR.ZS

2.21 Mortality

Life expectancy at birth ♀♂	SP.DYN.LE00.IN
Neonatal mortality rate	SH.DYN.NMRT
Infant mortality rate ♀♂	SP.DYN.IMRT.IN
Under-five mortality rate, Total ♀♂	SH.DYN.MORT
Under-five mortality rate, Male ♀♂	SH.DYN.MORT.MA
Under-five mortality rate, Female ♀♂	SH.DYN.MORT.FE
Adult mortality rate, Male ♀♂	SP.DYN.AMRT.MA
Adult mortality rate, Female ♀♂	SP.DYN.AMRT.FE

2.22 Health gaps by income

This table provides health survey data for the poorest and richest quintiles. ..[b]

♀♂ Data disaggregated by sex are available in the World Development Indicators database.
a. Derived from data elsewhere in the World Development Indicators database.
b. Available online only as part of the table, not as an individual indicator.

ENVIRONMENT

Front | User guide | World view | People | Environment

The World Bank Group's twin goals of eliminating extreme poverty and boosting shared prosperity to promote sustainable development require the efficient use of environmental resources. Whether the world can sustain itself depends largely on properly managing its natural resources. The indicators in the *Environment* section measure the use of resources and the way human activities affect the natural and built environment. They include measures of environmental goods (forest, water, and cultivable land) and of degradation (pollution, deforestation, loss of habitat, and loss of biodiversity). These indicators show that growing populations and expanding economies have placed greater demands on land, water, forests, minerals, and energy resources.

Economic growth and greater energy use are positively correlated. Access to electricity and the use of energy are vital in raising people's standard of living. But economic growth often has negative environmental consequences with disproportionate impacts on poor people. Recognizing this, the World Bank Group has joined the UN Sustainable Energy for All initiative, which calls on governments, businesses, and civil societies to achieve three goals by 2030: providing universal access to electricity and clean cooking fuels, doubling the share of the world's energy supply from renewable sources, and doubling the rate of improvement in energy efficiency. Several energy- and emissions-related indicators are presented in this section, covering data on access to electricity, energy use and efficiency, electricity production and use, and greenhouse gas emissions from various international sources.

Household and ambient air pollution place a major burden on people's health. About 40 percent of the world's population relies on dung, wood, crop waste, coal, or other solid fuels to meet basic energy needs. Previous assessments of global disease burden attributable to air pollution have been limited to urban areas or by coarse spatial resolution of concentration estimates. Recent developments in remote sensing and global chemical transport models and improvements in coverage of surface measurements facilitate virtually complete spatially resolved global air pollutant concentration estimates. This year's *Environment* section introduces the new global estimates of exposure to ambient air pollution, including population-weighted exposure to mean annual concentrations of fine particulate matter ($PM_{2.5}$) and the proportion of people who are exposed to ambient $PM_{2.5}$ concentrations that exceed World Health Organization guidelines. Produced by the Global Burden of Disease team at the Institute for Health Metrics and Evaluation, these improved estimates replace data on PM_{10} pollution in urban areas.

Other indicators in this section cover land use, agriculture and food production, forests and biodiversity, threatened species, water resources, climate variability, exposure to impact, resilience, urbanization, traffic and congestion, and natural resource rents. Where possible, the indicators come from international sources and have been standardized to facilitate comparison across countries. But ecosystems span national boundaries, and access to natural resources may vary within countries. For example, water may be abundant in some parts of a country but scarce in others, and countries often share water resources. Greenhouse gas emissions and climate change are measured globally, but their effects are experienced locally.

Highlights

Agricultural output has grown faster than the population since 1990

Population growth and food production (Index, 1990 = 100)

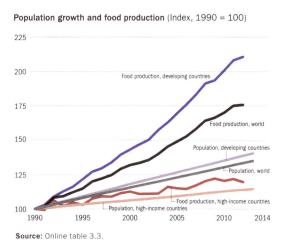

Food production, developing countries

Food production, world

Population, developing countries

Population, world

Population, high-income countries

Food production, high-income countries

Source: Online table 3.3.

Since 1990, food production has outpaced population growth in every region and income group. The pace has been considerably faster in developing economies, particularly those in Sub-Saharan Africa and East Asia and Pacific, than in high-income economies. Over the same period developing countries have boosted the area of land under cereal production 21 percent. Sub-Saharan African countries increased the area of land under cereal production 49 percent, to just under 100 million hectares in 2013. According to World Bank projections, there will likely be almost 9.5 billion people living on Earth by 2050, about 2 billion more than today. Most will live in cities, and the majority will depend on rural areas to feed them. Meeting the growing demand for food will require using agricultural inputs more efficiently and bringing more land into production. But intensive use of land and cultivation may cause further environmental degradation.

The number of threatened species is highest in Latin America and the Caribbean and Sub-Saharan Africa

Threatened species, by taxonomic group, 2014 (number of species)

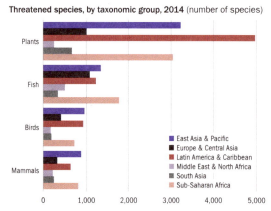

- East Asia & Pacific
- Europe & Central Asia
- Latin America & Caribbean
- Middle East & North Africa
- South Asia
- Sub-Saharan Africa

Source: International Union for the Conservation of Nature Red List of Threatened Species and online table 3.4.

As threats to biodiversity mount, the international community is increasingly focusing on conserving diversity, making the number of threatened species an important measure of the immediate need for conservation in an area. More than 74,000 species are on the International Union for Conservation of Nature Red List, but global analyses of the status of threatened species have been carried out for only a few groups of organisms: The status of virtually all known species has been assessed only for mammals (excluding whales and porpoises), birds (as listed for the area where their breeding or wintering ranges are located), and amphibians. East Asia and Pacific has the largest number of threatened mammal and bird species, Sub-Saharan Africa has the largest number of threatened fish species, and Latin America and the Caribbean has the most threatened plant species.

Agriculture accounts for 90 percent of water use in low-income countries

Share of freshwater withdrawals, most recent year available (%)

- Industrial
- Domestic
- Agricultural

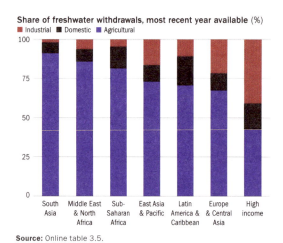

Source: Online table 3.5.

Water is crucial to economic growth and development and to the survival of both terrestrial and aquatic systems. Agriculture accounts for more than 70 percent of freshwater drawn from lakes, rivers, and underground sources and about 90 percent in low-income countries, where most of the water is used for irrigation. The volume of water on Earth is about 1,400 million cubic kilometers, only 3.1 percent of which, or about 43 million cubic kilometers, is freshwater. Due to increased demand, global per capita freshwater supplies have declined by nearly half over the past 45 years. As demand for water increases, more people will face water stress (having less than 1,700 cubic meters of water a year per person). Most of the people living in countries facing chronic and widespread water shortages are in developing country regions.

 Front User guide World view People Environment

Air pollution exceeds World Health Organization guidelines for 84 percent of the population

In many parts of the world exposure to air pollution is increasing at an alarming rate and has become the main environmental threat to health. In 2010 almost 84 percent of the world's population lived in areas where ambient concentrations of fine particulates with a diameter of fewer than 2.5 microns ($PM_{2.5}$) exceeded the World Health Organization's air quality guideline of 10 micrograms per cubic meter (annual average; WHO 2006). Exposure to ambient $PM_{2.5}$ pollution in 2010 resulted in more than 3.2 million premature deaths globally, according to the *Global Burden of Disease 2010*. Air pollution also carries substantial economic costs and represents a drag on development, particularly for developing countries, where average exposure to pollution has worsened since 1990, due largely to increases in East Asia and Pacific and South Asia. Globally, population-weighted exposure to $PM_{2.5}$ increased as much as 10 percent between 1990 and 2010.

Ambient population-weighted exposure to $PM_{2.5}$ pollution (micrograms per cubic meter)

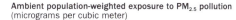
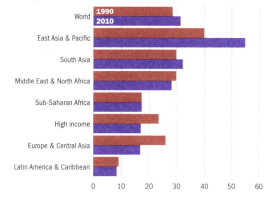

Source: Online table 3.13.

Some 2.5 billion people still lack access to improved sanitation facilities

Sanitation services in developing countries have improved over the last two decades. In 1990 only 35 percent of the people in developing countries had access to flush toilets or other forms of improved sanitation. By 2012, 57 percent did. But 2.5 billion people still lack access to improved sanitation, and the situation is worst in rural areas, where only 43 percent of the population in developing countries has access. East Asia and Pacific has made the most improvement, more than doubling access to improved sanitation since 1990—an impressive achievement, bringing access to basic sanitation facilities to more than 850 million additional people, mostly in China. But in the region more that 42 percent of people in rural areas still lack access to acceptable sanitation facilities, and there is wide variation within and across countries.

Share of population with access to improved sanitation facilities (%)

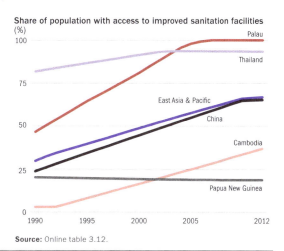

Source: Online table 3.12.

Natural resource rents account for 17 percent of Sub-Saharan Africa's GDP

In some countries earnings from natural resources, especially from fossil fuels and minerals, account for a sizable share of GDP, much of it in the form of economic rents—revenues above the cost of extracting natural resources. Natural resources give rise to economic rents because they are not produced. Rents from nonrenewable resources and from overharvesting forests indicate the liquidation of a country's capital stock. When countries use these rents to support current consumption rather than to invest in new capital to replace what is being used, they are, in effect, borrowing against their future. The Middle East and North Africa (more than 27 percent of GDP) and Sub-Saharan Africa (nearly 17 percent) are the most dependent on these revenues.

Natural resource rents, 2013 (% of GDP)

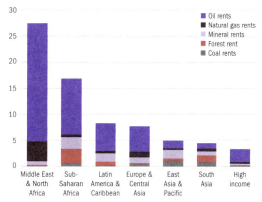

Source: Online table 3.15.

Biodiversity refers to the variety of life on Earth, Including the variety of plant and animal species, the genetic variability within each species, and the variety of different ecosystems. The Earth's biodiversity is the result of millions of years of evolution of life on the planet. The two most species-rich ecosystems are tropical forests and coral reefs. Tropical forests are under threat largely from conversion to other land uses, while coral reefs are experiencing increasing overexploitation and pollution. The pressure on biodiversity is driven largely by economic development and related demands. Several international conventions have been developed to conserve threatened species. One of the most widely used approaches for conserving habitat is to designate protected areas, such as national parks. The total area of protected sites has increased steadily in the past three decades.

Protected areas

NATIONALLY PROTECTED TERRESTRIAL AND MARINE AREAS AS A SHARE OF TOTAL TERRITORIAL AREA, 2012 (%)

- Less than 1.0
- 1.0–4.9
- 5.0–9.9
- 10.0–19.9
- 20.0 or more
- No data

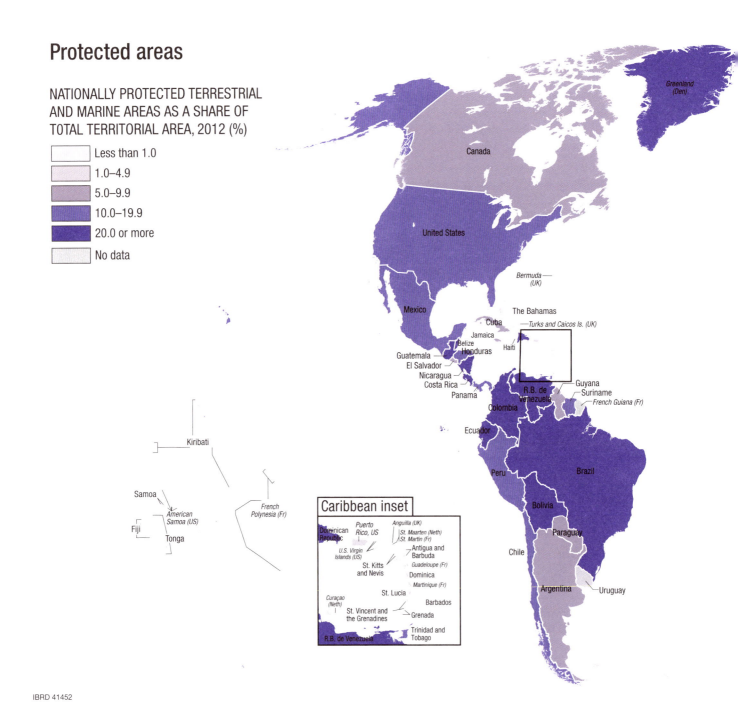

IBRD 41452

Over the last two decades the world's forests have shrunk by 142 million hectares—equivalent to more than 172 million soccer fields.

Protecting forests and other terrestrial and marine areas helps protect plant and animal habitats and preserve the diversity of species.

By 2012 more than 14 percent of the world's land and more than 12 percent of its marine areas had been protected, an increase of almost 6 percentage points in both categories since 1990.

Latin America and the Caribbean and Sub-Saharan Africa have the highest share of protected areas among developing country regions.

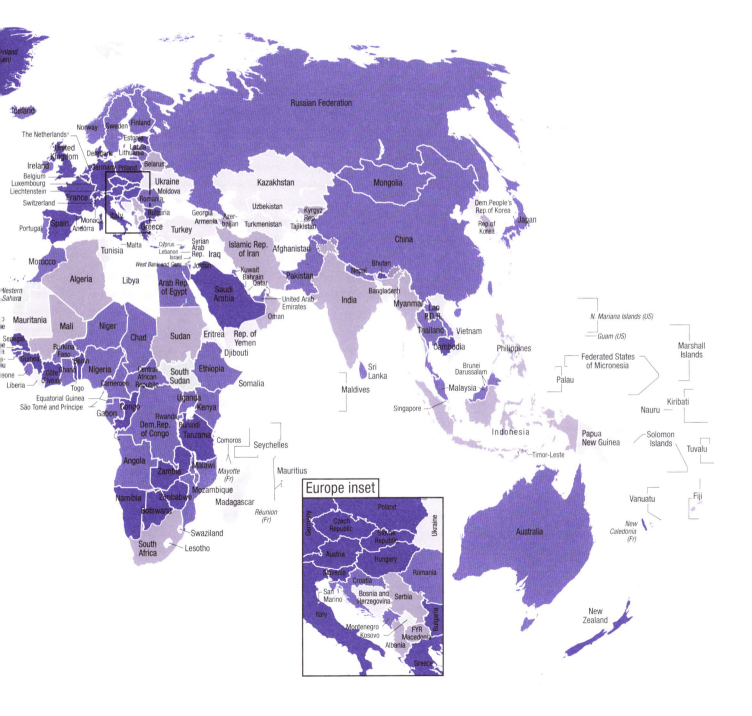

3 Environment

	Deforestation[a]	Nationally protected areas	Internal renewable freshwater resources[b]	Access to improved water source	Access to improved sanitation facilities	Urban population	Particulate matter concentration	Carbon dioxide emissions	Energy use	Electricity production
		Terrestrial and marine areas % of total territorial area					Mean annual exposure to PM$_{2.5}$ pollution micrograms per cubic meter			
	average annual %	% of total territorial area	Per capita cubic meters	% of total population	% of total population	% growth	micrograms per cubic meter	million metric tons	Per capita kilograms of oil equivalent	billion kilowatt hours
	2000–10	2012	2013	2012	2012	2012–13	2010	2010	2011	2011
Afghanistan	0.00	0.4	1,543	64	29	4.0	24	8.2	..	..
Albania	−0.10	9.5	9,284	96	91	1.8	14	4.3	748	4.2
Algeria	0.57	7.4	287	84	95	2.8	22	123.5	1,108	51.2
American Samoa	0.19	16.8	..	100	63	0.0	..	..	..	..
Andorra	0.00	9.8	3,984	100	100	0.5	13	0.5	..	..
Angola	0.21	12.1	6,893	54	60	5.0	11	30.4	673	5.7
Antigua and Barbuda	0.20	1.2	578	98	91	−1.0	17	0.5	..	..
Argentina	0.81	6.6	7,045	99	97	1.0	5	180.5	1,967	129.6
Armenia	1.48	8.1	2,304	100	91	0.0	19	4.2	916	7.4
Aruba	0.00	0.0	..	98	98	−0.2	..	2.3	..	..
Australia	0.37	15.0	21,272	100	100	1.9	6	373.1	5,501	252.6
Austria	−0.13	23.6	6,486	100	100	0.6	13	66.9	3,935	62.2
Azerbaijan	0.00	7.4	862	80	82	1.7	17	45.7	1,369	20.3
Bahamas, The	0.00	1.0	53	98	92	1.5	13	2.5	..	..
Bahrain	−3.55	6.8	3	100	99	1.1	49	24.2	7,353	13.8
Bangladesh	0.18	4.2	671	85	57	3.6	31	56.2	205	44.1
Barbados	0.00	0.1	281	100	..	0.1	19	1.5	..	..
Belarus	−0.43	8.3	3,930	100	94	0.6	11	62.2	3,114	32.2
Belgium	−0.16	24.5	1,073	100	100	0.5	19	108.9	5,349	89.0
Belize	0.67	26.4	45,978	99	91	1.9	6	0.4	..	..
Benin	1.04	25.5	998	76	14	3.7	22	5.2	385	0.2
Bermuda	0.00	5.1	..	..	..	0.3	..	0.5	..	..
Bhutan	−0.34	28.4	103,456	98	47	3.7	22	0.5	..	..
Bolivia	0.50	20.8	28,441	88	46	2.3	6	15.5	746	7.2
Bosnia and Herzegovina	0.00	1.5	9,271	100	95	0.2	12	31.1	1,848	15.3
Botswana	0.99	37.2	1,187	97	64	1.3	5	5.2	1,115	0.4
Brazil	0.50	26.0	28,254	98	81	1.2	5	419.8	1,371	531.8
Brunei Darussalam	0.44	29.6	20,345	..	..	1.8	5	9.2	9,427	3.7
Bulgaria	−1.53	35.4	2,891	100	100	−0.1	17	44.7	2,615	50.0
Burkina Faso	1.01	15.2	738	82	19	5.9	27	1.7	..	..
Burundi	1.40	4.9	990	75	48	5.6	11	0.3	..	..
Cabo Verde	−0.36	0.2	601	89	65	2.1	43	0.4	..	..
Cambodia	1.34	23.8	7,968	71	37	2.7	17	4.2	365	1.1
Cameroon	1.05	10.9	12,267	74	45	3.6	22	7.2	318	6.0
Canada	0.00	7.0	81,071	100	100	1.4	10	499.1	7,333	636.9
Cayman Islands	0.00	1.5	..	96	96	1.5	..	0.6	..	..
Central African Republic	0.13	18.0	30,543	68	22	2.6	19	0.3	..	..
Chad	0.66	16.6	1,170	51	12	3.4	33	0.5	..	..
Channel Islands	..	0.5	..	..	..	0.7	..	..	..	..
Chile	−0.25	15.0	50,228	99	99	1.1	8	72.3	1,940	65.7
China	−1.57	16.1	2,072	92	65	2.9	73	8,286.9	2,029	4,715.7
Hong Kong SAR, China	..	41.9	..	..	..	0.5	..	36.3	2,106	39.0
Macao SAR, China	..	..	..	..	..	1.7	..	1.0	..	..
Colombia	0.17	20.8	46,977	91	80	1.7	5	75.7	671	61.8
Comoros	9.34	4.0	1,633	95	35	2.7	5	0.1	..	..
Congo, Dem. Rep.	0.20	12.0	13,331	47	31	4.0	15	3.0	383	7.9
Congo, Rep.	0.07	30.4	49,914	75	15	3.2	14	2.0	393	1.3

 Front | User guide | World view | People | Environment

	Deforestation[a] average annual % 2000–10	Nationally protected areas Terrestrial and marine areas % of total territorial area 2012	Internal renewable freshwater resources[b] Per capita cubic meters 2013	Access to improved water source % of total population 2012	Access to improved sanitation facilities % of total population 2012	Urban population % growth 2012–13	Particulate matter concentration Mean annual exposure to PM$_{2.5}$ pollution micrograms per cubic meter 2010	Carbon dioxide emissions million metric tons 2010	Energy use Per capita kilograms of oil equivalent 2011	Electricity production billion kilowatt hours 2011
Costa Rica	−0.93	22.6	23,193	97	94	2.7	8	7.8	983	9.8
Côte d'Ivoire	−0.15	22.2	3,782	80	22	3.8	15	5.8	579	6.1
Croatia	−0.19	10.3	8,859	99	98	0.2	14	20.9	1,971	10.7
Cuba	−1.66	9.9	3,384	94	93	0.1	7	38.4	992	17.8
Curaçao	..	..	..	..	..	1.0	..	..	..	..
Cyprus	−0.09	17.1	684	100	100	0.9	19	7.7	2,121	4.9
Czech Republic	−0.08	22.4	1,251	100	100	0.0	16	111.8	4,138	86.8
Denmark	−1.14	23.6	1,069	100	100	0.6	12	46.3	3,231	35.2
Djibouti	0.00	0.2	344	92	61	1.6	27	0.5	..	..
Dominica	0.58	3.7	..	..	..	0.9	18	0.1	..	..
Dominican Republic	0.00	20.8	2,019	81	82	2.6	9	21.0	727	13.0
Ecuador	1.81	37.0	28,111	86	83	1.9	6	32.6	849	20.3
Egypt, Arab Rep.	−1.73	11.3	22	99	96	1.7	33	204.8	978	156.6
El Salvador	1.45	8.7	2,465	90	71	1.4	5	6.2	690	5.8
Equatorial Guinea	0.69	15.1	34,345	..	..	3.1	7	4.7	..	..
Eritrea	0.28	3.8	442	..	..	5.2	25	0.5	129	0.3
Estonia	0.12	23.2	9,643	99	95	−0.5	7	18.3	4,221	12.9
Ethiopia	1.08	18.4	1,296	52	24	4.9	15	6.5	381	5.2
Faeroe Islands	0.00	1.0	..	..	..	0.4	..	0.7	..	..
Fiji	−0.34	6.0	32,404	96	87	1.4	5	1.3	..	..
Finland	0.14	15.2	19,673	100	100	0.6	5	61.8	6,449	73.5
France	−0.39	28.7	3,033	100	100	0.7	14	361.3	3,869	556.9
French Polynesia	−3.97	0.1	..	100	97	0.9	..	0.9	..	..
Gabon	0.00	19.1	98,103	92	41	2.7	6	2.6	1,253	1.8
Gambia, The	−0.41	4.4	1,622	90	60	4.3	36	0.5	..	..
Georgia	0.09	3.7	12,955	99	93	0.2	12	6.2	790	10.2
Germany	0.00	49.0	1,327	100	100	0.6	16	745.4	3,811	602.4
Ghana	2.08	14.4	1,170	87	14	3.4	18	9.0	425	11.2
Greece	−0.81	21.5	5,260	100	99	−0.1	17	86.7	2,402	59.2
Greenland	0.00	40.6	..	100	100	−0.1	..	0.6	..	..
Grenada	0.00	0.3	..	97	98	0.3	15	0.3	..	..
Guam	0.00	5.3	..	100	90	1.5	..	..	..	..
Guatemala	1.40	29.8	7,060	94	80	3.4	12	11.1	691	8.1
Guinea	0.54	26.8	19,242	75	19	3.8	22	1.2	..	..
Guinea-Bissau	0.48	27.1	9,388	74	20	4.2	31	0.2	..	..
Guyana	0.00	5.0	301,396	98	84	0.8	6	1.7	..	..
Haiti	0.76	0.1	1,261	62	24	3.8	11	2.1	320	0.7
Honduras	2.06	16.2	11,196	90	80	3.2	7	8.1	609	7.1
Hungary	−0.62	23.1	606	100	100	0.4	16	50.6	2,503	36.0
Iceland	−4.99	13.3	525,074	100	100	1.1	6	2.0	17,964	17.2
India	−0.46	5.0	1,155	93	36	2.4	32	2,008.8	614	1,052.3
Indonesia	0.51	9.1	8,080	85	59	2.7	14	434.0	857	182.4
Iran, Islamic Rep.	0.00	7.0	1,659	96	89	2.1	30	571.6	2,813	239.7
Iraq	−0.09	0.4	1,053	85	85	2.7	30	114.7	1,266	54.2
Ireland	−1.53	12.8	10,658	100	99	0.7	9	40.0	2,888	27.7
Isle of Man	0.00	..	..	..	..	0.8	..	..	..	..
Israel	−0.07	14.7	93	100	100	1.9	26	70.7	2,994	59.6

3 Environment

	Deforestation[a]	Nationally protected areas	Internal renewable freshwater resources[b]	Access to improved water source	Access to improved sanitation facilities	Urban population	Particulate matter concentration	Carbon dioxide emissions	Energy use	Electricity production
	average annual %	Terrestrial and marine areas % of total territorial area	Per capita cubic meters	% of total population	% of total population	% growth	Mean annual exposure to PM$_{2.5}$ pollution micrograms per cubic meter	million metric tons	Per capita kilograms of oil equivalent	billion kilowatt hours
	2000–10	2012	2013	2012	2012	2012–13	2010	2010	2011	2011
Italy	−0.90	21.0	3,030	100	..	1.3	19	406.3	2,819	300.6
Jamaica	0.11	7.1	3,464	93	80	0.6	12	7.2	1,135	5.1
Japan	−0.05	11.0	3,377	100	100	0.5	22	1,170.7	3,610	1,042.7
Jordan	0.00	0.0	106	96	98	2.5	29	20.8	1,143	14.6
Kazakhstan	0.17	3.3	3,777	93	98	1.3	13	248.7	4,717	86.6
Kenya	0.33	11.6	467	62	30	4.4	6	12.4	480	7.8
Kiribati	0.00	20.2	..	67	40	1.8	6	0.1	..	..
Korea, Dem. People's Rep.	2.00	1.7	2,691	98	82	0.8	32	71.6	773	21.6
Korea, Rep.	0.11	5.3	1,291	98	100	0.6	38	567.6	5,232	520.1
Kosovo	..	..	..	..	..	..	..	..	1,411	5.8
Kuwait	−2.57	12.9	0	99	100	3.6	50	93.7	10,408	57.5
Kyrgyz Republic	−1.07	6.3	8,555	88	92	2.2	16	6.4	562	15.2
Lao PDR	0.49	16.7	28,125	72	65	4.9	22	1.9	..	..
Latvia	−0.34	17.6	8,317	98	79	−1.2	9	7.6	2,122	6.1
Lebanon	−0.45	0.5	1,074	100	..	1.1	24	20.4	1,449	16.4
Lesotho	−0.47	0.5	2,521	81	30	3.1	6	0.0	..	..
Liberia	0.67	2.4	46,576	75	17	3.2	9	0.8	..	..
Libya	0.00	0.1	113	..	97	1.0	37	59.0	2,186	27.6
Liechtenstein	0.00	43.1	..	..	..	0.5	..	..	..	..
Lithuania	−0.68	17.2	5,261	96	94	−1.1	10	13.6	2,406	4.2
Luxembourg	0.00	39.7	1,840	100	100	2.7	13	10.8	8,046	2.6
Macedonia, FYR	−0.41	7.3	2,563	99	91	0.1	17	10.9	1,484	6.9
Madagascar	0.45	4.7	14,700	50	14	4.7	5	2.0	..	..
Malawi	0.97	18.3	986	85	10	3.7	5	1.2	..	..
Malaysia	0.54	13.9	19,517	100	96	2.7	13	216.8	2,639	130.1
Maldives	0.00	..	87	99	99	4.5	16	1.1	..	..
Mali	0.61	6.0	3,921	67	22	5.0	34	0.6	..	..
Malta	0.00	2.2	119	100	100	1.1	21	2.6	2,060	2.2
Marshall Islands	0.00	0.7	..	95	76	0.5	8	0.1	..	..
Mauritania	2.66	1.2	103	50	27	3.5	65	2.2	..	..
Mauritius	1.00	0.7	2,186	100	91	−0.2	5	4.1	..	..
Mexico	0.30	13.7	3,343	95	85	1.6	17	443.7	1,560	295.8
Micronesia, Fed. Sets.	−0.04	0.1	..	89	57	0.3	5	0.1	..	..
Moldova	−1.77	3.8	281	97	87	0.0	14	4.9	936	5.8
Monaco	0.00	98.4	..	100	100	0.7	..	..	..	..
Mongolia	0.73	13.8	12,258	85	56	2.8	9	11.5	1,310	4.8
Montenegro	0.00	12.8	..	98	90	0.3	16	2.6	1,900	2.7
Morocco	−0.23	19.9	879	84	75	2.3	20	50.6	539	24.9
Mozambique	0.54	16.4	3,883	49	21	3.3	5	2.9	415	16.8
Myanmar	0.93	6.0	18,832	86	77	2.5	22	9.0	268	7.3
Namibia	0.97	42.6	2,674	92	32	4.2	4	3.2	717	1.4
Nepal	0.70	16.4	7,130	88	37	3.2	33	3.8	383	3.3
Netherlands	−0.14	31.5	655	100	100	1.1	19	182.1	4,638	113.0
New Caledonia	0.00	30.5	..	99	100	2.4	..	3.9	..	..
New Zealand	−0.01	21.3	73,614	100	..	0.8	6	31.6	4,144	44.5
Nicaragua	2.01	32.5	25,689	85	52	2.0	5	4.5	515	3.8
Niger	0.98	16.7	196	52	9	5.1	37	1.4	..	..

	Deforestation[a]	Nationally protected areas	Internal renewable freshwater resources[b]	Access to improved water source	Access to improved sanitation facilities	Urban population	Particulate matter concentration	Carbon dioxide emissions	Energy use	Electricity production
		Terrestrial and marine areas % of total territorial area	Per capita cubic meters	% of total population	% of total population	% growth	Mean annual exposure to PM$_{2.5}$ pollution micrograms per cubic meter	million metric tons	Per capita kilograms of oil equivalent	billion kilowatt hours
	average annual % 2000–10	2012	2013	2012	2012	2012–13	2010	2010	2011	2011
Nigeria	3.67	13.8	1,273	64	28	4.7	27	78.9	721	27.0
Northern Mariana Islands	0.53	19.9	..	98	80	1.0	..	..	..	..
Norway	−0.80	12.2	75,194	100	100	1.6	4	57.2	5,681	126.9
Oman	0.00	9.3	385	93	97	9.8	35	57.2	8,356	21.9
Pakistan	2.24	10.6	302	91	48	2.8	38	161.4	482	95.3
Palau	−0.18	28.2	..	95	100	1.7	..	0.2	..	..
Panama	0.36	14.1	35,350	94	73	2.1	5	9.6	1,085	7.9
Papua New Guinea	0.48	1.4	109,407	40	19	2.1	5	3.1	..	..
Paraguay	0.97	6.4	17,200	94	80	2.1	4	5.1	739	57.6
Peru	0.18	18.3	54,024	87	73	1.7	10	57.6	695	39.2
Philippines	−0.75	5.1	4,868	92	74	1.3	7	81.6	426	69.2
Poland	−0.31	34.8	1,392	..	..	−0.2	16	317.3	2,629	163.1
Portugal	−0.11	14.7	3,634	100	100	0.4	13	52.4	2,187	51.9
Puerto Rico	−1.76	4.6	1,964	..	99	−1.1	..	..	..	..
Qatar	0.00	2.4	26	100	100	5.7	69	70.5	17,419	30.7
Romania	−0.32	19.2	2,117	..	..	−0.1	17	78.7	1,778	62.0
Russian Federation	0.00	11.3	30,056	97	71	0.3	10	1,740.8	5,113	1,053.0
Rwanda	−2.38	10.5	807	71	64	6.4	14	0.6	..	..
Samoa	0.00	2.3	..	99	92	−0.2	5	0.2	..	..
San Marino	0.00	..	..	..	..	0.7	..	..	..	..
São Tomé and Príncipe	0.00	0.0	11,296	97	34	3.6	5	0.1	..	..
Saudi Arabia	0.00	29.9	83	97	100	2.1	62	464.5	6,738	250.1
Senegal	0.49	24.2	1,825	74	52	3.6	41	7.1	264	3.0
Serbia	−0.99	6.3	1,173	99	97	−0.4	16	46.0	2,237	38.0
Seychelles	0.00	1.3	..	96	97	1.6	5	0.7	..	..
Sierra Leone	0.69	10.3	26,264	60	13	2.8	18	0.7	..	..
Singapore	0.00	3.4	111	100	100	1.6	20	13.5	6,452	46.0
Sint Maarten	..	..	..	..	..	1.5	..	..	..	..
Slovak Republic	−0.06	36.1	2,328	100	100	−0.3	15	36.1	3,214	28.3
Slovenia	−0.16	54.9	9,063	100	100	0.0	15	15.3	3,531	15.9
Solomon Islands	0.25	1.1	79,646	81	29	4.3	6	0.2	..	..
Somalia	1.07	0.5	572	32	24	4.1	8	0.6	..	..
South Africa	0.00	6.6	843	95	74	2.4	8	460.1	2,742	259.6
South Sudan	..	..	2,302	57	9	5.2	..	..	..	..
Spain	−0.68	25.3	2,385	100	100	0.0	14	269.7	2,686	289.0
Sri Lanka	1.12	15.4	2,578	94	92	0.8	9	12.7	499	11.6
St. Kitts and Nevis	0.00	0.8	443	98	..	1.3	..	0.2	..	..
St. Lucia	−0.07	2.5	..	94	65	0.8	18	0.4	..	..
St. Martin	0.00	..	..	..	..	..	..	..	..	..
St. Vincent & the Grenadines	−0.27	1.2	..	95	..	0.7	17	0.2	..	..
Sudan	0.08[c]	7.1[c]	81	56	24	2.5	26[c]	14.2[c]	355	8.6
Suriname	0.01	15.2	183,579	95	80	0.8	5	2.4	..	..
Swaziland	−0.84	3.0	2,113	74	58	1.3	5	1.0	..	..
Sweden	−0.30	13.9	17,812	100	100	1.0	6	52.5	5,190	150.3
Switzerland	−0.38	26.3	4,995	100	100	1.2	14	38.8	3,207	62.9
Syrian Arab Republic	−1.29	0.7	312	90	96	2.7	26	61.9	910	41.1
Tajikistan	0.00	4.8	7,732	72	94	2.7	17	2.9	306	16.2

3 Environment

	Deforestation[a] average annual % 2000–10	Nationally protected areas Terrestrial and marine areas % of total territorial area 2012	Internal renewable freshwater resources[b] Per capita cubic meters 2013	Access to improved water source % of total population 2012	Access to improved sanitation facilities % of total population 2012	Urban population % growth 2012–13	Particulate matter concentration Mean annual exposure to PM$_{2.5}$ pollution micrograms per cubic meter 2010	Carbon dioxide emissions million metric tons 2010	Energy use Per capita kilograms of oil equivalent 2011	Electricity production billion kilowatt hours 2011
Tanzania	1.13	31.7	1,705	53	12	5.4	5	6.8	448	5.3
Thailand	0.02	16.4	3,350	96	93	3.0	21	295.3	1,790	156.0
Timor-Leste	1.40	6.2	6,961	71	39	4.8	5	0.2	..	..
Togo	5.13	24.2	1,687	60	11	3.8	21	1.5	427	0.1
Tonga	0.00	9.5	..	99	91	0.6	5	0.2	..	..
Trinidad and Tobago	0.32	10.1	2,863	94	92	–1.2	4	50.7	15,691	8.9
Tunisia	–1.86	4.8	385	97	90	1.3	19	25.9	890	16.1
Turkey	–1.11	2.1	3,029	100	91	2.0	17	298.0	1,539	229.4
Turkmenistan	0.00	3.2	268	71	99	2.0	48	53.1	4,839	17.2
Turks and Caicos Islands	0.00	3.6	..	..	..	2.5	..	0.2	..	..
Tuvalu	0.00	0.3	..	98	83	1.9	..	..	..	..
Uganda	2.56	11.5	1,038	75	34	5.4	10	3.8	..	..
Ukraine	–0.21	4.5	1,167	98	94	0.1	13	304.8	2,766	194.9
United Arab Emirates	–0.24	15.5	16	100	98	1.9	80	167.6	7,407	99.1
United Kingdom	–0.31	23.4	2,262	100	100	1.0	14	493.5	2,973	364.9
United States	–0.13	15.1	8,914	99	100	0.9	13	5,433.1	7,032	4,326.6
Uruguay	–2.14	2.6	27,061	100	96	0.5	6	6.6	1,309	10.3
Uzbekistan	–0.20	3.4	540	87	100	1.7	22	104.4	1,628	52.4
Vanuatu	0.00	0.5	..	91	58	3.4	5	0.1	..	..
Venezuela, RB	0.60	49.5	26,476	..	..	1.5	8	201.7	2,380	122.1
Vietnam	–1.65	4.7	4,006	95	75	3.1	30	150.2	697	99.2
Virgin Islands (U.S.)	0.80	2.8	..	100	96	–0.4	..	..	..	..
West Bank and Gaza	–0.10	0.6	195	82	94	3.3	25	2.4	..	..
Yemen, Rep.	0.00	1.1	86	55	53	4.0	30	21.9	312	6.2
Zambia	0.33	37.8	5,516	63	43	4.3	6	2.4	621	11.5
Zimbabwe	1.88	27.2	866	80	40	2.5	5	9.4	697	8.9
World	**0.11 w**	**14.0 w**	**6,055 s**	**89 w**	**64 w**	**2.1 w**	**31 w**	**33,615.4[d] w**	**1,890 w**	**22,158.5 w**
Low income	0.61	13.6	4,875	69	37	3.9	19	222.9	359	190.6
Middle income	0.13	14.3	4,920	90	60	2.4	37	16,554.9	1,280	9,794.1
Lower middle income	0.31	11.0	3,047	88	47	2.6	27	3,833.4	686	2,226.3
Upper middle income	0.04	15.8	6,910	93	74	2.3	47	12,721.1	1,893	7,566.7
Low & middle income	0.22	14.2	4,913	87	57	2.6	34	16,777.5	1,179	10,005.1
East Asia & Pacific	–0.44	13.7	4,376	91	67	2.8	55	9,570.5	1,671	5,410.8
Europe & Central Asia	–0.48	5.2	2,710	95	94	1.1	17	1,416.7	2,080	908.6
Latin America & Carib.	0.46	21.2	22,124	94	81	1.5	8	1,553.7	1,292	1,348.0
Middle East & N. Africa	–0.15	5.9	656	90	88	2.3	28	1,277.9	1,376	654.4
South Asia	–0.29	5.9	1,186	91	40	2.6	32	2,252.6	555	1,215.8
Sub-Saharan Africa	0.48	16.3	4,120	64	30	4.1	17	703.8	681	445.2
High income	–0.03	13.8	11,269	99	96	0.8	17	14,901.7	4,877	12,198.4
Euro area	–0.31	26.7	2,991	100	100	0.6	16	2,480.0	3,485	2,298.3

a. Negative values indicate an increase in forest area. b. River flows from other countries are not included because of data unreliability. c. Includes South Sudan. d. Includes emissions not allocated to specific countries.

 Front User guide World view People Environment

About the data

Environmental resources are needed to promote growth and poverty reduction, but growth can create new stresses on the environment. Deforestation, loss of biologically diverse habitat, depletion of water resources, pollution, urbanization, and ever increasing demand for energy production are some of the factors that must be considered in shaping development strategies.

Loss of forests

Forests provide habitat for many species and act as carbon sinks. If properly managed they also provide a livelihood for people who manage and use forest resources. FAO (2010) provides information on forest cover in 2010 and adjusted estimates of forest cover in 1990 and 2000. Data presented here do not distinguish natural forests from plantations, a breakdown the FAO provides only for developing countries. Thus, data may underestimate the rate at which natural forest is disappearing in some countries.

Habitat protection and biodiversity

Deforestation is a major cause of loss of biodiversity, and habitat conservation is vital for stemming this loss. Conservation efforts have focused on protecting areas of high biodiversity. The World Conservation Monitoring Centre (WCMC) and the United Nations Environment Programme (UNEP) compile data on protected areas. Differences in definitions, reporting practices, and reporting periods limit cross-country comparability. Nationally protected areas are defined using the six International Union for Conservation of Nature (IUCN) categories for areas of at least 1,000 hectares—scientific reserves and strict nature reserves with limited public access, national parks of national or international significance and not materially affected by human activity, natural monuments and natural landscapes with unique aspects, managed nature reserves and wildlife sanctuaries, protected landscapes (which may include cultural landscapes), and areas managed mainly for the sustainable use of natural systems to ensure long-term protection and maintenance of biological diversity—as well as terrestrial protected areas not assigned to an IUCN category. Designating an area as protected does not mean that protection is in force. For small countries with protected areas smaller than 1,000 hectares, the size limit in the definition leads to underestimation of protected areas. Due to variations in consistency and methods of collection, data quality is highly variable across countries. Some countries update their information more frequently than others, some have more accurate data on extent of coverage, and many underreport the number or extent of protected areas.

Freshwater resources

The data on freshwater resources are derived from estimates of runoff into rivers and recharge of groundwater. These estimates are derived from different sources and refer to different years, so cross-country comparisons should be made with caution. Data are collected intermittently and may hide substantial year-to-year variations

in total renewable water resources. Data do not distinguish between seasonal and geographic variations in water availability within countries. Data for small countries and countries in arid and semiarid zones are less reliable than data for larger countries and countries with greater rainfall.

Water and sanitation

A reliable supply of safe drinking water and sanitary disposal of excreta are two of the most important means of improving human health and protecting the environment. Improved sanitation facilities prevent human, animal, and insect contact with excreta.

Data on access to an improved water source measure the percentage of the population with ready access to water for domestic purposes and are estimated by the World Health Organization (WHO)/United Nations Children's Fund (UNICEF) Joint Monitoring Programme for Water Supply and Sanitation based on surveys and censuses. The coverage rates are based on information from service users on household use rather than on information from service providers, which may include nonfunctioning systems. Access to drinking water from an improved source does not ensure that the water is safe or adequate, as these characteristics are not tested at the time of survey. While information on access to an improved water source is widely used, it is extremely subjective; terms such as "safe," "improved," "adequate," and "reasonable" may have different meanings in different countries despite official WHO definitions (see *Definitions*). Even in high-income countries treated water may not always be safe to drink. Access to an improved water source is equated with connection to a supply system; it does not account for variations in the quality and cost of the service.

Urbanization

There is no consistent and universally accepted standard for distinguishing urban from rural areas and, by extension, calculating their populations. Most countries use a classification related to the size or characteristics of settlements. Some define areas based on the presence of certain infrastructure and services. Others designate areas based on administrative arrangements. Because data are based on national definitions, cross-country comparisons should be made with caution.

Air pollution

Air pollution places a major burden on world health. More than 40 percent of the world's people rely on wood, charcoal, dung, crop waste, or coal to meet basic energy needs. Cooking with solid fuels creates harmful smoke and particulates that fill homes and the surrounding environment. Household air pollution from cooking with solid fuels is responsible for 3.9 million premature deaths a year—about one every 8 seconds. In many places, including cities but also nearby rural areas, exposure to air pollution exposure is the main environmental threat to health. Long-term exposure to high levels of fine particulates in the air contributes to a range of health

effects, including respiratory diseases, lung cancer, and heart disease, resulting in 3.2 million premature deaths annually. Not only does exposure to air pollution endanger the health of the world's people, it also carries huge economic costs and represents a drag on development, particularly for low- and middle-income countries and vulnerable segments of the population such as children and the elderly.

Data on exposure to ambient air pollution are derived from estimates of annual concentrations of very fine particulates produced for the Global Burden of Disease. Estimates of annual concentrations are generated by combining data from atmospheric chemistry transport models and satellite observations of aerosols in the atmosphere. Modeled concentrations are calibrated against observations from ground-level monitoring of particulates in more than 460 locations around the world. Exposure to concentrations of particulates in both urban and rural areas is weighted by population and is aggregated at the national level.

Pollutant concentrations are sensitive to local conditions, and even monitoring sites in the same city may register different levels. Direct monitoring of ambient $PM_{2.5}$ is still rare in many parts of the world, and measurement protocols and standards are not the same for all countries. These data should be considered only a general indication of air quality, intended for cross-country comparisons of the relative risk of particulate matter pollution.

Carbon dioxide emissions

Carbon dioxide emissions are the primary source of greenhouse gases, which contribute to global warming, threatening human and natural habitats. Fossil fuel combustion and cement manufacturing are the primary sources of anthropogenic carbon dioxide emissions, which the U.S. Department of Energy's Carbon Dioxide Information Analysis Center (CDIAC) calculates using data from the United Nations Statistics Division's World Energy Data Set and the U.S. Bureau of Mines's Cement Manufacturing Data Set. Carbon dioxide emissions, often calculated and reported as elemental carbon, were converted to actual carbon dioxide mass by multiplying them by 3.667 (the ratio of the mass of carbon to that of carbon dioxide). Although estimates of global carbon dioxide emissions are probably accurate within 10 percent (as calculated from global average fuel chemistry and use), country estimates may have larger error bounds. Trends estimated from a consistent time series tend to be more accurate than individual values. Each year the CDIAC recalculates the entire time series since 1949, incorporating recent findings and corrections. Estimates exclude fuels supplied to ships and aircraft in international transport because of the difficulty of apportioning the fuels among benefiting countries.

Energy use

In developing economies growth in energy use is closely related to growth in the modern sectors—industry, motorized transport, and urban areas—but also reflects climatic, geographic, and economic factors. Energy use has been growing rapidly in low- and middle-income economies, but high-income economies still use more than four times as much energy per capita.

Total energy use refers to the use of primary energy before transformation to other end-use fuels (such as electricity and refined petroleum products). It includes energy from combustible renewables and waste—solid biomass and animal products, gas and liquid from biomass, and industrial and municipal waste. Biomass is any plant matter used directly as fuel or converted into fuel, heat, or electricity. Data for combustible renewables and waste are often based on small surveys or other incomplete information and thus give only a broad impression of developments and are not strictly comparable across countries. The International Energy Agency (IEA) reports include country notes that explain some of these differences (see *Data sources*). All forms of energy—primary energy and primary electricity—are converted into oil equivalents. A notional thermal efficiency of 33 percent is assumed for converting nuclear electricity into oil equivalents and 100 percent efficiency for converting hydroelectric power.

Electricity production

Use of energy is important in improving people's standard of living. But electricity generation also can damage the environment. Whether such damage occurs depends largely on how electricity is generated. For example, burning coal releases twice as much carbon dioxide—a major contributor to global warming—as does burning an equivalent amount of natural gas. Nuclear energy does not generate carbon dioxide emissions, but it produces other dangerous waste products.

The IEA compiles data and data on energy inputs used to generate electricity. Data for countries that are not members of the Organisation for Economic Co-operation and Development (OECD) are based on national energy data adjusted to conform to annual questionnaires completed by OECD member governments. In addition, estimates are sometimes made to complete major aggregates from which key data are missing, and adjustments are made to compensate for differences in definitions. The IEA makes these estimates in consultation with national statistical offices, oil companies, electric utilities, and national energy experts. It occasionally revises its time series to reflect political changes. For example, the IEA has constructed historical energy statistics for countries of the former Soviet Union. In addition, energy statistics for other countries have undergone continuous changes in coverage or methodology in recent years as more detailed energy accounts have become available. Breaks in series are therefore unavoidable.

Definitions

• **Deforestation** is the permanent conversion of natural forest area to other uses, including agriculture, ranching, settlements, and infrastructure. Deforested areas do not include areas logged but intended for regeneration or areas degraded by fuelwood gathering, acid precipitation, or forest fires. • **Nationally protected areas** are terrestrial and marine protected areas as a percentage of total territorial area and include all nationally designated protected areas with known location and extent. All overlaps between different designations and categories, buffered points, and polygons are removed, and all undated protected areas are dated. • **Internal renewable freshwater resources** are the average annual flows of rivers and groundwater from rainfall in the country. Natural incoming flows originating outside a country's borders and overlapping water resources between surface runoff and groundwater recharge are excluded. • **Access to an improved water source** is the percentage of the population using an improved drinking water source. An improved drinking water source includes piped water on premises (piped household water connection located inside the user's dwelling, plot or yard), public taps or standpipes, tube wells or boreholes, protected dug wells, protected springs, and rainwater collection. • **Access to improved sanitation facilities** is the percentage of the population using improved sanitation facilities. Improved sanitation facilities are likely to ensure hygienic separation of human excreta from human contact. They include flush/pour flush toilets (to piped sewer system, septic tank, or pit latrine), ventilated improved pit latrines, pit latrines with slab, and composting toilets. • **Urban population growth** is the annual rate of change of urban population assuming exponential change. Urban population is the proportion of midyear population of areas defined as urban in each country, which is obtained by the United Nations, multiplied by the World Bank estimate of total population. • **Population-weighted exposure to ambient PM$_{2.5}$ pollution** is defined as exposure to fine suspended particulates of less than 2.5 microns in diameter that are capable of penetrating deep into the respiratory tract and causing severe health damage. Data are aggregated at the national level and include both rural and urban areas. Exposure is calculated by weighting mean annual concentrations of PM$_{2.5}$ by population. • **Carbon dioxide emissions** are emissions from the burning of fossil fuels and the manufacture of cement and include carbon dioxide produced during consumption of solid, liquid, and gas fuels and gas flaring. • **Energy use** refers to the use of primary energy before transformation to other end use fuels, which equals indigenous production plus imports and stock changes, minus exports and fuels supplied to ships and aircraft engaged in international transport. • **Electricity production** is measured at the terminals of all alternator sets in a station. In addition to hydropower, coal, oil, gas, and nuclear power generation, it covers generation by geothermal, solar, wind, and tide and wave energy as well as that from combustible renewables and waste. Production includes the output of electric plants designed to produce electricity only, as well as that of combined heat and power plants.

Data sources

Data on deforestation are from FAO (2010) and the FAO's website. Data on protected areas, derived from the UNEP and WCMC online databases, are based on data from national authorities, national legislation, and international agreements. Data on freshwater resources are from the FAO's AQUASTAT database. Data on access to water and sanitation are from the WHO/UNICEF Joint Monitoring Programme for Water Supply and Sanitation (www.wssinfo.org). Data on urban population are from the United Nations Population Division (2014). Data on particulate matter concentrations are from the Global Burden of Disease 2010 study (www.healthdata.org/gbd /data) by the Institute for Health Metrics and Evaluation (see Lim and others 2012). See Brauer and others (2012) for the data and methods used to estimate ambient PM$_{2.5}$ exposure. Data on carbon dioxide emissions are from CDIAC online databases. Data on energy use and electricity production are from IEA online databases and its annual *Energy Statistics of Non-OECD Countries, Energy Balances of Non-OECD Countries, Energy Statistics of OECD Countries,* and *Energy Balances of OECD Countries.*

References

Brauer, M., M. Amman, R.T. Burnett, A. Cohen, F. Dentener, et al. 2012. "Exposure Assessment for Estimation of the Global Burden of Disease Attributable to Outdoor Air Pollution." *Environmental Science & Technology* 46: 652–60.

CDIAC (Carbon Dioxide Information Analysis Center). n.d. Online database. [http://cdiac.ornl.gov/home.html]. Oak Ridge National Laboratory, Environmental Science Division, Oak Ridge, TN.

FAO (Food and Agriculture Organization of the United Nations). 2010. *Global Forest Resources Assessment 2010.* Rome.

———. n.d. AQUASTAT. Online database. [www.fao.org/nr/water /aquastat/data/query/index.html]. Rome.

IEA (International Energy Agency). Various years. *Energy Balances of Non-OECD Countries.* Paris.

———. Various years. *Energy Balances of OECD Countries.* Paris.

———. Various years. *Energy Statistics of Non-OECD Countries.* Paris.

———. Various years. *Energy Statistics of OECD Countries.* Paris.

Lim, S.S., T. Vos, A.D. Flaxman, G. Danaei, K. Shibuya, et al. 2012. "A Comparative Risk Assessment of Burden of Disease and Injury Attributable to 67 Risk Factors and Risk Factor Clusters in 21 Regions, 1990–2010: A Systematic Analysis for the Global Burden of Disease Study 2010." *Lancet* 380(9859): 2224–60.

UNEP (United Nations Environment Programme) and WCMC (World Conservation Monitoring Centre). 2013. Online databases. [www .unep-wcmc.org/datasets-tools–reports_15.html?&types=Data,We bsite,Tool&ctops=]. Cambridge, UK.

United Nations Population Division. 2014. *World Urbanization Prospects: The 2014 Revision.* [http://esa.un.org/unpd/wup/]. New York: United Nations, Department of Economic and Social Affairs.

WHO (World Health Organization). 2006. *WHO Air Quality Guidelines for Particulate Matter, Ozone, Nitrogen Dioxide, and Sulfur Dioxide: Global Update 2005, Summary of Risk Assessment.* [http://whqlibdoc.who .int/hq/2006/WHO_SDE_PHE_OEH_06.02_eng.pdf].

3 Environment

To access the World Development Indicators online tables, use the URL http://wdi.worldbank.org/table/ and the table number (for example, http://wdi.worldbank.org/table/3.1). To view a specific indicator online, use the URL http://data.worldbank.org/indicator/ and the indicator code (for example, http://data.worldbank.org/indicator/SP.RUR.TOTL.ZS).

3.1 Rural environment and land use

Rural population	SP.RUR.TOTL.ZS
Rural population growth	SP.RUR.TOTL.ZG
Land area	AG.LND.TOTL.K2
Forest area	AG.LND.FRST.ZS
Permanent cropland	AG.LND.CROP.ZS
Arable land, % of land area	AG.LND.ARBL.ZS
Arable land, hectares per person	AG.LND.ARBL.HA.PC

3.2 Agricultural inputs

Agricultural land, % of land area	AG.LND.AGRI.ZS
Agricultural land, % irrigated	AG.LND.IRIG.AG.ZS
Average annual precipitation	AG.LND.PRCP.MM
Land under cereal production	AG.LND.CREL.HA
Fertilizer consumption, % of fertilizer production	AG.CON.FERT.PT.ZS
Fertilizer consumption, kilograms per hectare of arable land	AG.CON.FERT.ZS
Agricultural employment	SL.AGR.EMPL.ZS
Tractors	AG.LND.TRAC.ZS

3.3 Agricultural output and productivity

Crop production index	AG.PRD.CROP.XD
Food production index	AG.PRD.FOOD.XD
Livestock production index	AG.PRD.LVSK.XD
Cereal yield	AG.YLD.CREL.KG
Agriculture value added per worker	EA.PRD.AGRI.KD

3.4 Deforestation and biodiversity

Forest area	AG.LND.FRST.K2
Average annual deforestation	..a,b
Threatened species, Mammals	EN.MAM.THRD.NO
Threatened species, Birds	EN.BIR.THRD.NO
Threatened species, Fishes	EN.FSH.THRD.NO
Threatened species, Higher plants	EN.HPT.THRD.NO
Terrestrial protected areas	ER.LND.PTLD.ZS
Marine protected areas	ER.MRN.PTMR.ZS

3.5 Freshwater

Internal renewable freshwater resources	ER.H2O.INTR.K3
Internal renewable freshwater resources, Per capita	ER.H2O.INTR.PC
Annual freshwater withdrawals, cu. m	ER.H2O.FWTL.K3
Annual freshwater withdrawals, % of internal resources	ER.H2O.FWTL.ZS
Annual freshwater withdrawals, % for agriculture	ER.H2O.FWAG.ZS
Annual freshwater withdrawals, % for industry	ER.H2O.FWIN.ZS
Annual freshwater withdrawals, % of domestic	ER.H2O.FWDM.ZS
Water productivity, GDP/water use	ER.GDP.FWTL.M3.KD
Access to an improved water source, % of rural population	SH.H2O.SAFE.RU.ZS
Access to an improved water source, % of urban population	SH.H2O.SAFE.UR.ZS

3.6 Energy production and use

Energy production	EG.EGY.PROD.KT.OE
Energy use	EG.USE.COMM.KT.OE
Energy use, Average annual growth	..a,b
Energy use, Per capita	EG.USE.PCAP.KG.OE
Fossil fuel	EG.USE.COMM.FO.ZS
Combustible renewable and waste	EG.USE.CRNW.ZS
Alternative and nuclear energy production	EG.USE.COMM.CL.ZS

3.7 Electricity production, sources, and access

Electricity production	EG.ELC.PROD.KH
Coal sources	EG.ELC.COAL.ZS
Natural gas sources	EG.ELC.NGAS.ZS
Oil sources	EG.ELC.PETR.ZS
Hydropower sources	EG.ELC.HYRO.ZS
Renewable sources	EG.ELC.RNWX.ZS
Nuclear power sources	EG.ELC.NUCL.ZS
Access to electricity	EG.ELC.ACCS.ZS

3.8 Energy dependency, efficiency and carbon dioxide emissions

Net energy imports	EG.IMP.CONS.ZS
GDP per unit of energy use	EG.GDP.PUSE.KO.PP.KD
Carbon dioxide emissions, Total	EN.ATM.CO2E.KT
Carbon dioxide emissions, Carbon intensity	EN.ATM.CO2E.EG.ZS
Carbon dioxide emissions, Per capita	EN.ATM.CO2E.PC
Carbon dioxide emissions, kilograms per 2011 PPP $ of GDP	EN.ATM.CO2E.PP.GD.KD

3.9 Trends in greenhouse gas emissions

Carbon dioxide emissions, Total	EN.ATM.CO2E.KT
Carbon dioxide emissions, % change	..a,b
Methane emissions, Total	EN.ATM.METH.KT.CE
Methane emissions, % change	..a,b

Methane emissions, From energy processes	EN.ATM.METH.EG.ZS
Methane emissions, Agricultural	EN.ATM.METH.AG.ZS
Nitrous oxide emissions, Total	EN.ATM.NOXE.KT.CE
Nitrous oxide emissions, % change	..[a,b]
Nitrous oxide emissions, Energy and industry	EN.ATM.NOXE.EI.ZS
Nitrous oxide emissions, Agriculture	EN.ATM.NOXE.AG.ZS
Other greenhouse gas emissions, Total	EN.ATM.GHGO.KT.CE
Other greenhouse gas emissions, % change	..[a,b]

3.10 Carbon dioxide emissions by sector

Electricity and heat production	EN.CO2.ETOT.ZS
Manufacturing industries and construction	EN.CO2.MANF.ZS
Residential buildings and commercial and public services	EN.CO2.BLDG.ZS
Transport	EN.CO2.TRAN.ZS
Other sectors	EN.CO2.OTHX.ZS

3.11 Climate variability, exposure to impact, and resilience

Average daily minimum/maximum temperature	..[b]
Projected annual temperature	..[b]
Projected annual cool days/cold nights	..[b]
Projected annual hot days/warm nights	..[b]
Projected annual precipitation	..[b]
Land area with an elevation of 5 meters or less	AG.LND.EL5M.ZS
Population living in areas with elevation of 5 meters or less	EN.POP.EL5M.ZS
Population affected by droughts, floods, and extreme temperatures	EN.CLC.MDAT.ZS
Disaster risk reduction progress score	EN.CLC.DRSK.XQ

3.12 Urbanization

Urban population	SP.URB.TOTL
Urban population, % of total population	SP.URB.TOTL.IN.ZS
Urban population, Average annual growth	SP.URB.GROW

Population in urban agglomerations of more than 1 million	EN.URB.MCTY.TL.ZS
Population in the largest city	EN.URB.LCTY.UR.ZS
Access to improved sanitation facilities, % of urban population	SH.STA.ACSN.UR
Access to improved sanitation facilities, % of rural population	SH.STA.ACSN.RU

3.13 Traffic and congestion

Motor vehicles, Per 1,000 people	IS.VEH.NVEH.P3
Motor vehicles, Per kilometer of road	IS.VEH.ROAD.K1
Passenger cars	IS.VEH.PCAR.P3
Road density	IS.ROD.DNST.K2
Road sector energy consumption, % of total consumption	IS.ROD.ENGY.ZS
Road sector energy consumption, Per capita	IS.ROD.ENGY.PC
Diesel fuel consumption	IS.ROD.DESL.PC
Gasoline fuel consumption	IS.ROD.SGAS.PC
Pump price for super grade gasoline	EP.PMP.SGAS.CD
Pump price for diesel	EP.PMP.DESL.CD
$PM_{2.5}$ pollution	EN.ATM.PM25.MC.M3

3.14 Air pollution

This table provides air pollution data for major cities.	..[b]

3.15 Contribution of natural resources to gross domestic product

Total natural resources rents	NY.GDP.TOTL.RT.ZS
Oil rents	NY.GDP.PETR.RT.ZS
Natural gas rents	NY.GDP.NGAS.RT.ZS
Coal rents	NY.GDP.COAL.RT.ZS
Mineral rents	NY.GDP.MINR.RT.ZS
Forest rents	NY.GDP.FRST.RT.ZS

a. Derived from data elsewhere in the World Development Indicators database.
b. Available online only as part of the table, not as an individual indicator.

ECONOMY

The *Economy* section provides a picture of the global economy and the economic activity of more than 200 countries and territories. It includes measures of macroeconomic performance and stability as well as broader measures of income and savings adjusted for pollution, depreciation, and resource depletion.

The world economy grew 2.6 percent in 2014 to reach $77 trillion in current prices, and growth is projected to accelerate to 3 percent in 2015. The share that developing economies account for increased to 32.9 percent in 2014, from 32.1 percent in 2013 in current prices. Developing economies grew an estimated 4.4 percent in 2014 and are projected to grow 4.8 percent in 2015. Growth in high-income economies has been updated from earlier forecasts to 1.8 percent in 2014 and 2.2 percent in 2015.

The structures of economies change over time. GDP is a well recognized and frequently quoted indicator of an economy's size and strength. To measure changes over time, or growth, it is necessary to strip out any effect of price changes and look at changes in the volume of output. This is done by valuing the production at an earlier year's (base year) prices, referred to as constant price estimates. Countries conduct a periodic statistical re-evaluation, known as a national accounts revision exercise, that assesses the importance of different sectors to the aggregate economy and prices. These exercises are a recommended practice to ensure that official GDP estimates use an accurate picture of the economy's structure.

In 2014 several African countries revised their national accounts estimates by incorporating new data sources to ensure coverage of economic activities, including new activities, new standards and methods (such as the 2008 System of National Accounts), and a new base year for constant price estimates. In general, African economies tend to have large informal sectors and economic activities that are not always well captured by existing statistics. As census and survey data for these activities have become available, estimates for economic activities previously not covered in national accounts have been included to better reflect the true size and structure of the economies. For many countries, incorporating new activities has led to upward adjustments to GDP.

Adjusted net savings has been included in *World Development Indicators* since 1999. It measures the change in a country's real wealth, including manufactured, natural, and human capital. Years of negative adjusted net savings suggest that a country's economy is on an unsustainable path. This year the methodology has been adjusted to improve accounting of the economic costs of air pollution. In previous editions the scope of pollution damages included in adjusted net savings was limited to outdoor air pollution in urban areas with more than 100,000 people, but it now covers outdoor air pollution and household air pollution in urban and rural areas. Health costs previously estimated for exposure to airborne particles with a diameter of 10 micrometers or less (PM_{10}) are now measured for exposure to finer particles that are more closely associated with health effects ($PM_{2.5}$). And pollution damages are now calculated as productivity losses in the workforce due to premature death and illness. These costs represent only a part of the total welfare losses from pollution, but they are more amenable to the standard national accounting framework.

Highlights

Economic growth slowed in developing countries

GDP growth (%)

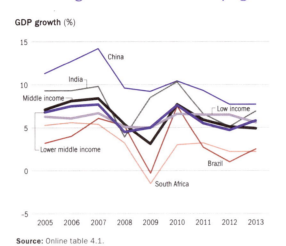

Source: Online table 4.1.

In recent years GDP growth has decelerated considerably in almost all developing countries. The average GDP growth rate of developing economies declined 1.8 percentage points between 2010 and 2013 thanks mostly to large middle-income countries such as Brazil, China, India, and South Africa, where growth fell an average of 3 percentage points. Low-income countries performed better than middle-income countries, whose growth rates fell around 1 percentage point. Latin America and the Caribbean saw GDP growth drop significantly (3.4 percentage points), as did South Asia (2.5 percentage points).

Inflation remains high across most of South Asia

Inflation (%)

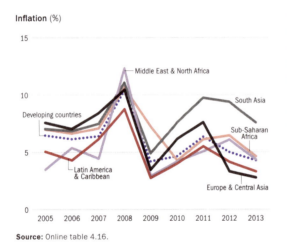

Source: Online table 4.16.

In 2013 South Asia's median inflation rate, 7.6 percent as measured by the consumer price index, was the highest of all regions and 5 percentage points above the world median, even after falling from the 2012 rate. Even in countries where inflation is falling, the rate remains higher than in other countries. India's average inflation rate was 10.9 percent, followed closely by Nepal at 9 percent. In all other South Asian countries inflation hovered between 7 and 8 percent, except the Maldives (2.3 percent).

Many economies in Africa are larger than previously thought

Revisions in 2013 nominal GDP, selected countries (%)

Nigeria
Congo, Dem. Rep.
Tanzania
Kenya
Zambia
Uganda
Namibia
South Africa
Mozambique
Rwanda
Equatorial Guinea

-25   0   25   50   75   100

Source: Online table 4.2.

Nigeria, Africa's most populous country, is also its largest economy. Last year, as part of a statistical review of national accounts, it adjusted its estimate of 2013 GDP up 91 percent, from $273 billion to $521 billion. This was the first major revision of Nigeria's GDP estimate in almost two decades, changing the base year from 1990 to 2010. The most notable improvements include incorporating small business activity and fast-growing industries (such as mobile telecoms, real estate, and the film industry). Several other countries in Sub-Saharan Africa also improved the quality of their GDP estimates, including the Democratic Republic of the Congo (up 62 percent), Tanzania (up 31 percent), Kenya (up 25 percent, to become the region's fourth largest economy), Zambia (up 20 percent), Uganda (up 15 percent), and Namibia (up 14 percent). Two countries revised their GDP estimates down: Rwanda (3 percent) and Equatorial Guinea (9 percent).

 Front   User guide   World view   People   Environment

How Mercosur and the Pacific Alliance compare

The Pacific Alliance is a Latin American trade bloc that officially launched in 2012 among Chile, Colombia, Mexico, and Peru. Together the four Pacific Alliance countries have a combined population of 218.6 million and GDP of $2.1 trillion. The Southern Common Market (Mercosur), another bloc in the region, was created in 1991 and includes Argentina, Brazil, Paraguay, Uruguay, and Venezuela. Together the five Mercosur countries have 282.4 million inhabitants and GDP of $3.3 trillion. The Pacific Alliance saw average GDP growth of 3.3 percent over 2011–13, surpassing the overall GDP growth of 2.7 percent in Latin America and the 2.0 percent growth of Mercosur. In addition, Pacific Alliance exports increased an average of 3.5 percent, compared with constant exports in Mercosur.

Annual GDP growth (%)

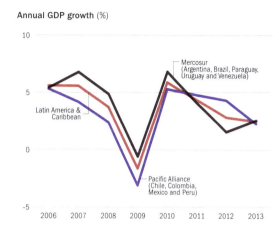

Source: Online table 4.1.

Developing countries have a higher share of world GDP

Purchasing power parity (PPP) estimates based on the 2011 round of the International Comparison Program were incorporated into *World Development Indicators* in 2014, replacing the extrapolated PPP estimates based on the 2005 round. When comparing the 2011 results to the 2005 results, high-income countries' share in the world economy is about 4.5 percentage points smaller, lower middle-income countries' share is 3.4 percentage points larger, and upper middle-income countries' share is 0.9 percentage point larger. Compared with estimates based on market exchange rates, lower middle-income and low-income countries' PPP-based shares are more than double, upper middle-income countries' share is more than 30 percent greater, and high-income countries' share decreases to half of the world economy from two-thirds.

GDP as a share of the world economy, 2011 (%)

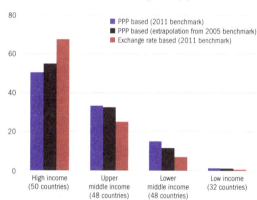

Source: International Comparison Program and World Development Indicators database.

Different starting points but similarly low levels of sustainability in Sub-Saharan Africa

Gross national savings, a measure of natural resources available for investment, averaged about 16 percent of gross national income for upper middle-income countries in Sub-Saharan Africa, compared with 3–6 percent in the region's low- and lower middle-income countries. Upper middle-income countries are investing substantially more in human capital, with much higher current public expenditure on education. These countries depend heavily on extractive industries, which are both capital and resource intensive, so their savings were nearly zero after adjusting for natural resource depletion and the depreciation of manufactured capital. In the region's low-income countries overharvest of timber resources accounted for the largest downward adjustment in savings for 2013. Much of this was due to harvesting wood fuel, as the majority of people in these countries rely on solid fuels for cooking, with the resulting emissions causing the majority of pollution damage.

Share of gross national income, Sub-Saharan Africa, 2013 (%)

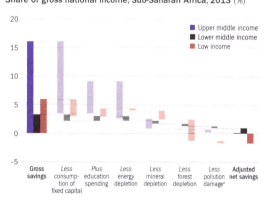

a. Data are for 2010, the most recent year available.
Source: Online table 4.11.

Economic growth reduces poverty. As a result, fast-growing developing countries are closing the income gap with high-income economies. But growth must be sustained over the long term, and the gains from growth must be shared to make lasting improvements to the well-being of all people.

In 2009 the financial crisis, which began in 2007 and spread from high-income to low-income economies in 2008, became the most severe global recession in 50 years and affected sustained development around the world. The average annual growth of gross domestic product (GDP) per capita in developing countries, while still faster than in high-income countries, slowed from 5 percent in 2000–09 (the pre-crisis period) to 4.5 percent in 2009–13 (the post-crisis period). High-income countries grew an average of 1.3 percent after the crisis, down from 1.5 percent before crisis. The Middle East and North Africa saw the largest drop: Average annual GDP growth fell 2.6 percentage points from before the pre-crisis period.

Economic growth

AVERAGE ANNUAL GROWTH OF
GDP PER CAPITA, 2009–13 (%)

- Less than 0.0
- 0.0–1.9
- 2.0–3.9
- 4.0–5.9
- 6.0 or more
- No data

IBRD 41453

Mongolia recorded the highest average GDP per capita
growth in 2009–13 among developing countries at 10.8 percent, thanks to stronger mineral production led by copper and gold in the Oyu Tolgoi mine.

Turkmenistan's average GDP per capita growth of
10.2 percent over 2009–13 was sustained by vast hydrocarbon resources and considerable government infrastructure spending.

Panama is the fastest growing country in Latin America
and the Caribbean, driven by a steady rise in investments, including the large Panama Canal expansion, and business-friendly regulations.

After a decade of economic decline and hyperinflation,
Zimbabwe has seen a recovery since 2009, supported by better economic policies, which have moved the country from a 7.5 percent annual average decrease in GDP per capita pre-crisis to 7.3 percent growth post-crisis.

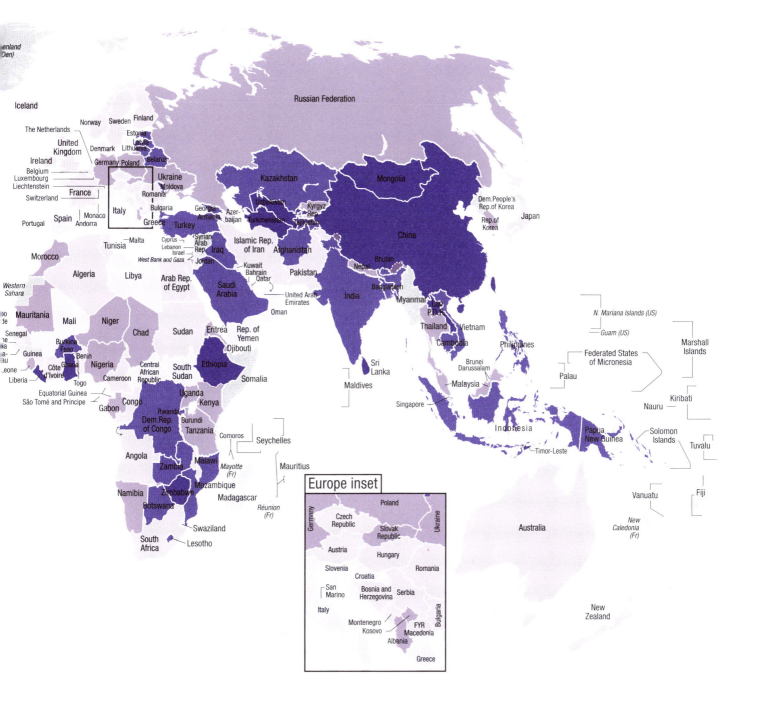

4 Economy

	Gross domestic product			Gross savings	Adjusted net savings	Current account balance	Central government cash surplus or deficit	Central government debt	Consumer price index	Broad money
	average annual % growth			% of GDP	% of GNI	% of GDP	% of GDP	% of GDP	% growth	% of GDP
	1990–2000	2000–09	2009–13	2013	2013ᵃ	2013	2012	2012	2013	2013
Afghanistan	..	8.5	8.1	−21.2	−34.8	−33.0	−0.6	..	7.6	33.0
Albania	3.8	5.5	2.3	18.2	4.4	−10.7	..	..	1.9	84.1
Algeria	1.9	4.2	3.1	45.3	24.7	0.4	−0.3	..	3.3	62.7
American Samoa	..	..	..							
Andorra	3.2	5.9	..	..	..	..			..	..
Angola	1.6	13.8	4.8	18.5	−20.1	6.7	6.7	..	8.8	36.7
Antigua and Barbuda	3.5	4.9	−0.9	7.8	..	−17.0	−1.3	..	1.1	98.2
Argentina	4.3	4.9ᵇ	5.2ᵇ	16.2	8.3	−0.8	..	..	..ᵇ	27.2
Armenia	−1.9	10.6	4.7	13.7	1.6	−8.0	−1.4	..	5.8	36.2
Aruba	3.9	−0.1	..	..	..	−10.1	..	..	−2.4	68.3
Australia	3.6	3.3	2.7	24.6	9.3	−3.2	−3.0	40.5	2.4	106.4
Austriaᶜ	2.5	1.9	1.6	25.6	12.9	1.0	−2.4	78.5	2.0	..
Azerbaijan	−6.3	17.9	2.8	40.9	14.1	16.6	6.1	6.4	2.4	33.4
Bahamas, The	2.6	1.0	1.1	11.3	8.4	−19.2	−4.1	47.5	0.4	74.8
Bahrain	5.0	6.0	3.6	27.6	17.6	7.8	−0.5	35.6	3.2	74.3
Bangladesh	4.8	5.9	6.2	38.8	26.8	1.6	−0.8	..	7.5	61.3
Barbados	2.1	1.8	0.4	..	..	..	−8.0	96.8	1.8	..
Belarus	−1.6	8.2	3.9	28.5	21.5	−10.5	0.1	25.2	18.3	30.4
Belgiumᶜ	2.2	1.8	1.1	20.9	7.0	−3.5	−3.5	89.4	1.1	..
Belize	4.5	4.2	2.7	9.9	−6.5	−4.4	−0.2	74.5	0.7	76.2
Benin	4.6	3.9	4.2	13.8	−1.6	−7.6	1.7	..	1.0	41.8
Bermuda	2.9	2.3	−3.4	..	..	16.9	..	..	..	..
Bhutan	5.2	8.4	6.6	25.5	9.4	−28.6	..	..	7.0	57.0
Bolivia	4.0	4.0	5.3	23.9	7.3	3.8	..	..	5.7	76.7
Bosnia and Herzegovina	..	5.0	0.6	12.3	..	−5.9	−1.6	..	−0.1	61.2
Botswana	4.9	4.4	6.0	39.4	29.0	12.0	1.4	19.0	5.9	40.9
Brazil	2.7	3.6	3.1	13.7	3.1	−3.6	−2.0	..	6.2	79.9
Brunei Darussalam	2.1	1.4	1.5	..	..	33.5	..	..	0.4	70.3
Bulgaria	−0.3	5.3	1.1	23.4	10.6	1.8	−0.8	17.5	0.9	83.8
Burkina Faso	5.5	5.9	7.7	..	..	..	−3.0	..	0.5	28.9
Burundi	−2.9	3.3	4.1	17.8	−18.4	−9.3	..	..	8.0	21.8
Cabo Verde	12.1	7.3	2.0	29.7	21.5	−3.9	−10.1	..	1.5	88.1
Cambodia	7.0	9.2	7.0	8.5	−3.8	−10.5	−4.4	..	2.9	53.6
Cameroon	1.8	3.3	4.4	10.2	−6.0	−3.8	..	..	1.9	20.9
Canada	3.1	2.1	2.3	21.0	6.0	−3.0	−0.2	53.5	0.9	..
Cayman Islands	..	..	..						..	..
Central African Republic	1.8	3.8	−5.3	..	..	..	0.7	..	1.5	28.1
Chad	2.2	11.4	6.1	..	..	..	..	..	0.1	12.8
Channel Islands	..	0.5	..	..	..	..	..	..	..	..
Chile	6.6	4.2	5.3	20.4	4.2	−3.4	0.5	..	1.8	82.2
China	10.6	10.9	8.7	51.3	29.5	2.0	..	..	2.6	194.5
Hong Kong SAR, China	3.6	4.8	3.8	25.6	..	1.9	..	..	4.4	352.7
Macao SAR, China	2.2	11.9	16.8	58.2	..	43.2	24.1	..	5.5	106.7
Colombia	2.8	4.6	4.9	19.7	2.1	−3.2	2.8	65.3	2.0	45.8
Comoros	1.2	2.5	2.8	14.6	−3.2	−7.5	..	..	2.3	40.5
Congo, Dem. Rep.	−4.9	5.1	7.3	9.5	−28.1	−8.8	2.3	..	1.6	11.4
Congo, Rep.	1.0	4.0	4.6	..	..	..	..	..	6.0	32.0

 Front | User guide | World view | People | Environment

	Gross domestic product			Gross savings	Adjusted net savings	Current account balance	Central government cash surplus or deficit	Central government debt	Consumer price index	Broad money
	average annual % growth			% of GDP	% of GNI	% of GDP	% of GDP	% of GDP	% growth	% of GDP
	1990–2000	2000–09	2009–13	2013	2013ª	2013	2012	2012	2013	2013
Costa Rica	5.3	5.1	4.6	16.1	15.9	−5.1	−4.0	..	5.2	49.2
Côte d'Ivoire	3.2	1.0	3.8	..	..	..	−2.8	..	2.6	35.7
Croatia	3.1	3.7	−1.3	19.3	4.8	1.2	−3.4	..	2.2	69.8
Cuba	−0.7	6.4	2.5	..	..	..	..	..	..	..
Curaçao	..	..	..	..	..	..	..	..	..	..
Cyprusᶜ	4.2	3.4ᵈ	−1.5	..	..	−1.9	−6.4	131.0	−0.4	..
Czech Republic	1.4	4.1	0.7	23.6	4.8	−1.4	−2.3	40.8	1.4	77.0
Denmark	2.8	1.2	0.4	25.9	14.2	7.1	−3.8	47.2	0.8	72.1
Djibouti	−2.0	4.0	4.4	..	..	−21.2	..	..	2.4	85.2
Dominica	2.0	3.4	−0.4	−1.9	..	−14.0	−11.1	..	0.0	93.2
Dominican Republic	6.3	5.1	4.2	18.8	15.5	−4.0	−2.5	..	4.8	34.9
Ecuador	2.2	4.5	5.5	27.2	9.4	−1.4	..	..	2.7	32.0
Egypt, Arab Rep.	4.4	4.9	2.6	13.0	2.2	−2.7	−10.6	..	9.5	79.1
El Salvador	4.8	2.4	1.8	9.1	4.7	−6.5	−0.8	47.8	0.8	44.8
Equatorial Guinea	36.7	15.7	1.2	..	..	..	..	..	6.4	23.5
Eritrea	6.5	0.2	5.4	..	..	..	..	..	..	110.8
Estoniaᶜ	6.5	5.2	4.7	25.1	13.0	−1.2	−0.1	10.4	2.8	..
Ethiopia	3.8	8.5	10.5	31.1	9.9	−6.9	−1.3	..	8.1	..
Faeroe Islands	..	..	..	..	..	..	..	..	..	..
Fiji	2.7	1.6	2.6	..	..	−14.5	..	..	2.9	80.6
Finlandᶜ	2.9	2.4	0.7	19.7	6.2	−0.9	−1.0	51.0	1.5	..
Franceᶜ	2.0	1.5	1.2	20.1	6.8	−1.4	−4.6	100.9	0.9	..
French Polynesia	..	..	..	..	..	..	..	..	..	..
Gabon	2.3	1.9	6.3	..	..	..	..	..	0.5	22.7
Gambia, The	3.0	3.2	2.6	25.8	2.0	6.4	..	..	5.7	55.8
Georgia	−7.1ᵉ	7.4ᵉ	5.9ᵉ	19.0ᵉ	8.7ᵉ	−5.7	−0.5	32.5	−0.5	36.6
Germanyᶜ	1.7	1.0	2.0	25.8	12.1	6.9	0.1	55.2	1.5	..
Ghana	4.3	5.8	10.2	20.7	10.1	−11.8	−3.9	..	11.6	29.1
Greeceᶜ	2.4	3.2	−6.4	11.2	−5.0	0.6	−9.4	163.6	−0.9	..
Greenland	1.9	1.7	..	..	..	..	..	..	..	..
Grenada	3.2	3.1	0.3	−5.9	..	−25.5	−5.5	..	0.0	90.8
Guam	..	..	..	..	..	..	..	..	..	..
Guatemala	4.2	3.7	3.5	11.8	4.2	−2.7	−2.3	24.3	4.3	47.1
Guinea	4.2	2.7	3.2	−17.0	−50.4	−18.9	..	..	11.9	36.4
Guinea-Bissau	0.6	2.4	2.9	..	..	−8.7	..	..	0.7	39.4
Guyana	5.4	0.7	5.0	..	−0.3	−14.2	..	..	1.8	67.1
Haiti	..	0.7	2.2	23.1	17.8	−6.4	..	..	5.9	44.4
Honduras	3.2	4.9	3.6	13.4	8.7	−8.9	−3.2	..	5.2	52.9
Hungary	1.9	2.8	0.6	23.9	9.3	4.1	−2.6	84.7	1.7	61.5
Iceland	2.8	4.3	1.1	20.4	12.4	8.9	−3.3	112.6	3.9	84.8
India	6.0	7.6	6.9	31.8	19.6	−2.6	−3.8	50.3	10.9	77.4
Indonesia	4.2	5.3	6.2	29.0	22.1	−3.4	..	..	6.4	41.1
Iran, Islamic Rep.	3.1	5.4	1.7	..	..	..	..	..	39.3	..
Iraq	10.3	3.8	8.1	30.4	..	13.7	..	..	1.9	33.4
Irelandᶜ	7.5	3.5	0.7	20.7	18.2	6.2	−7.6	120.5	0.5	..
Isle of Man	6.4	6.2	..	..	..	..	..	..	..	..
Israel	7.6	3.6	4.0	20.9	12.6	2.4	−5.4	..	1.5	..

4 Economy

	Gross domestic product			Gross savings	Adjusted net savings	Current account balance	Central government cash surplus or deficit	Central government debt	Consumer price index	Broad money
	average annual % growth			% of GDP	% of GNI	% of GDP	% of GDP	% of GDP	% growth	% of GDP
	1990–2000	2000–09	2009–13	2013	2013[a]	2013	2012	2012	2013	2013
Italy[c]	1.6	0.6	–0.6	19.0	4.2	1.0	–3.0	126.2	1.2	..
Jamaica	..	..	..	8.7	..	–9.2	–4.0	..	9.3	50.3
Japan	1.0	0.9	1.6	21.8	2.8	0.7	–8.0	196.0	0.4	247.8
Jordan	5.0	7.1	2.6	18.0	13.4	–10.0	–8.3	66.8	5.5	124.5
Kazakhstan	–4.1	8.8	6.4	23.9	–1.9	–0.1	..	..	5.8	32.9
Kenya	2.2	4.3	6.0	11.3	6.0	–8.4	–3.9	..	5.7	41.3
Kiribati	4.0	1.5	2.2	..	..	–8.7	14.8	..	..	..
Korea, Dem. People's Rep.	..	..	..	..	..	..	..	..	..	..
Korea, Rep.	6.2	4.4	3.7	34.6	19.0	6.1	1.7	..	1.3	134.5
Kosovo	..	5.3	3.3	21.3	..	–6.4	..	..	1.8	44.8
Kuwait	4.9	7.2	5.7	59.5	..	39.7	27.9	..	2.7	57.6
Kyrgyz Republic	–4.1	4.6	3.7	12.5	–2.1	–23.3	–6.5	..	6.6	..
Lao PDR	6.4	7.0	8.2	16.7	–4.1	–3.3	–0.8	..	6.4	..
Latvia	–1.5	6.2	3.8	25.9	14.2	–0.8	0.5	41.1	0.0	43.0
Lebanon	5.3	5.3	3.0	20.7	6.1	–24.8	–8.8	..	..	250.1
Lesotho	3.8	3.6	5.3	36.5	..	–3.3	..	..	4.9	38.4
Liberia	4.1	4.3	10.3	24.5	–14.7	–27.5	–2.6	32.7	7.6	38.2
Libya	..	5.4	–8.6	..	..	–0.1	..	..	2.6	70.9
Liechtenstein	6.2	2.5	..	..	..	..	..	..	..	..
Lithuania	–2.5	6.3	3.8	16.9	8.2	1.5	–3.1	49.4	1.1	47.3
Luxembourg[c]	4.4	3.2	2.1	14.4	6.4	5.3	–0.6	20.0	1.7	..
Macedonia, FYR	–0.8	3.4	1.9	30.7	15.8	–1.9	–4.0	..	2.8	59.7
Madagascar	2.0	3.6	1.9	..	..	..	–1.7	..	5.8	23.8
Malawi	3.7	4.5	4.2	7.9	–15.0	–18.9	..	..	27.3	38.7
Malaysia	7.0	5.1	5.7	30.4	15.4	3.7	–4.5	53.3	2.1	143.8
Maldives	..	8.1	4.5	..	..	–7.7	–8.7	73.5	2.3	67.0
Mali	4.1	5.7	2.3	18.1	0.4	–6.2	0.0	..	–0.6	33.6
Malta[c]	5.2	1.8	2.2	12.1	..	0.9	–3.2	85.9	1.4	..
Marshall Islands	0.4	1.4	3.2	..	..	..	..	..	..	..
Mauritania	–1.3	4.6	5.5	34.7	–15.9	–30.3	..	..	4.1	35.4
Mauritius	5.2	3.8	3.6	12.7	1.7	–9.9	–0.6	37.2	3.5	99.8
Mexico	3.3	2.2	3.6	20.6	6.5	–2.1	..	..	3.8	33.3
Micronesia, Fed. Sts.	1.8	–0.3	0.4	..	..	..	..	..	..	46.1
Moldova	–9.6[f]	5.6[f]	5.0[f]	19.3[f]	15.2[f]	–5.0	–2.0	24.3	4.6	62.4
Monaco	1.9	4.2	..	..	..	..	..	..	..	..
Mongolia	1.0	7.5	12.5	34.1	13.9	–27.7	–8.4	..	8.6	53.9
Montenegro	..	4.7	1.3	4.5	..	–14.7	..	..	2.2	52.2
Morocco	2.9[g]	4.9[g]	3.9[g]	26.6[g]	13.8[g]	–7.6	–6.0	59.7	1.9	112.3
Mozambique	6.1	7.6	7.3	17.9	7.1	–37.7	–2.7	..	4.3	46.0
Myanmar	..	..	..	..	..	..	..	..	5.5	..
Namibia	3.3	5.3	5.3	17.5	14.3	–4.1	–11.9	35.5	5.6	54.5
Nepal	4.9	3.7	4.2	43.1	36.7	6.0	–0.6	33.9	9.0	85.6
Netherlands[c]	3.2	1.8	0.1	26.7	14.4	10.2	–3.3	67.9	2.5	..
New Caledonia	..	..	..	..	..	..	..	..	..	..
New Zealand	3.5	2.9	2.1	16.3	8.3	–3.2	–0.5	69.0	1.3	..
Nicaragua	3.7	3.4	4.8	18.2	13.1	–11.4	0.5	..	7.1	35.4
Niger	2.4	4.1	6.4	21.0	0.4	–16.6	..	..	2.3	24.1

 Front User guide World view People Environment

	Gross domestic product			Gross savings	Adjusted net savings	Current account balance	Central government cash surplus or deficit	Central government debt	Consumer price index	Broad money
	average annual % growth			% of GDP	% of GNI	% of GDP	% of GDP	% of GDP	% growth	% of GDP
	1990–2000	2000–09	2009–13	2013	2013[a]	2013	2012	2012	2013	2013
Nigeria	1.9	10.0	5.4	33.3	19.4	4.4	–1.3	10.4	8.5	21.5
Northern Mariana Islands	..	..	..						..	..
Norway	3.9	1.9	1.5	37.5	19.9	11.2	14.6	20.9	2.1	..
Oman	4.5	2.8	3.5	..	..	6.4	–0.4	5.0	1.2	38.2
Pakistan	3.8	5.1	3.1	21.0	10.7	–1.9	–8.0		7.7	40.9
Palau	2.4	0.7	3.9	..	..	..	..	..	..	..
Panama	4.7	6.8	9.1	25.2	23.8	–11.5	..	..	4.0	60.5
Papua New Guinea	3.8	3.8	8.3	..	..	–14.9	..	..	5.0	52.3
Paraguay	3.0	3.2	6.2	17.3	8.5	2.1	–1.0	..	2.7	48.6
Peru	4.5	5.9	6.6	23.8	11.3	–4.5	2.0	19.2	2.8	43.0
Philippines	3.3	4.9	6.1	43.2	26.9	3.8	–1.9	51.5	3.0	69.7
Poland	4.7	4.3	3.0	18.3	10.3	–1.4	–3.6	..	1.0	59.0
Portugal[c]	2.8	0.8	–1.5	16.5	3.5	0.5	–6.8	122.8	0.3	..
Puerto Rico	3.6	0.3	–2.0	..	..	..	..	..	..	..
Qatar	11.1	13.5	10.2	61.8	30.1	30.8	2.9	..	3.1	61.8
Romania	–0.6	5.8	1.3	21.8	20.9	–0.9	–2.5	..	4.0	38.3
Russian Federation	–4.7	6.0	3.5	24.2	10.6	1.6	2.7	9.4	6.8	55.8
Rwanda	–0.2	7.7	7.4	19.6	5.3	–7.5	–4.0	..	8.0	..
Samoa	2.6	3.6	1.8	..	..	–5.7	0.0	..	0.6	40.8
San Marino	5.8	3.2	..	..	..	..	..	..	1.6	..
São Tomé and Príncipe	..	5.3	4.4	18.0	..	–25.8	–12.2	..	7.1	37.5
Saudi Arabia	2.1	5.9	6.6	43.6	21.2	17.7	..	..	3.5	55.9
Senegal	3.0	4.3	3.1	21.8	12.9	–7.9	–5.3	..	0.7	42.8
Serbia	0.7	5.5	0.7	10.7	..	–6.1	–6.1	..	7.7	44.3
Seychelles	4.4	2.4	5.4	19.7	..	–15.8	5.3	80.2	4.3	53.7
Sierra Leone	–3.0	7.3	5.5	28.1	13.2	–9.3	–5.6	..	10.3	20.8
Singapore	7.2	6.0	6.3	47.4	..	18.3	8.7	110.9	2.4	133.0
Sint Maarten	..	..	..	..	..	..	..	..	..	..
Slovak Republic[c]	4.5	5.8	2.5	21.8	3.6	2.1	–4.5	53.5	1.4	..
Slovenia[c]	4.3	3.7	–0.6	24.9	8.9	6.1	–3.5	..	1.8	..
Solomon Islands	3.4	3.9	6.8	..	..	–4.5	..	..	5.4	43.0
Somalia	..	..	..	..	..	..	..	..	..	..
South Africa	2.1	4.0	2.7	14.4	1.2	–5.6	–4.5	..	3.3	71.1
South Sudan	..	..	..	..	..	..	..	..	47.3	..
Spain[c]	2.7	2.9	–1.1	21.1	8.0	0.8	–8.8	65.9	1.4	..
Sri Lanka	5.3	5.5	7.4	25.7	21.1	–3.9	–6.1	79.2	6.9	39.4
St. Kitts and Nevis	4.6	3.4	0.3	20.5	..	–8.2	11.2	..	0.7	156.5
St. Lucia	3.5	2.8	–0.4	16.8	..	–7.5	–6.5	..	1.5	91.5
St. Martin	..	..	..	..	..	..	..	..	..	..
St. Vincent & the Grenadines	3.1	4.2	–0.2	–4.7	..	–29.6	–2.1	..	0.8	73.6
Sudan	5.5[h]	7.0[h]	–4.6[i]	13.6	8.6	–6.7	..	..	30.0	21.0
Suriname	0.8	5.2	4.1	..	..	–3.7	–1.2	..	1.9	51.5
Swaziland	3.2	2.5	1.3	19.9	12.6	6.3	..	..	5.6	30.6
Sweden	2.3	2.4	2.2	28.8	17.9	6.0	–0.3	35.3	0.0	85.7
Switzerland	1.2	2.2	1.8	37.5	20.7	14.2	0.6	24.3	–0.2	182.3
Syrian Arab Republic	5.1	5.0	..	..	..	..	..	..	36.7	..
Tajikistan	–10.4	8.5	7.2	16.6	13.0	–3.2	..	..	5.0	21.0

4 Economy

	Gross domestic product			Gross savings	Adjusted net savings	Current account balance	Central government cash surplus or deficit	Central government debt	Consumer price index	Broad money
	average annual % growth			% of GDP	% of GNI	% of GDP	% of GDP	% of GDP	% growth	% of GDP
	1990–2000	2000–09	2009–13	2013	2013[a]	2013	2012	2012	2013	2013
Tanzania[j]	3.0	6.9	6.6	17.3	11.7	–10.8	–5.3	..	7.9	23.1
Thailand	4.2	4.6	4.2	28.5	11.8	–0.7	–2.2	..	2.2	134.5
Timor-Leste	..	3.4	11.0	249.0	..	216.3	..	..	11.2	32.0
Togo	3.5	2.2	5.1	..	..	..	–6.1	..	1.8	45.2
Tonga	2.6	0.8	1.9	18.1	..	–9.6	..	..	0.7	44.0
Trinidad and Tobago	3.2	7.4	0.3	..	..	12.2	–1.6	..	5.2	60.7
Tunisia	4.7	4.7	2.4	13.0	–2.7	–8.3	–5.0	44.5	6.1	66.7
Turkey	3.9	4.9	5.9	13.1	9.4	–7.9	–0.6	45.1	7.5	60.7
Turkmenistan	–3.2	8.0	11.6	..	..	..	..	..	..	..
Turks and Caicos Islands	..	..	..	..	..	..	..	..	..	..
Tuvalu	3.2	1.2	2.2	..	..	..	..	..	..	..
Uganda	7.0	7.8	5.9	21.5	4.7	–8.1	–2.1	33.2	5.5	20.8
Ukraine	–9.3	5.7	2.8	10.4	–5.4	–9.3	–4.0	33.5	–0.3	62.5
United Arab Emirates	4.8	5.3	4.2	..	..	..	–0.2	..	1.1	61.2
United Kingdom	2.6	2.2	1.4	12.8	4.0	–4.3	–5.5	97.2	2.6	150.9
United States	3.6	2.1	2.1	17.4	5.0	–2.4	–7.6	94.3	1.5	88.4
Uruguay	3.9	3.1	5.8	17.2	9.0	–5.4	–2.1	44.5	8.6	46.2
Uzbekistan	–0.2	6.9	8.2	..	..	..	..	..	..	..
Vanuatu	3.4	3.9	1.6	20.5	..	–3.7	–2.3	..	1.4	70.9
Venezuela, RB	1.6	5.1	2.9	25.6	13.4	2.9	..	..	40.6	44.8
Vietnam	7.9	6.8	5.8	32.0	16.3	5.5	..	..	6.6	117.0
Virgin Islands (U.S.)	..	..	..	..	..	..	..	..	..	..
West Bank and Gaza	14.3	2.7	6.0	5.6	..	–20.3	..	..	..	15.6
Yemen, Rep.	5.6	4.0	–2.7	..	..	–4.3	..	..	11.0	39.1
Zambia	1.6	7.2	7.3	..	..	0.7	4.1	..	7.0	21.4
Zimbabwe	2.5	–7.2	9.9	..	..	..	..	..	1.6	..
World	**2.9 w**	**2.9 w**	**2.8 w**	**22.5 w**	**10.9 w**					
Low income	2.7	5.4	6.3	24.9	9.4					
Middle income	4.3	6.4	5.8	31.0	18.7					
Lower middle income	3.5	6.4	5.7	28.6	17.2					
Upper middle income	4.6	6.4	5.9	31.8	18.9					
Low & middle income	4.3	6.4	5.8	31.0	18.6					
East Asia & Pacific	8.5	9.4	8.1	46.3	27.7					
Europe & Central Asia	0.2	5.4	4.3	17.0	7.6					
Latin America & Carib.	3.1	3.6	3.8	17.7	5.5					
Middle East & N. Africa	3.9	4.9	2.3	..	8.1					
South Asia	5.6	7.2	6.6	30.7	18.9					
Sub-Saharan Africa	2.3	5.7	4.2	19.4	6.3					
High income	2.6	2.1	1.8	20.8	7.7					
Euro area	2.1	1.5	0.6	22.0	8.7					

a. Includes data on pollution damage for 2010, the most recent year available. b. Data for Argentina are officially reported by the National Statistics and Censuses Institute of Argentina. The International Monetary Fund has, however, issued a declaration of censure and called on Argentina to adopt remedial measures to address the quality of official GDP and consumer price index data. Alternative data sources have shown significantly lower real growth and higher inflation than the official data since 2008. In this context, the World Bank is also using alternative data sources and estimates for the surveillance of macroeconomic developments in Argentina. c. As members of the European Monetary Union, these countries share a single currency, the euro. d. Refers to the area controlled by the government of the Republic of Cyprus. e. Excludes Abkhazia and South Ossetia. f. Excludes Transnistria. g. Includes Former Spanish Sahara. h. Includes South Sudan. i. Includes South Sudan until July 9, 2011. j. Covers mainland Tanzania only.

About the data

Economic data are organized by several different accounting conventions: the system of national accounts, the balance of payments, government finance statistics, and international finance statistics. There has been progress in unifying the concepts in the system of national accounts, balance of payments, and government finance statistics, but there are many national variations in the implementation of these standards. For example, even though the United Nations recommends using the 2008 System of National Accounts (2008 SNA) methodology in compiling national accounts, many are still using earlier versions, some as old as 1968. The International Monetary Fund (IMF) has recently published a new balance of payments methodology (BPM6), but many countries are still using the previous version. Similarly, the standards and definitions for government finance statistics were updated in 2001, but several countries still report using the 1986 version. For individual country information about methodology used, refer to *Primary data documentation*.

Economic growth

An economy's growth is measured by the change in the volume of its output or in the real incomes of its residents. The 2008 SNA offers three plausible indicators for calculating growth: the volume of gross domestic product (GDP), real gross domestic income, and real gross national income. Only growth in GDP is reported here.

Growth rates of GDP and its components are calculated using the least squares method and constant price data in the local currency for countries and using constant price U.S. dollar series for regional and income groups. Local currency series are converted to constant U.S. dollars using an exchange rate in the common reference year. The growth rates are average annual and compound growth rates. Methods of computing growth are described in *Statistical methods*. Forecasts of growth rates come from World Bank (2014).

Rebasing national accounts

Rebasing of national accounts can alter the measured growth rate of an economy and lead to breaks in series that affect the consistency of data over time. When countries rebase their national accounts, they update the weights assigned to various components to better reflect current patterns of production or uses of output. The new base year should represent normal operation of the economy—it should be a year without major shocks or distortions. Some developing countries have not rebased their national accounts for many years. Using an old base year can be misleading because implicit price and volume weights become progressively less relevant and useful.

To obtain comparable series of constant price data for computing aggregates, the World Bank rescales GDP and value added by industrial origin to a common reference year. This year's *World Development Indicators* switches the reference year to 2005. Because rescaling changes the implicit weights used in forming regional and income group aggregates, aggregate growth rates in this year's edition are not comparable with those from earlier editions with different base years.

Rescaling may result in a discrepancy between the rescaled GDP and the sum of the rescaled components. To avoid distortions in the growth rates, the discrepancy is left unallocated. As a result, the weighted average of the growth rates of the components generally does not equal the GDP growth rate.

Adjusted net savings

Adjusted net savings measure the change in a country's real wealth after accounting for the depreciation and depletion of a full range of assets in the economy. If a country's adjusted net savings are positive and the accounting includes a sufficiently broad range of assets, economic theory suggests that the present value of social welfare is increasing. Conversely, persistently negative adjusted net savings indicate that the present value of social welfare is decreasing, suggesting that an economy is on an unsustainable path.

Adjusted net savings are derived from standard national accounting measures of gross savings by making four adjustments. First, estimates of fixed capital consumption of produced assets are deducted to obtain net savings. Second, current public expenditures on education are added to net savings (in standard national accounting these expenditures are treated as consumption). Third, estimates of the depletion of a variety of natural resources are deducted to reflect the decline in asset values associated with their extraction and harvest. And fourth, deductions are made for damages from carbon dioxide emissions and local air pollution. Damages from local air pollution include damages from exposure to household air pollution and ambient concentrations of very fine particulate matter in urban and rural areas. By accounting for the depletion of natural resources and the degradation of the environment, adjusted net savings go beyond the definition of savings or net savings in the SNA.

Balance of payments

The balance of payments records an economy's transactions with the rest of the world. Balance of payments accounts are divided into two groups: the current account, which records transactions in goods, services, primary income, and secondary income, and the capital and financial account, which records capital transfers, acquisition or disposal of nonproduced, nonfinancial assets, and transactions in financial assets and liabilities. The current account balance is one of the most analytically useful indicators of an external imbalance.

A primary purpose of the balance of payments accounts is to indicate the need to adjust an external imbalance. Where to draw the line for analytical purposes requires a judgment concerning the imbalance that best indicates the need for adjustment. There are a number of definitions in common use for this and related analytical purposes. The trade balance is the difference between exports and imports of goods. From an analytical view it is arbitrary to distinguish goods from services. For example, a unit of foreign exchange earned by a freight company strengthens the balance of payments to the same extent as the foreign exchange earned by a goods exporter.

 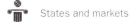

Even so, the trade balance is useful because it is often the most timely indicator of trends in the current account balance. Customs authorities are typically able to provide data on trade in goods long before data on trade in services are available.

Beginning in August 2012, the International Monetary Fund implemented the Balance of Payments Manual 6 (BPM6) framework in its major statistical publications. The World Bank implemented BPM6 in its online databases and publications from April 2013. Balance of payments data for 2005 onward will be presented in accord with the BPM6. The historical BPM5 data series will end with data for 2008, which can be accessed through the *World Development Indicators* archives.

The complete balance of payments methodology can be accessed through the International Monetary Fund website (www.imf.org /external/np/sta/bop/bop.htm).

Government finance

Central government cash surplus or deficit, a summary measure of the ongoing sustainability of government operations, is comparable to the national accounting concept of savings plus net capital transfers receivable, or net operating balance in the 2001 update of the IMF's *Government Finance Statistics Manual.*

The 2001 manual, harmonized with the 1993 SNA, recommends an accrual accounting method, focusing on all economic events affecting assets, liabilities, revenues, and expenses, not just those represented by cash transactions. It accounts for all changes in stocks, so stock data at the end of an accounting period equal stock data at the beginning of the period plus flows over the period. The 1986 manual considered only debt stocks.

For most countries central government finance data have been consolidated into one account, but for others only budgetary central government accounts are available. Countries reporting budgetary data are noted in *Primary data documentation.* Because budgetary accounts may not include all central government units (such as social security funds), they usually provide an incomplete picture. In federal states the central government accounts provide an incomplete view of total public finance.

Data on government revenue and expense are collected by the IMF through questionnaires to member countries and by the Organisation for Economic Co-operation and Development (OECD). Despite IMF efforts to standardize data collection, statistics are often incomplete, untimely, and not comparable across countries.

Government finance statistics are reported in local currency. The indicators here are shown as percentages of GDP. Many countries report government finance data by fiscal year; see *Primary data documentation* for information on fiscal year end by country.

Financial accounts

Money and the financial accounts that record the supply of money lie at the heart of a country's financial system. There are several commonly used definitions of the money supply. The narrowest, M1, encompasses currency held by the public and demand deposits with banks. M2 includes M1 plus time and savings deposits with banks that require prior notice for withdrawal. M3 includes M2 as well as various money market instruments, such as certificates of deposit issued by banks, bank deposits denominated in foreign currency, and deposits with financial institutions other than banks. However defined, money is a liability of the banking system, distinguished from other bank liabilities by the special role it plays as a medium of exchange, a unit of account, and a store of value.

A general and continuing increase in an economy's price level is called inflation. The increase in the average prices of goods and services in the economy should be distinguished from a change in the relative prices of individual goods and services. Generally accompanying an overall increase in the price level is a change in the structure of relative prices, but it is only the average increase, not the relative price changes, that constitutes inflation. A commonly used measure of inflation is the consumer price index, which measures the prices of a representative basket of goods and services purchased by a typical household. The consumer price index is usually calculated on the basis of periodic surveys of consumer prices. Other price indices are derived implicitly from indexes of current and constant price series.

Consumer price indexes are produced more frequently and so are more current. They are constructed explicitly, using surveys of the cost of a defined basket of consumer goods and services. Nevertheless, consumer price indexes should be interpreted with caution. The definition of a household, the basket of goods, and the geographic (urban or rural) and income group coverage of consumer price surveys can vary widely by country. In addition, weights are derived from household expenditure surveys, which, for budgetary reasons, tend to be conducted infrequently in developing countries, impairing comparability over time. Although useful for measuring consumer price inflation within a country, consumer price indexes are of less value in comparing countries.

Definitions

• **Gross domestic product (GDP)** at purchaser prices is the sum of gross value added by all resident producers in the economy plus any product taxes (less subsidies) not included in the valuation of output. It is calculated without deducting for depreciation of fabricated capital assets or for depletion and degradation of natural resources. Value added is the net output of an industry after adding up all outputs and subtracting intermediate inputs. • **Gross savings** are the difference between gross national income and public and private consumption, plus net current transfers. • **Adjusted net savings** measure the change in value of a specified set of assets, excluding capital gains. Adjusted net savings are net savings plus education expenditure minus energy depletion, mineral depletion, net forest depletion, and carbon dioxide and particulate emissions damage. • **Current account balance** is the sum of net exports of goods and services, net primary income, and net secondary income. • **Central**

government cash surplus or deficit is revenue (including grants) minus expense, minus net acquisition of nonfinancial assets. In editions before 2005 nonfinancial assets were included under revenue and expenditure in gross terms. This cash surplus or deficit is close to the earlier overall budget balance (still missing is lending minus repayments, which are included as a financing item under net acquisition of financial assets). • **Central government debt** is the entire stock of direct government fixed-term contractual obligations to others outstanding on a particular date. It includes domestic and foreign liabilities such as currency and money deposits, securities other than shares, and loans. It is the gross amount of government liabilities reduced by the amount of equity and financial derivatives held by the government. Because debt is a stock rather than a flow, it is measured as of a given date, usually the last day of the fiscal year. • **Consumer price index** reflects changes in the cost to the average consumer of acquiring a basket of goods and services that may be fixed or may change at specified intervals, such as yearly. The Laspeyres formula is generally used. • **Broad money** (IFS line 35L..ZK) is the sum of currency outside banks; demand deposits other than those of the central government; the time, savings, and foreign currency deposits of resident sectors other than the central government; bank and traveler's checks; and other securities such as certificates of deposit and commercial paper.

Data sources

Data on GDP for most countries are collected from national statistical organizations and central banks by visiting and resident World Bank missions; data for selected high-income economies are from the OECD. Data on gross savings are from World Bank national accounts data files. Data on adjusted net savings are based on a conceptual underpinning by Hamilton and Clemens (1999). Data on consumption of fixed capital are from the United Nations Statistics Division's National Accounts Statistics: Main Aggregates and Detailed Tables, the Organization for Economic Co-operation and Development's National Accounts Statistics database, and the Penn World Table (Feenstra, Inklaar, and Timmler 2013), with missing data estimated by World Bank staff. Data on education expenditure are from the United Nations Educational, Scientific and Cultural Organization Institute for Statistics, with missing data estimated by World Bank staff. Data on forest, energy, and mineral depletion are based on the sources and methods described in World Bank (2011). Additional data on energy commodity production and reserves are from the United States Energy Information Administration. Estimates of damages from carbon dioxide emissions follow the method of Fankhauser (1994) using data from the International Energy Agency's CO2 Emissions from Fuel Combustion Statistics database. Data on exposure to household air pollution and ambient particulate matter pollution are from the Institute for Health Metrics and Evaluation's Global Burden of Disease 2010 study. Data on current account balances are from the IMF's Balance of Payments Statistics Yearbook and International Financial Statistics. Data on central government finances are from the IMF's Government Finance Statistics database. Data on the consumer price index are from the IMF's International Financial Statistics. Data on broad money are from the IMF's monthly International Financial Statistics and annual International Financial Statistics Yearbook.

References

Asian Development Bank. 2012. *Asian Development Outlook 2012 Update: Services and Asia's Future Growth.* Manila.

De la Torre, Augusto, Eduardo Levy Yeyati, Samuel Pienknagura. 2013. *Latin America's Deceleration and the Exchange Rate Buffer.* Semiannual Report, Office of the Chief Economist. Washington, DC: World Bank.

Fankhauser, Samuel. 1994. "The Social Costs of Greenhouse Gas Emissions: An Expected Value Approach." *Energy Journal* 15 (2): 157–84.

Feenstra, Robert C., Robert Inklaar, and Marcel P. Timmer. 2013. "The Next Generation of the Penn World Table." [www.ggdc.net/pwt].

Hamilton, Kirk, and Michael Clemens. 1999. "Genuine Savings Rates in Developing Countries." *World Bank Economic Review* 13 (2): 333–56.

IMF (International Monetary Fund). 2001. *Government Finance Statistics Manual.* Washington, DC.

Institute for Health Metrics and Evaluation. 2010. Global Burden of Disease data. University of Washington, Seattle. [https://www.healthdata.org/gbd/data].

International Energy Agency. Various years. IEA CO2 Emissions from Fuel Combustion Statistics database. [http://dx.doi.org/10.1787/co2-data-en]. Paris.

Organisation for Economic Co-operation and Development. Various years. National Accounts Statistics database. [http://dx.doi.org/10.1787/na-data-en]. Paris.

United Nations Statistics Division. Various years. *National Accounts Statistics: Main Aggregates and Detailed Tables. Parts 1 and 2.* New York: United Nations.

United States Energy Information Administration. Various years. International Energy Statistics database. [http://www.eia.gov/cfapps/ipdbproject/IEDIndex3.cfm]. Washington, DC.

World Bank. 2011. *The Changing Wealth of Nations: Measuring Sustainable Development for the New Millennium.* Washington, DC.

———. 2015. *Global Economic Prospects: Having Fiscal Space and Using It.* Washington, DC.

———. Various years. *World Development Indicators.* Washington, DC.

4 Economy

To access the World Development Indicators online tables, use the URL http://wdi.worldbank.org/table/ and the table number (for example, http://wdi.worldbank.org/table/4.1). To view a specific indicator online, use the URL http://data.worldbank.org/indicator/ and the indicator code (for example, http://data.worldbank.org/indicator/NY.GDP.MKTP.KD.ZG).

4.1 Growth of output

Gross domestic product	NY.GDP.MKTP.KD.ZG
Agriculture	NV.AGR.TOTL.KD.ZG
Industry	NV.IND.TOTL.KD.ZG
Manufacturing	NV.IND.MANF.KD.ZG
Services	NV.SRV.TETC.KD.ZG

4.2 Structure of output

Gross domestic product	NY.GDP.MKTP.CD
Agriculture	NV.AGR.TOTL.ZS
Industry	NV.IND.TOTL.ZS
Manufacturing	NV.IND.MANF.ZS
Services	NV.SRV.TETC.ZS

4.3 Structure of manufacturing

Manufacturing value added	NV.IND.MANF.CD
Food, beverages and tobacco	NV.MNF.FBTO.ZS.UN
Textiles and clothing	NV.MNF.TXTL.ZS.UN
Machinery and transport equipment	NV.MNF.MTRN.ZS.UN
Chemicals	NV.MNF.CHEM.ZS.UN
Other manufacturing	NV.MNF.OTHR.ZS.UN

4.4 Structure of merchandise exports

Merchandise exports	TX.VAL.MRCH.CD.WT
Food	TX.VAL.FOOD.ZS.UN
Agricultural raw materials	TX.VAL.AGRI.ZS.UN
Fuels	TX.VAL.FUEL.ZS.UN
Ores and metals	TX.VAL.MMTL.ZS.UN
Manufactures	TX.VAL.MANF.ZS.UN

4.5 Structure of merchandise imports

Merchandise imports	TM.VAL.MRCH.CD.WT
Food	TM.VAL.FOOD.ZS.UN
Agricultural raw materials	TM.VAL.AGRI.ZS.UN
Fuels	TM.VAL.FUEL.ZS.UN
Ores and metals	TM.VAL.MMTL.ZS.UN
Manufactures	TM.VAL.MANF.ZS.UN

4.6 Structure of service exports

Commercial service exports	TX.VAL.SERV.CD.WT
Transport	TX.VAL.TRAN.ZS.WT
Travel	TX.VAL.TRVL.ZS.WT
Insurance and financial services	TX.VAL.INSF.ZS.WT
Computer, information, communications, and other commercial services	TX.VAL.OTHR.ZS.WT

4.7 Structure of service imports

Commercial service imports	TM.VAL.SERV.CD.WT
Transport	TM.VAL.TRAN.ZS.WT
Travel	TM.VAL.TRVL.ZS.WT
Insurance and financial services	TM.VAL.INSF.ZS.WT
Computer, information, communications, and other commercial services	TM.VAL.OTHR.ZS.WT

4.8 Structure of demand

Household final consumption expenditure	NE.CON.PETC.ZS
General government final consumption expenditure	NE.CON.GOVT.ZS
Gross capital formation	NE.GDI.TOTL.ZS
Exports of goods and services	NE.EXP.GNFS.ZS
Imports of goods and services	NE.IMP.GNFS.ZS
Gross savings	NY.GNS.ICTR.ZS

4.9 Growth of consumption and investment

Household final consumption expenditure	NE.CON.PRVT.KD.ZG
Household final consumption expenditure, Per capita	NE.CON.PRVT.PC.KD.ZG
General government final consumption expenditure	NE.CON.GOVT.KD.ZG
Gross capital formation	NE.GDI.TOTL.KD.ZG
Exports of goods and services	NE.EXP.GNFS.KD.ZG
Imports of goods and services	NE.IMP.GNFS.KD.ZG

4.10 Toward a broader measure of national income

Gross domestic product, $	NY.GDP.MKTP.CD
Gross domestic product, % growth	NY.GDP.MKTP.KD.ZG
Gross national income, $	NY.GNP.MKTP.CD
Gross national income, % growth	NY.GNP.MKTP.KD.ZG
Consumption of fixed capital	NY.ADJ.DKAP.GN.ZS
Natural resource depletion	NY.ADJ.DRES.GN.ZS
Adjusted net national income, $	NY.ADJ.NNTY.CD
Adjusted net national income, % growth	NY.ADJ.NNTY.KD.ZG

4.11 Toward a broader measure of savings

Gross savings	NY.ADJ.ICTR.GN.ZS
Consumption of fixed capital	NY.ADJ.DKAP.GN.ZS
Education expenditure	NY.ADJ.AEDU.GN.ZS
Net forest depletion	NY.ADJ.DFOR.GN.ZS
Energy depletion	NY.ADJ.DNGY.GN.ZS
Mineral depletion	NY.ADJ.DMIN.GN.ZS
Carbon dioxide damage	NY.ADJ.DCO2.GN.ZS
Local pollution damage	NY.ADJ.DPEM.GN.ZS
Adjusted net savings	NY.ADJ.SVNG.GN.ZS

 Front | User guide | World view | People | Environment

4.12 Central government finances

Revenue	GC.REV.XGRT.GD.ZS
Expense	GC.XPN.TOTL.GD.ZS
Cash surplus or deficit	GC.BAL.CASH.GD.ZS
Net incurrence of liabilities, Domestic	GC.FIN.DOMS.GD.ZS
Net incurrence of liabilities, Foreign	GC.FIN.FRGN.GD.ZS
Debt and interest payments, Total debt	GC.DOD.TOTL.GD.ZS
Debt and interest payments, Interest	GC.XPN.INTP.RV.ZS

4.13 Central government expenditure

Goods and services	GC.XPN.GSRV.ZS
Compensation of employees	GC.XPN.COMP.ZS
Interest payments	GC.XPN.INTP.ZS
Subsidies and other transfers	GC.XPN.TRFT.ZS
Other expense	GC.XPN.OTHR.ZS

4.14 Central government revenues

Taxes on income, profits and capital gains	GC.TAX.YPKG.RV.ZS
Taxes on goods and services	GC.TAX.GSRV.RV.ZS
Taxes on international trade	GC.TAX.INTT.RV.ZS
Other taxes	GC.TAX.OTHR.RV.ZS
Social contributions	GC.REV.SOCL.ZS
Grants and other revenue	GC.REV.GOTR.ZS

4.15 Monetary indicators

Broad money	FM.LBL.BMNY.ZG
Claims on domestic economy	FM.AST.DOMO.ZG.M3
Claims on central governments	FM.AST.CGOV.ZG.M3
Interest rate, Deposit	FR.INR.DPST
Interest rate, Lending	FR.INR.LEND
Interest rate, Real	FR.INR.RINR

4.16 Exchange rates and price

Official exchange rate	PA.NUS.FCRF
Purchasing power parity (PPP) conversion factor	PA.NUS.PPP
Ratio of PPP conversion factor to market exchange rate	PA.NUS.PPPC.RF
Real effective exchange rate	PX.REX.REER
GDP implicit deflator	NY.GDP.DEFL.KD.ZG
Consumer price index	FP.CPI.TOTL.ZG
Wholesale price index	FP.WPI.TOTL

4.17 Balance of payments current account

Goods and services, Exports	BX.GSR.GNFS.CD
Goods and services, Imports	BM.GSR.GNFS.CD
Balance on primary income	BN.GSR.FCTY.CD
Balance on secondary income	BN.TRF.CURR.CD
Current account balance	BN.CAB.XOKA.CD
Total reserves	FI.RES.TOTL.CD

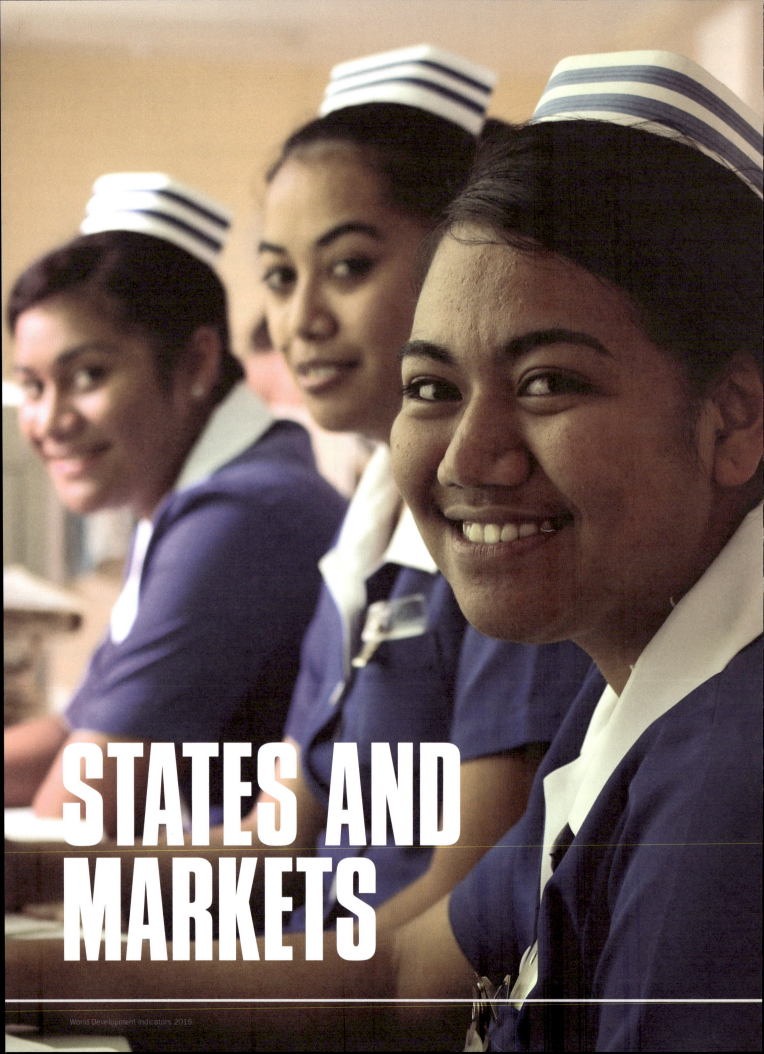

STATES AND
MARKETS

States and markets includes indicators of private investment and performance, the public sector's role in nurturing investment and growth, and the quality and availability of infrastructure essential for growth. These indicators measure the business environment, government functions, financial system development, infrastructure, information and communication technology, science and technology, government and policy performance, and conditions in fragile countries with weak institutions.

Doing Business measures business regulations that affect domestic small and medium-size firms in 11 areas across 189 economies. It provides quantitative measures of regulations for starting a business, dealing with construction permits, getting electricity, registering property, getting credit, protecting minority investors, paying taxes, trading across borders, enforcing contracts, and resolving insolvency. It also measures labor market regulations.

Since 2004, Doing Business has captured more than 2,400 regulatory reforms that make it easier to do business. From June 1, 2013, to June 1, 2014, 123 economies implemented at least one reform in measured areas—230 in total. More than 63 percent of these reforms reduced the complexity and cost of regulatory processes; the rest strengthened legal institutions. More than 80 percent of the economies covered by Doing Business saw their distance to frontier score improve—it is now easier to do business in most parts of the world. Singapore continues to have the most business-friendly regulations.

Doing Business 2015 introduces three improvements: a revised calculation of the ease of doing business ranking, an expanded sample of cities covered in large economies, and a broader scope of indicator sets.

First, the report changes the basis for the ranking, from the percentile rank to the distance to frontier score, which benchmarks economies with respect to a measure of regulatory best practice—showing the gap between each economy's performance and the best performance on each indicator. This measure captures more information than the percentile rank because it shows not only how economies are ordered on their performance on the indicators, but also how far apart they are.

Second, the report extends its coverage to include the second largest business city in economies with a population of more than 100 million (Bangladesh, Brazil, China, India, Indonesia, Japan, Mexico, Nigeria, Pakistan, the Russian Federation, and the United States).

Third, the report expands the data in 3 of the 11 topics covered, with plans to expand on 5 topics next year. These improvements provide a new conceptual framework in which the emphasis on regulatory efficiency is complemented by greater emphasis on regulatory quality. *Doing Business 2015* introduces a new measure of quality in the resolving insolvency indicator set and expands the measures of quality in the getting credit and protecting minority investors' indicator sets. *Doing Business 2016* will add measures of regulatory quality to the indicator sets for dealing with construction permits, getting electricity, registering property, paying taxes, and enforcing contracts. The results so far suggest that efficiency and quality go hand in hand.

This year *States and markets* contains a new table, table 5.14 on statistical capacity. The main Statistical Capacity Indicator and its subcategories assess the changes in national statistical capacity, thus helping national statistics offices and governments identify gaps in their capability to collect, produce, and use data.

Highlights

Asia dominates the information and communications technology goods trade

Information and communication technology goods as a share of goods exported and imported, 2012 (%)

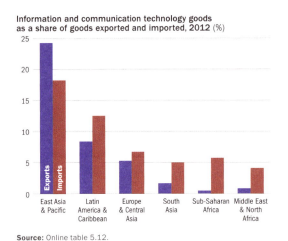

Source: Online table 5.12.

Information and communications technology (ICT) goods—products such as mobile phones, smartphones, laptops, tablets, integrated circuits, and various other parts and components—now account for more than 10 percent of merchandise trade worldwide. Seven of the top ten export economies in 2012 and six of the top ten import economies were in East Asia and Pacific. According to the United Nations Conference on Trade and Development, Asia's rising share in the manufacture and trade of ICT goods has been fueled by the cross-border transport of intermediate goods within intraregional production networks, which resulted in considerable flows between developing countries. In monetary terms China led the ICT goods trade in 2012 with exports of $508 billion and imports of $356 billion, followed by the United States with exports of $139 billion and imports of $299 billion.

Private investment goes primarily to energy and telecommunications

Private investment in developing countries, by sector ($ billions)
■ Water ■ Transport ■ Telecommunications ■ Energy

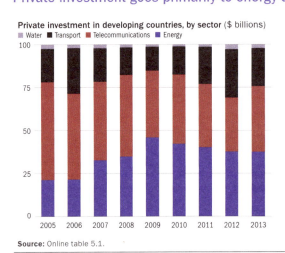

Source: Online table 5.1.

Infrastructure is a key element in the enabling environment for economic growth. The continuing global recession will curtail maintenance and new investment in infrastructure as governments face shrinking budgets and declining private financial flows. In 2013 private participation in infrastructure in developing countries fell 23 percent from 2012, to $150.3 billion. Investment in the energy sector dropped 23 percent from $73.6 billion in 2012 to $56.4 billion in 2013, and investment in the telecom sector dropped 6 percent to $57.3 billion. In 2013 the transport and water sectors both saw a 40 percent decline in private investment. Between 2005 and 2013 the transport sector accounted for an average of 20 percent of total private investment ($34.0 billion in 2013). The water and sanitation sector remained low at average of 2 percent, or $3.2 billion a year.

Research and development expenditures are rising steadily in selected economies

Research and development expenditures (% of GDP)

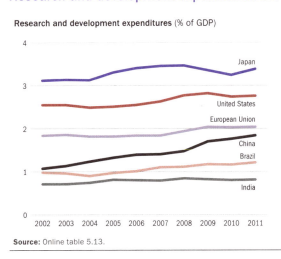

Source: Online table 5.13.

Research and development (R&D) intensity, measured by the resources spent on R&D activities as a share of GDP, has risen gradually since 2002. In 2011 high-income countries spent 2.5 percent of GDP on R&D activities, compared with developing countries' 1.2 percent. In some developing countries the rise in gross domestic expenditure on R&D has been related to strong economic growth—for example, climbing more than 70 percent since 2002 to 1.84 percent in 2011 in China. The United Nations Educational, Scientific and Cultural Organization reported that developing countries, including Brazil, China, and India, are witnessing sustained domestic growth and moving upstream in the value chain (UNESCO 2010). These economies once served as a repository for the outsourcing of manufacturing activities and now undertake autonomous technology development, product development, design, and applied research.

 Front   User guide   World view   People   Environment

Regulation places a heavy burden on businesses in Latin America and the Caribbean

Firms in Latin America and the Caribbean report that their senior managers spend more time dealing with the requirements of government regulations than firms in other regions. According to Enterprise Surveys, in Latin America and the Caribbean 14 percent of senior management's time is spent dealing with regulation, double the 7 percent in Sub-Saharan Africa and 6 percent in East Asia and Pacific and close to triple the less than 5 percent in the Middle East and North Africa and South Asia. However, the time varies greatly within regions. Firms in smaller Caribbean countries spend 6 percent of management time on regulations, compared with 16 percent for firms in the rest of the region. Smaller economies tend to rely on trade, and their efforts focus on maintaining a business-friendly environment.

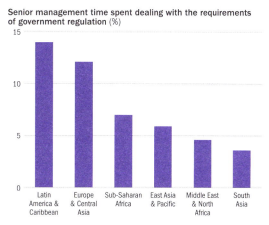

Senior management time spent dealing with the requirements of government regulation (%)

Source: Online table 5.2.

Managing the public sector effectively and adopting good policy are not easy

The links among weak institutions, poor development outcomes, and the risk of conflict are often evident in countries with fragile situations. A capable and accountable state creates opportunities for poor people, provides better services, and improves development outcomes. A total of 39 Sub-Saharan African countries have been part of the World Bank's Country Policy and Institutional Assessment exercise, which determines eligibility for the World Bank's International Development Association lending. In 2013, 7 countries showed improvement in the public sector and institutions cluster score from 2012, 9 countries were downgraded, and 23 remained unchanged. Cabo Verde (4.1 on a scale of 1, low, to 6, high) and Tanzania (3.4) were the top performers, and Chad and the Democratic Republic of the Congo improved the most, with both increasing their scores 0.2 point, from 2.2 to 2.4.

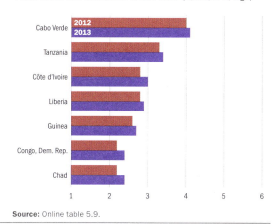

Public sector and institutions cluster score (1, low, to 6, high)

Source: Online table 5.9.

The statistical capacity of developing countries has improved steadily over the last 10 years

The Statistical Capacity Indicator is a useful monitoring and tracking tool for assessing changes in national statistical capacity, as well as for helping governments identify gaps in their capability to collect, produce, and use data. The combined Statistical Capacity Indicator of all developing countries has improved since assessment began in 2004, from 65 to 68 (on a scale of 0, low, to 100, high). The average scores increased from 58 to 62 for countries eligible for International Development Association funding (see http://data.worldbank.org/about/country-and-lending-groups) and from 73 to 75 for those eligible for International Bank for Reconstruction and Development funding. However, continued efforts are needed to help countries adhere to international statistical standards and methods and to improve data availability and periodicity.

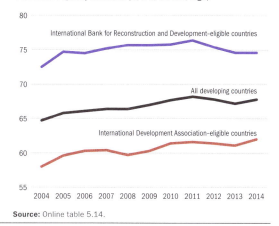

Statistical Capacity Indicator (0, low, to 100, high)

Source: Online table 5.14.

The digital and information revolution has changed the way the world learns, communicates, does business, and treats illnesses. Information and communication technologies offer vast opportunities for progress in all walks of life in all countries—opportunities for economic growth, improved health, better service delivery, learning through distance education, and social and cultural advances. The Internet delivers information to schools and hospitals, improves public and private services, and increases productivity and participation. Through mobile phones, Internet access is expanding in developing countries. The mobility, ease of use, flexible deployment, and declining rollout costs of wireless technologies enable mobile communications to reach rural populations. According to the International Telecommunication Union, by the end of 2014 the number of Internet users worldwide will have reached 3 billion.

Internet users

INDIVIDUALS USING THE INTERNET
AS A SHARE OF POPULATION, 2013

- Fewer than 20
- 20–39
- 40–59
- 60–79
- 80 or more
- No data

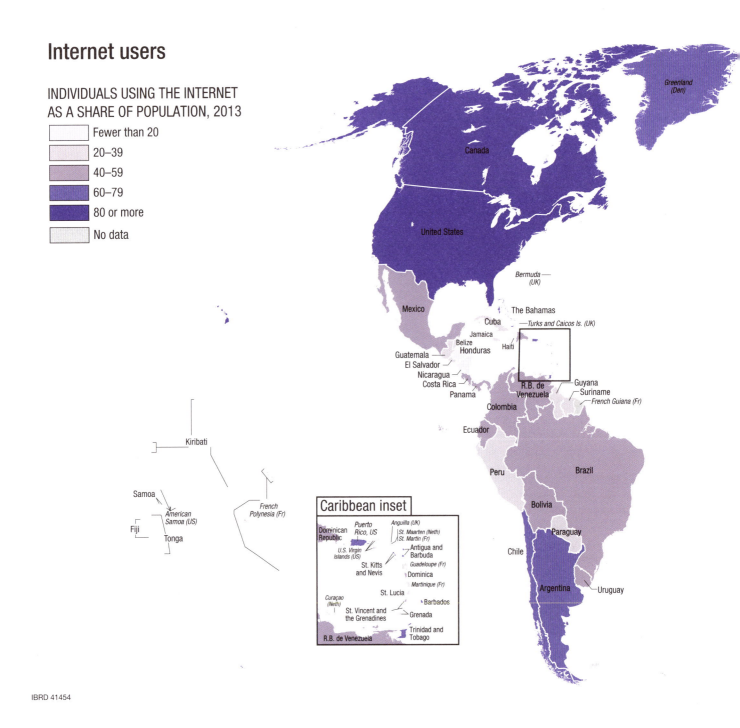

Caribbean inset

IBRD 41454

Latin America and the Caribbean and Europe and Central
Asia have the highest Internet user penetration rate among developing country regions: 46 percent in 2013.

In Sub-Saharan Africa 17 percent of the population was
online at the end of 2013, up from 10 percent in 2010.

The number of people using the Internet continues to
grow worldwide. Some 2.7 billion people—38 percent of the population—were online in 2013.

The number of Internet users in developing countries
tripled from 440 million in 2006 to 1.7 billion in 2013.

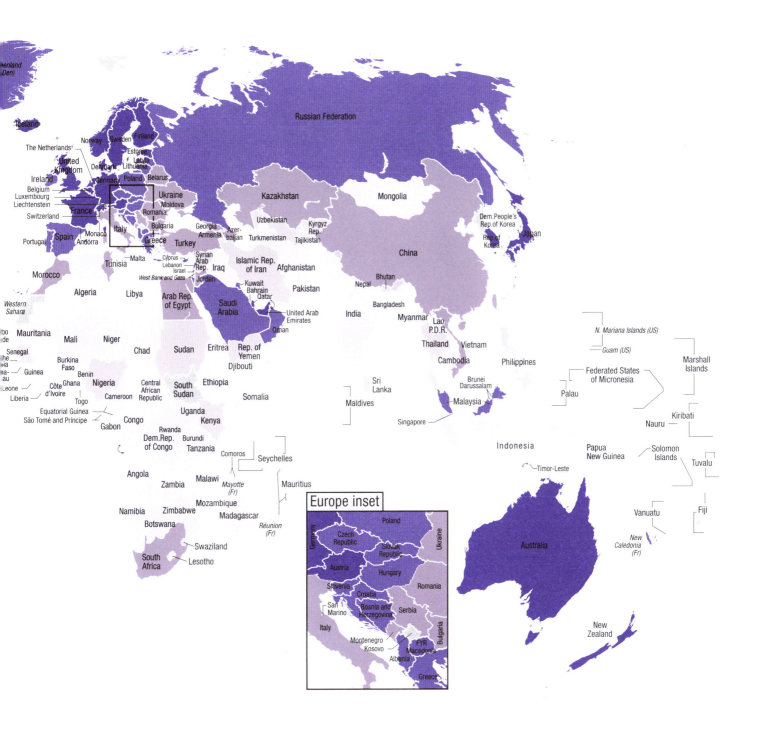

5 States and markets

	Business entry density	Time required to start a business	Domestic credit provided by financial sector	Tax revenue collected by central government	Military expenditures	Electric power consumption per capita	Mobile cellular subscriptions[a]	Individuals using the Internet[a]	High-technology exports	Statistical Capacity Indicator
	per 1,000 people ages 15–64	days	% of GDP	% of GDP	% of GDP	kilowatt-hours	per 100 people	% of population	% of manufactured exports	(0, low, to 100, high)
	2012	June 2014	2013	2012	2013	2011	2013	2013	2013	2014
Afghanistan	0.15	7	–3.9	7.5[b]	6.4	..	71	6	..	54.4
Albania	0.88	5	66.9	..	1.3	2,195	116	60	0.5	75.6
Algeria	0.53	22	3.0	37.4	5.0	1,091	101	17	0.2	52.2
American Samoa	..	..	..	..	..	..	..	..	..	..
Andorra	..	..	..	..	..	..	81	94	..	..
Angola	..	66	18.9	18.8[b]	4.9	248	62	19	..	48.9
Antigua and Barbuda	..	21	90.0	18.6[b]	..	..	127	63	0.0	58.9
Argentina	0.47	25	33.3	..	0.7	2,967	163	60	9.8	83.0
Armenia	1.55	3	46.0	18.7[b]	4.1	1,755	112	46	2.9	87.8
Aruba	..	..	56.0	..	..	..	135	79	10.2	..
Australia	12.16	3	159.1	21.4	1.6	10,712	107	83	12.9	..
Austria	0.50	22	127.9	18.3	0.8	8,388	156	81	13.7	..
Azerbaijan	0.70	5	25.5	13.0[b]	4.7	1,705	108	59	13.4	70.0
Bahamas, The	..	24	104.9	15.5[b]	..	..	76	72	0.0	..
Bahrain	..	9	78.6	1.1	3.8	10,018	166	90	0.2	..
Bangladesh	0.09	20	57.9	8.7[b]	1.2	259	74	7	0.2	80.0
Barbados	..	18	..	25.2	..	..	108	75	15.3	..
Belarus	1.14	9	39.9	15.1[b]	1.3	3,628	119	54	4.4	87.8
Belgium	2.48	4	111.2	24.9	1.0	8,021	111	82	11.4	..
Belize	4.31	43	58.3	22.6[b]	1.0	..	53	32	0.0	55.6
Benin	..	12	21.5	15.6	1.0	..	93	5	1.2	65.6
Bermuda	..	..	..	..	..	..	144	95	12.4	..
Bhutan	0.20	17	50.2	..	..	..	72	30	0.0	78.9
Bolivia	0.56	49	50.4	..	1.5	623	98	40	9.4	76.7
Bosnia and Herzegovina	0.70	37	67.7	20.9	1.1	3,189	91	68	2.3	72.2
Botswana	12.30	60	13.6	27.1[b]	2.0	1,603	161	15	0.4	51.1
Brazil	2.17	84	110.1	15.4[b]	1.4	2,438	135	52	9.6	75.6
Brunei Darussalam	..	101	20.8	..	2.6	8,507	112	65	15.2	..
Bulgaria	9.03	18	71.1	19.0[b]	1.5	4,864	145	53	8.0	84.4
Burkina Faso	0.15	13	22.8	15.0	1.3	..	66	4	13.7	71.1
Burundi	..	5	23.9	..	2.2	..	25	1	2.7	54.4
Cabo Verde	..	10	82.8	17.8[b]	0.5	..	100	38	0.6	68.9
Cambodia	..	101	40.3	11.6	1.6	164	134	6	0.2	76.7
Cameroon	..	15	15.5	..	1.3	256	70	6	3.7	56.7
Canada	1.07	5	..	11.7	1.0	16,473	81	86	14.0	..
Cayman Islands	..	..	..	..	..	..	168	74	..	..
Central African Republic	..	22	36.7	9.5	..	..	29	4	0.0	58.9
Chad	..	60	7.0	..	2.0	..	36	2	..	63.3
Channel Islands	..	..	..	..	..	..	..	..	..	..
Chile	5.69	6	115.5	19.0	2.0	3,568	134	67	4.8	95.6
China	..	31	163.0	10.6[b]	2.1[c]	3,298	89	46	27.0	70.0
Hong Kong SAR, China	28.12	3	224.0	..	..	5,949	237	74	16.2	..
Macao SAR, China	..	..	–10.7	37.0[b]	..	..	304	66	0.0	..
Colombia	2.00	11	70.1	13.2	3.4	1,123	104	52	7.4	81.1
Comoros	..	15	26.9	..	..	..	47	7	..	40.0
Congo, Dem. Rep.	0.02	16	7.3	8.4[b]	1.3	105	42	2	..	57.0
Congo, Rep.	..	53	–7.2	..	..	172	105	7	1.6	47.8

	Business entry density per 1,000 people ages 15–64 2012	Time required to start a business days June 2014	Domestic credit provided by financial sector % of GDP 2013	Tax revenue collected by central government % of GDP 2012	Military expenditures % of GDP 2013	Electric power consumption per capita kilowatt-hours 2011	Mobile cellular subscriptions[a] per 100 people 2013	Individuals using the Internet[a] % of population 2013	High-technology exports % of manufactured exports 2013	Statistical Capacity Indicator (0, low, to 100, high) 2014
Costa Rica	3.55	24	56.5	13.6	..	1,844	146	46	43.3	77.8
Côte d'Ivoire	..	7	26.9	14.2	1.5	212	95	3	1.3	46.7
Croatia	2.82	15	94.1	19.6[b]	1.7	3,901	115	67	8.6	83.3
Cuba	..	..	..	..	3.3	1,327	18	26	..	..
Curaçao	..	..	..	..	..	..	128	..	..	..
Cyprus	22.51	8	335.8	25.5	2.1	4,271	96	65	7.2	..
Czech Republic	2.96	19	67.0	13.4[b]	1.0	6,289	128	74	14.8	..
Denmark	4.36	6	199.6	33.4	1.4	6,122	127	95	14.3	..
Djibouti	..	14	33.9	..	..	..	28	10	..	45.6
Dominica	..	12	61.9	21.8[b]	..	..	130	59	8.8	55.6
Dominican Republic	1.05	20	47.7	12.2	0.6	893	88	46	2.7	78.9
Ecuador	..	56	29.6	..	3.0	1,192	111	40	4.4	70.0
Egypt, Arab Rep.	..	8	86.2	13.2[b]	1.7	1,743	122	50	0.5	90.0
El Salvador	0.48	17	72.1	14.5	1.1	830	136	23	4.4	91.1
Equatorial Guinea	..	135	–3.5	..	..	..	67	16	..	34.0
Eritrea	..	84	98.3	..	..	49	6	1	..	31.1
Estonia	..	5	71.6	16.3	1.9	6,314	160	80	10.6	86.7
Ethiopia	..	15	..	9.2[b]	0.8	52	27	2	2.4	61.1
Faeroe Islands	..	..	..	..	..	..	121	90	..	..
Fiji	..	59	121.8	..	1.4	..	106	37	2.2	71.1
Finland	2.32	14	104.9	20.0	1.2	15,738	172	92	7.2	..
France	2.88	5	130.8	21.4	2.2	7,292	98	82	25.9	..
French Polynesia	..	..	..	..	..	..	86	57	7.8	..
Gabon	..	50	11.7	..	1.3	907	215	9	..	42.2
Gambia, The	..	26	50.1	..	..	..	100	14	7.3	66.7
Georgia	4.86	2	42.9	24.1[b]	2.7	1,918	115	43	2.5	82.2
Germany	1.29	15	113.5	11.5	1.3	7,081	121	84	16.1	..
Ghana	0.90	14	34.8	14.9[b]	0.5	344	108	12	6.1	62.2
Greece	0.77	13	134.3	22.4	2.5	5,380	117	60	7.5	..
Greenland	..	..	..	..	..	..	106	66	8.0	..
Grenada	..	15	80.0	18.7[b]	..	..	126	35	..	44.4
Guam	..	..	..	..	..	..	..	65	..	..
Guatemala	0.52	19	40.6	10.8[b]	0.5	539	140	20	4.7	68.9
Guinea	0.23	8	32.2	..	..	..	63	2	..	52.2
Guinea-Bissau	..	9	18.6	..	1.7	..	74	3	..	43.3
Guyana	..	19	55.3	..	1.1	..	69	33	0.0	58.9
Haiti	0.06	97	20.4	..	..	32	69	11	..	47.8
Honduras	..	14	57.3	14.7	1.2	708	96	18	2.4	73.3
Hungary	4.75	5	64.7	22.9	0.9	3,895	116	73	16.3	85.6
Iceland	8.17	4	130.9	22.3	0.1	52,374	108	97	15.5	..
India	0.12	28	77.2	10.8[b]	2.4	684	71	15	8.1	81.1
Indonesia	0.29	53	45.6	..	0.9	680	125	16	7.1	83.3
Iran, Islamic Rep.	..	12	..	..	2.1	2,649	84	31	4.1	73.3
Iraq	0.13	29	–1.4	..	3.4	1,343	96	9	..	46.7
Ireland	4.50	6	186.1	22.0	0.5	5,701	103	78	22.4	..
Isle of Man	45.27	..	..	..	..	..	..	..	..	..
Israel	2.96	13	..	22.1	5.6	6,926	123	71	15.6	..

5 States and markets

	Business entry density	Time required to start a business	Domestic credit provided by financial sector	Tax revenue collected by central government	Military expenditures	Electric power consumption per capita	Mobile cellular subscriptions[a]	Individuals using the Internet[a]	High-technology exports	Statistical Capacity Indicator
	per 1,000 people ages 15–64	days	% of GDP	% of GDP	% of GDP	kilowatt-hours	per 100 people	% of population	% of manufactured exports	(0, low, to 100, high)
	2012	June 2014	2013	2012	2013	2011	2013	2013	2013	2014
Italy	1.91	5	161.8	22.4	1.5	5,515	159	58	7.3	..
Jamaica	1.11	15	51.4	27.1	0.8	1,553	102	38	0.7	78.9
Japan	1.15	11	366.5	10.1	1.0	7,848	118	86	16.8	..
Jordan	0.98	12	111.9	15.3	3.6	2,289	142	44	1.6	74.4
Kazakhstan	1.71	10	39.1	..	1.2	4,893	185	54	36.9	88.9
Kenya	..	30	42.8	15.9[b]	1.6	155	72	39	..	54.4
Kiribati	0.11	31	..	16.1[b]	..	..	17	12	38.5	35.6
Korea, Dem. People's Rep.	..	..	..	..	..	739	10	0	..	..
Korea, Rep.	2.03	4	155.9	14.4[b]	2.6	10,162	111	85	27.1	..
Kosovo	1.22	11	23.3	..	..	2,947	..	..	..	33.3
Kuwait	..	31	47.9	0.7[b]	3.2	16,122	190	75	1.4	..
Kyrgyz Republic	0.92	8	..	18.1[b]	3.2	1,642	121	23	5.3	86.7
Lao PDR	0.10	92	..	14.8[b]	0.2	..	68	13	..	73.3
Latvia	11.63	13	58.6	13.8[b]	1.0	3,264	228	75	13.0	86.7
Lebanon	..	9	187.6	15.5	4.4	3,499	81	71	2.2	62.2
Lesotho	1.49	29	1.7	..	2.1	..	86	5	..	72.2
Liberia	..	5	38.7	20.9[b]	0.7	..	59	5	..	46.7
Libya	..	35	−51.1	..	3.6	3,926	165	17	..	28.9
Liechtenstein	..	..	..	..	..	..	104	94	..	..
Lithuania	4.71	4	51.0	13.4	0.8	3,530	151	68	10.3	83.3
Luxembourg	20.98	19	163.9	25.5	0.5	15,530	149	94	8.1	..
Macedonia, FYR	3.60	2	52.4	16.7[b]	1.2	3,881	106	61	3.7	84.4
Madagascar	0.05	8	15.6	10.1	0.5	..	37	2	0.6	62.2
Malawi	..	38	31.2	..	1.4	..	32	5	6.0	75.6
Malaysia	2.28	6	142.6	16.1[b]	1.5	4,246	145	67	43.5	74.4
Maldives	..	9	86.9	15.5[b]	..	..	181	44	..	66.7
Mali	..	11	20.9	15.6	1.4	..	129	2	1.2	66.7
Malta	13.61	35	146.7	27.0	0.6	4,689	130	69	38.6	..
Marshall Islands	..	17	..	..	..	..	..	12	..	46.7
Mauritania	..	9	39.1	..	3.6	..	103	6	..	59.0
Mauritius	7.40	6	122.4	19.0	0.2	..	123	39	0.6	85.6
Mexico	0.88	6	49.5	..	0.6	2,092	86	43	15.9	85.6
Micronesia, Fed. Sts.	..	16	−27.2	..	..	..	30	28	..	36.7
Moldova	..	6	44.0	18.6[b]	0.3	1,470	106	49	2.4	94.4
Monaco	..	..	..	..	..	..	94	91	..	..
Mongolia	..	11	63.6	18.2[b]	1.1	1,577	124	18	15.9	83.3
Montenegro	10.66	10	61.0	..	1.6	5,747	160	57	..	75.6
Morocco	..	11	115.5	24.5	3.9	826	129	56	6.4	78.9
Mozambique	..	13	29.3	20.8[b]	..	447	48	5	13.4	74.4
Myanmar	..	72	..	..	..	110	13	1	..	46.7
Namibia	0.85	66	49.7	23.1	3.0	1,549	118	14	1.7	48.9
Nepal	0.66	17	69.1	13.9[b]	1.4	106	77	13	0.3	65.6
Netherlands	4.44	4	193.0	19.7	1.2	7,036	114	94	20.4	..
New Caledonia	..	..	..	..	..	..	94	66	10.6	..
New Zealand	15.07	1	..	29.3	1.0	9,444	106	83	10.3	..
Nicaragua	..	13	44.8	14.8[b]	0.8	522	112	16	0.4	65.6
Niger	..	15	11.8	..	1.1	..	39	2	52.4	67.8

 Front User guide World view People Environment

	Business entry density per 1,000 people ages 15–64 2012	Time required to start a business days June 2014	Domestic credit provided by financial sector % of GDP 2013	Tax revenue collected by central government % of GDP 2012	Military expenditures % of GDP 2013	Electric power consumption per capita kilowatt-hours 2011	Mobile cellular subscriptions[a] per 100 people 2013	Individuals using the Internet[a] % of population 2013	High-technology exports % of manufactured exports 2013	Statistical Capacity Indicator (0, low, to 100, high) 2014
Nigeria	0.91	31	22.3	1.6	0.5	149	73	38	2.7	72.2
Northern Mariana Islands	..	..	..	..	..	..	..	..	..	..
Norway	7.83	5	..	27.3	1.4	23,174	116	95	19.1	..
Oman	..	7	35.7	2.5[b]	11.5	6,292	155	66	3.4	..
Pakistan	0.04	19	49.0	10.1[b]	3.5	449	70	11	1.9	74.4
Palau	..	28	..	..	..	..	86	..	..	36.7
Panama	14.10	6	67.6	..	..	1,829	163	43	0.0	82.0
Papua New Guinea	..	53	48.8	..	0.6	..	41	7	3.5	46.7
Paraguay	..	35	38.3	12.8[b]	1.6	1,228	104	37	7.5	71.1
Peru	3.83	26	22.0	16.5[b]	1.4	1,248	98	39	3.6	99.0
Philippines	0.27	34	51.9	12.9[b]	1.3	647	105	37	47.1	77.8
Poland	..	30	65.8	16.0	1.8	3,832	149	63	7.9	78.9
Portugal	3.62	3	183.3	20.3	2.1	4,848	113	62	4.3	..
Puerto Rico	..	6	..	..	..	..	84	74	..	..
Qatar	1.74	9	73.9	14.7[b]	..	15,755	153	85	0.0	..
Romania	4.12	8	52.0	18.8	1.3	2,639	106	50	5.7	87.8
Russian Federation	4.30	11	48.3	15.1	4.2	6,486	153	61	10.0	84.0
Rwanda	1.07	7	..	13.7[b]	1.1	..	57	9	4.4	78.9
Samoa	1.04	9	40.8	0.0[b]	..	..	..	15	0.6	53.3
San Marino	..	40	..	..	..	..	117	51	..	..
São Tomé and Príncipe	3.75	4	28.8	14.0	..	..	65	23	14.1	68.9
Saudi Arabia	..	21	−7.9	..	9.0	8,161	184	61	0.7	..
Senegal	0.27	6	35.1	19.2	0.0	187	93	21	0.7	73.3
Serbia	1.68	12	49.5	19.7[b]	2.0	4,490	119	52	..	92.3
Seychelles	..	38	35.2	31.2[b]	0.9	..	147	50	..	62.2
Sierra Leone	0.32	12	14.5	11.7[b]	0.0	..	66	2	..	58.9
Singapore	8.04	3	112.6	14.0[b]	3.3	8,404	156	73	47.0	..
Sint Maarten	..	..	..	..	..	..	..	..	..	..
Slovak Republic	5.11	12	..	12.2	1.0	5,348	114	78	10.3	83.3
Slovenia	4.36	6	82.8	17.5[b]	1.1	6,806	110	73	6.2	..
Solomon Islands	..	9	20.3	..	..	..	58	8	12.6	53.3
Somalia	..	..	..	..	..	..	49	2	..	20.0
South Africa	6.54	19	182.2	25.5	1.1	4,606	146	49	5.5	74.4
South Sudan	0.73	14	..	..	9.3	..	25	..	..	29.4
Spain	2.71	13	205.1	7.1	0.9	5,530	107	72	7.7	..
Sri Lanka	0.51	11	47.4	12.0[b]	2.7	490	95	22	1.0	78.9
St. Kitts and Nevis	5.69	19	65.9	20.2[b]	..	..	142	80	0.1	52.2
St. Lucia	3.00	15	123.1	23.0[b]	..	..	116	35	..	66.7
St. Martin	..	..	..	..	..	..	..	..	..	..
St. Vincent & the Grenadines	1.37	10	58.4	23.0[b]	..	..	115	52	0.1	55.6
Sudan	..	36	24.0	..	..	143	73	23	0.7	43.3
Suriname	1.63	84	31.5	19.4[b]	..	..	161	37	6.5	63.3
Swaziland	..	30	18.4	..	3.0	..	71	25	..	60.0
Sweden	6.41	16	138.1	20.7	1.1	14,030	124	95	14.0	..
Switzerland	2.53	10	173.4	9.8	0.7	7,928	137	87	26.5	..
Syrian Arab Republic	0.04	13	..	..	..	1,715	56	26	..	44.4
Tajikistan	0.26	39	19.0	..	..	1,714	92	16	..	75.6

5 States and markets

	Business entry density per 1,000 people ages 15–64 2012	Time required to start a business days June 2014	Domestic credit provided by financial sector % of GDP 2013	Tax revenue collected by central government % of GDP 2012	Military expenditures % of GDP 2013	Electric power consumption per capita kilowatt-hours 2011	Mobile cellular subscriptions[a] per 100 people 2013	Individuals using the Internet[a] % of population 2013	High-technology exports % of manufactured exports 2013	Statistical Capacity Indicator (0, low, to 100, high) 2014
Tanzania	..	26	24.3	16.1[b]	1.1	92	56	4	5.4	72.2
Thailand	0.86	28	173.3	16.5	1.5	2,316	140	29	20.1	83.3
Timor-Leste	2.76	10	-53.6	..	2.3	..	57	1	9.8	64.4
Togo	0.12	10	36.0	16.4	1.6	..	63	5	0.2	64.4
Tonga	1.91	16	27.1	..	..	..	55	35	6.5	50.0
Trinidad and Tobago	..	12	33.7	28.3[b]	..	6,332	145	64	..	62.2
Tunisia	1.52	11	83.4	21.0[b]	2.0	1,297	116	44	4.9	72.0
Turkey	0.79	7	84.3	20.4	2.3	2,709	93	46	1.9	84.4
Turkmenistan	..	..	..	..	..	2,444	117	10	..	43.3
Turks and Caicos Islands	..	..	..	..	..	..	..	..	1.9	..
Tuvalu	..	..	..	..	..	..	34	37	..	33.3
Uganda	1.17	32	14.2	11.0[b]	1.9	..	44	16	1.9	64.4
Ukraine	0.92	21	95.7	18.2[b]	2.9	3,662	138	42	5.9	91.1
United Arab Emirates	1.38	8	76.5	0.4	5.0	9,389	172	88	..	..
United Kingdom	11.04	6	184.1	25.3	2.2	5,472	125	90	16.3	..
United States	..	6	240.5	10.2	3.8	13,246	96	84	17.8	..
Uruguay	2.98	7	36.3	19.3[b]	1.9	2,810	155	58	8.7	90.0
Uzbekistan	0.64	8	..	..	..	1,626	74	38	..	54.4
Vanuatu	..	35	68.7	16.0[b]	..	..	50	11	54.0	43.3
Venezuela, RB	..	144	52.5	..	1.2	3,313	102	55	2.3	81.1
Vietnam	..	34	108.2	..	2.2	1,073	131	44	28.2	76.7
Virgin Islands (U.S.)	..	..	..	..	..	..	..	45	..	..
West Bank and Gaza	..	44	..	..	..	..	74	47	..	82.0
Yemen, Rep.	..	40	33.9	..	3.9	193	69	20	0.4	56.0
Zambia	1.36	7	27.5	16.0[b]	1.4	599	72	15	2.4	60.0
Zimbabwe	..	90	..	..	2.6	757	96	19	3.6	57.8
World	**3.83 u**	**22 u**	**166.5 w**	**14.3 w**	**2.3 w**	**3,045 w**	**93 w**	**38 w**	**17.8 w**	**.. u**
Low income	0.33	29	35.8	11.8	1.5	219	55	7	4.1	60.5
Middle income	2.20	24	108.4	13.2	1.9	1,816	92	33	19.1	70.8
Lower middle income	1.10	22	61.9	10.9	1.9	736	85	21	11.1	68.8
Upper middle income	3.01	26	121.3	14.0	1.9	2,932	100	45	21.2	72.8
Low & middle income	1.86	25	106.9	13.1	1.9	1,646	87	29	18.9	67.8
East Asia & Pacific	1.34	35[d]	149.8	11.2	1.9	2,582	96	39	26.8	71.4
Europe & Central Asia	2.19	11[d]	68.3	19.6	2.1	2,954	112	46	10.4	78.1
Latin America & Carib.	2.38	34[d]	72.5	..	1.3	1,985	114	46	12.0	77.1
Middle East & N. Africa	0.55	20[d]	46.8	..	3.3	1,696	101	34	2.0	63.4
South Asia	0.25	16[d]	71.6	10.7	2.5	605	71	14	7.5	72.4
Sub-Saharan Africa	2.09	25[d]	61.0	14.0	1.3	535	66	17	4.3	58.7
High income	7.47	15	196.6	14.2	2.5	8,906	121	78	17.2	..
Euro area	6.62	11	143.2	17.1	1.5	6,599	123	76	15.9	..

a. Data are from the International Telecommunication Union's (ITU) World Telecommunication/ICT Indicators database. Please cite ITU for third party use of these data. b. Data were reported on a cash basis and have been adjusted to the accrual framework of the International Monetary Fund's *Government Finance Statistics Manual 2001.* c. Differs from the official value published by the government of China (1.3 percent; see National Bureau of Statistics of China, www.stats.gov.cn). d. Differs from data reported on the Doing Business website because the regional aggregates on the Doing Business website include developed economies.

 Front | User guide | World view | People | Environment

About the data

Entrepreneurial activity

The rate new businesses are added to an economy is a measure of its dynamism and entrepreneurial activity. Data on business entry density are from the World Bank's 2013 Entrepreneurship Database, which includes indicators for more than 150 countries for 2004–12. Survey data are used to analyze firm creation, its relationship to economic growth and poverty reduction, and the impact of regulatory and institutional reforms. Data on total registered businesses were collected from national registrars of companies. For cross-country comparability, only limited liability corporations that operate in the formal sector are included. For additional information on sources, methodology, calculation of entrepreneurship rates, and data limitations see www.doingbusiness.org/data/exploretopics/entrepreneurship.

Data on time required to start a business are from the Doing Business database, whose indicators measure business regulation, gauge regulatory outcomes, and measure the extent of legal protection of property, the flexibility of employment regulation, and the tax burden on businesses. The fundamental premise is that economic activity requires good rules and regulations that are efficient, accessible, and easy to implement. Some indicators give a higher score for more regulation, such as stricter disclosure requirements in related-party transactions, and others give a higher score for simplified regulations, such as a one-stop shop for completing business startup formalities. There are 11 sets of indicators covering starting a business, registering property, dealing with construction permits, getting electricity, enforcing contracts, getting credit, protecting investors, paying taxes, trading across borders, resolving insolvency, and employing workers. The indicators are available at www.doingbusiness.org.

Doing Business data are collected with a standardized survey that uses a simple business case to ensure comparability across economies and over time—with assumptions about the legal form of the business, its size, its location, and nature of its operation. Surveys in 189 countries are administered through more than 10,700 local experts, including lawyers, business consultants, accountants, freight forwarders, government officials, and other professionals who routinely administer or advise on legal and regulatory requirements.

Over the next two years Doing Business will introduce important improvements in 8 of the 10 sets of Doing Business indicators to provide a new conceptual framework in which the emphasis on efficiency of regulation is complemented by increased emphasis on quality of regulation. Moreover, Doing Business will change the basis for the ease of doing business ranking, from the percentile rank to the distance to frontier score. The distance to frontier score benchmarks economies with respect to a measure of regulatory best practice—showing the gap between each economy's performance and the best performance on each indicator. This measure captures more information than the simple rankings previously used as the basis because it shows not only how economies are ordered on their performance on the indicators, but also how far apart they are.

The Doing Business methodology has limitations that should be considered when interpreting the data. First, the data collected refer to businesses in the economy's largest business city and may not represent regulations in other locations of the economy. To address this limitation, subnational indicators are being collected for selected economies, and coverage has been extended to the second largest business city in economies with a population of more than 100 million. Subnational indicators point to significant differences in the speed of reform and the ease of doing business across cities in the same economy. Second, the data often focus on a specific business form—generally a limited liability company of a specified size—and may not represent regulation for other types of businesses such as sole proprietorships. Third, transactions described in a standardized business case refer to a specific set of issues and may not represent all the issues a business encounters. Fourth, the time measures involve an element of judgment by the expert respondents. When sources indicate different estimates, the Doing Business time indicators represent the median values of several responses given under the assumptions of the standardized case. Fifth, the methodology assumes that a business has full information on what is required and does not waste time when completing procedures. In constructing the indicators, it is assumed that entrepreneurs know about all regulations and comply with them. In practice, entrepreneurs may not be aware of all required procedures or may avoid legally required procedures altogether.

Financial systems

The development of an economy's financial markets is closely related to its overall development. Well functioning financial systems provide good and easily accessible information. That lowers transaction costs, which in turn improves resource allocation and boosts economic growth. Data on the access to finance, availability of credit, and cost of service improve understanding of the state of financial development. Credit is an important link in money transmission; it finances production, consumption, and capital formation, which in turn affect economic activity. The availability of credit to households, private companies, and public entities shows the depth of banking and financial sector development in the economy.

Domestic credit provided by the financial sector as a share of GDP measures banking sector depth and financial sector development in terms of size. Data are taken from the financial corporation survey of the International Monetary Fund's (IMF) *International Financial Statistics* or, when unavailable, from its depository corporation survey. The financial corporation survey includes monetary authorities (the central bank), deposit money banks, and other banking institutions, such as finance companies, development banks, and savings and loan institutions. In a few countries governments may hold international reserves as deposits in the banking system rather than in the central bank. Claims on the central government are a net item (claims on the central government minus central government deposits) and thus may be negative, resulting in a negative value for domestic credit provided by the financial sector.

5 States and markets

Tax revenues

Taxes are the main source of revenue for most governments. Tax revenue as a share of GDP provides a quick overview of the fiscal obligations and incentives facing the private sector across countries. The table shows only central government data, which may significantly understate the total tax burden, particularly in countries where provincial and municipal governments are large or have considerable tax authority.

Low ratios of tax revenue to GDP may reflect weak administration and large-scale tax avoidance or evasion. Low ratios may also reflect a sizable parallel economy with unrecorded and undisclosed incomes. Tax revenue ratios tend to rise with income, with higher income countries relying on taxes to finance a much broader range of social services and social security than lower income countries are able to.

Military expenditures

Although national defense is an important function of government, high expenditures for defense or civil conflicts burden the economy and may impede growth. Military expenditures as a share of GDP are a rough indicator of the portion of national resources used for military activities. As an "input" measure, military expenditures are not directly related to the "output" of military activities, capabilities, or security. Comparisons across countries should take into account many factors, including historical and cultural traditions, the length of borders that need defending, the quality of relations with neighbors, and the role of the armed forces in the body politic.

Data are from the Stockholm International Peace Research Institute (SIPRI), whose primary source of military expenditure data is official data provided by national governments. These data are derived from budget documents, defense white papers, and other public documents from official government agencies, including government responses to questionnaires sent by SIPRI, the United Nations Office for Disarmament Affairs, or the Organization for Security and Co-operation in Europe. Secondary sources include international statistics, such as those of the North Atlantic Treaty Organization (NATO) and the IMF's *Government Finance Statistics Yearbook*. Other secondary sources include country reports of the Economist Intelligence Unit, country reports by IMF staff, and specialist journals and newspapers.

In the many cases where SIPRI cannot make independent estimates, it uses country-provided data. Because of differences in definitions and the difficulty of verifying the accuracy and completeness of data, data are not always comparable across countries. However, SIPRI puts a high priority on ensuring that the data series for each country is comparable over time. More information on SIPRI's military expenditure project can be found at www.sipri.org/research/armaments/milex.

Infrastructure

The quality of an economy's infrastructure, including power and communications, is an important element in investment decisions and economic development. The International Energy Agency (IEA) collects data on electric power consumption from national energy agencies and adjusts the values to meet international definitions. Consumption by auxiliary stations, losses in transformers that are considered integral parts of those stations, and electricity produced by pumping installations are included. Where data are available, electricity generated by primary sources of energy—coal, oil, gas, nuclear, hydro, geothermal, wind, tide and wave, and combustible renewables—are included. Consumption data do not capture the reliability of supplies, including breakdowns, load factors, and frequency of outages.

The International Telecommunication Union (ITU) estimates that there were 6.7 billion mobile subscriptions globally in 2013. No technology has ever spread faster around the world. Mobile communications have a particularly important impact in rural areas. The mobility, ease of use, flexible deployment, and relatively low and declining rollout costs of wireless technologies enable them to reach rural populations with low levels of income and literacy. The next billion mobile subscribers will consist mainly of the rural poor.

Operating companies have traditionally been the main source of telecommunications data, so information on subscriptions has been widely available for most countries. This gives a general idea of access, but a more precise measure is the penetration rate—the share of households with access to telecommunications. During the past few years more information on information and communication technology use has become available from household and business surveys. Also important are data on actual use of telecommunications services. The quality of data varies among reporting countries as a result of differences in regulations covering data provision and availability.

High-technology exports

The method for determining high-technology exports was developed by the Organisation for Economic Co-operation and Development in collaboration with Eurostat. It takes a "product approach" (rather than a "sectoral approach") based on research and development intensity (expenditure divided by total sales) for groups of products from Germany, Italy, Japan, the Netherlands, Sweden, and the United States. Because industrial sectors specializing in a few high-technology products may also produce low-technology products, the product approach is more appropriate for international trade. The method takes only research and development intensity into account, but other characteristics of high technology are also important, such as knowhow, scientific personnel, and technology embodied in patents. Considering these characteristics would yield a different list (see Hatzichronoglou 1997).

Statistical capacity

Statistical capacity is a country's ability to collect, analyze, and disseminate high-quality data about its population and economy. When statistical capacity improves and policymakers use accurate statistics to inform their decisions, this results in better development policy design and outcomes. The Statistical Capacity Indicator is an essential tool for monitoring and tracking the statistical capacity of developing countries and helps national statistics offices worldwide identify gaps in their capabilities to collect, produce, and use data.

Definitions

• **Business entry density** is the number of newly registered limited liability corporations per 1,000 people ages 15–64. • **Time required to start a business** is the number of calendar days to complete the procedures for legally operating a business using the fastest procedure, independent of cost. • **Domestic credit provided by financial sector** is all credit to various sectors on a gross basis, except to the central government, which is net. The financial sector includes monetary authorities, deposit money banks, and other banking institutions for which data are available. • **Tax revenue collected by central government** is compulsory transfers to the central government for public purposes. Certain compulsory transfers such as fines, penalties, and most social security contributions are excluded. Refunds and corrections of erroneously collected tax revenue are treated as negative revenue. The analytic framework of the IMF's *Government Finance Statistics Manual 2001* (GFSM 2001) is based on accrual accounting and balance sheets. For countries still reporting government finance data on a cash basis, the IMF adjusts reported data to the GFSM 2001 accrual framework. These countries are footnoted in the table. • **Military expenditures** are SIPRI data derived from NATO's former definition (in use until 2002), which includes all current and capital expenditures on the armed forces, including peacekeeping forces; defense ministries and other government agencies engaged in defense projects; paramilitary forces, if judged to be trained and equipped for military operations; and military space activities. Such expenditures include military and civil personnel, including retirement pensions and social services for military personnel; operation and maintenance; procurement; military research and development; and military aid (in the military expenditures of the donor country). Excluded are civil defense and current expenditures for previous military activities, such as for veterans benefits, demobilization, and weapons conversion and destruction. This definition cannot be applied for all countries, however, since that would require more detailed information than is available about military budgets and off-budget military expenditures (for example, whether military budgets cover civil defense, reserves and auxiliary forces, police and paramilitary forces, and military pensions). • **Electric power consumption per capita** is the production of power plants and combined heat and power plants less transmission, distribution, and transformation losses and own use by heat and power plants, divided by midyear population. • **Mobile cellular subscriptions** are the number of subscriptions to a public mobile telephone service that provides access to the public switched telephone network using cellular technology. Postpaid subscriptions and active prepaid accounts (that is, accounts that have been used during the last three months) are included. The indicator applies to all mobile cellular subscriptions that offer voice communications and excludes subscriptions for data cards or USB modems, subscriptions to public mobile data services, private-trunked mobile

radio, telepoint, radio paging, and telemetry services. • **Individuals using the Internet** are the percentage of individuals who have used the Internet (from any location) in the last 12 months. Internet can be used via a computer, mobile phone, personal digital assistant, games machine, digital television, or similar device. • **High-technology exports** are products with high research and development intensity, such as in aerospace, computers, pharmaceuticals, scientific instruments, and electrical machinery. • **Statistical Capacity Indicator** is the composite score assessing the capacity of a country's statistical system. It is based on a diagnostic framework that assesses methodology, data sources, and periodicity and timeliness. Countries are scored against 25 criteria in these areas, using publicly available information and country input. The overall statistical capacity score is then calculated as simple average of all three area scores on a scale of 0–100.

Data sources

Data on business entry density are from the World Bank's Entrepreneurship Database (www.doingbusiness.org/data/exploretopics/entrepreneurship). Data on time required to start a business are from the World Bank's Doing Business project (www.doingbusiness.org). Data on domestic credit are from the IMF's *International Financial Statistics*. Data on central government tax revenue are from the IMF's *Government Finance Statistics*. Data on military expenditures are from SIPRI's Military Expenditure Database (www.sipri.org/research/armaments/milex/milex_database/milex_database). Data on electricity consumption are from the IEA's *Energy Statistics of Non-OECD Countries, Energy Balances of Non-OECD Countries*, and *Energy Statistics of OECD Countries* and from the United Nations Statistics Division's *Energy Statistics Yearbook*. Data on mobile cellular phone subscriptions and individuals using the Internet are from the ITU's World Telecommunication/ICT Indicators database. Data on high-technology exports are from the United Nations Statistics Division's Commodity Trade (Comtrade) database. Data on Statistical Capacity Indicator are from the World Bank's Bulletin Board on Statistical Capacity (http://bbsc.worldbank.org).

References

Claessens, Stijn, Daniela Klingebiel, and Sergio L. Schmukler. 2002. "Explaining the Migration of Stocks from Exchanges in Emerging Economies to International Centers." Policy Research Working Paper 2816, World Bank, Washington, DC.

Hatzichronoglou, Thomas. 1997. "Revision of the High-Technology Sector and Product Classification." STI Working Paper 1997/2. Organisation for Economic Co-operation and Development, Directorate for Science, Technology, and Industry, Paris.

UNESCO (United Nations Educational, Scientific and Cultural Organization). 2010. *Science Report.* Paris.

5 States and markets

To access the World Development Indicators online tables, use the URL http://wdi.worldbank.org/table/ and the table number (for example, http://wdi.worldbank.org/table/5.1). To view a specific indicator online, use the URL http://data.worldbank.org/indicator/ and the indicator code (for example, http://data.worldbank.org/indicator/IE.PPI.TELE.CD).

5.1 Private sector in the economy

Telecommunications investment	IE.PPI.TELE.CD
Energy investment	IE.PPI.ENGY.CD
Transport investment	IE.PPI.TRAN.CD
Water and sanitation investment	IE.PPI.WATR.CD
Domestic credit to private sector	FS.AST.PRVT.GD.ZS
Businesses registered, New	IC.BUS.NREG
Businesses registered, Entry density	IC.BUS.NDNS.ZS

5.2 Business environment: enterprise surveys

Time dealing with government regulations	IC.GOV.DURS.ZS
Average number of times meeting with tax officials	IC.TAX.METG
Time required to obtain operating license	IC.FRM.DURS
Bribery incidence	IC.FRM.BRIB.ZS
Losses due to theft, robbery, vandalism, and arson	IC.FRM.CRIM.ZS
Firms competing against unregistered firms	IC.FRM.CMPU.ZS
Firms with female top manager	IC.FRM.FEMM.ZS
Firms using banks to finance working capital	IC.FRM.BKWC.ZS
Value lost due to electrical outages	IC.FRM.OUTG.ZS
Internationally recognized quality certification ownership	IC.FRM.ISOC.ZS
Average time to clear exports through customs	IC.CUS.DURS.EX
Firms offering formal training	IC.FRM.TRNG.ZS

5.3 Business environment: Doing Business indicators

Number of procedures to start a business	IC.REG.PROC
Time required to start a business	IC.REG.DURS
Cost to start a business	IC.REG.COST.PC.ZS
Number of procedures to register property	IC.PRP.PROC
Time required to register property	IC.PRP.DURS
Number of procedures to build a warehouse	IC.WRH.PROC
Time required to build a warehouse	IC.WRH.DURS
Time required to get electricity	IC.ELC.TIME
Number of procedures to enforce a contract	IC.LGL.PROC
Time required to enforce a contract	IC.LGL.DURS
Business disclosure index	IC.BUS.DISC.XQ
Time required to resolve insolvency	IC.ISV.DURS

5.4 Stock markets

Market capitalization, $	CM.MKT.LCAP.CD
Market capitalization, % of GDP	CM.MKT.LCAP.GD.ZS
Value of shares traded	CM.MKT.TRAD.GD.ZS
Turnover ratio	CM.MKT.TRNR
Listed domestic companies	CM.MKT.LDOM.NO
S&P/Global Equity Indices	CM.MKT.INDX.ZG

5.5 Financial access, stability, and efficiency

Strength of legal rights index	IC.LGL.CRED.XQ
Depth of credit information index	IC.CRD.INFO.XQ
Depositors with commercial banks	FB.CBK.DPTR.P3
Borrowers from commercial banks	FB.CBK.BRWR.P3
Commercial bank branches	FB.CBK.BRCH.P5
Automated teller machines	FB.ATM.TOTL.P5
Bank capital to assets ratio	FB.BNK.CAPA.ZS
Ratio of bank nonperforming loans to total gross loans	FB.AST.NPER.ZS
Domestic credit to private sector by banks	FD.AST.PRVT.GD.ZS
Interest rate spread	FR.INR.LNDP
Risk premium on lending	FR.INR.RISK

5.6 Tax policies

Tax revenue collected by central government	GC.TAX.TOTL.GD.ZS
Number of tax payments by businesses	IC.TAX.PAYM
Time for businesses to prepare, file and pay taxes	IC.TAX.DURS
Business profit tax	IC.TAX.PRFT.CP.ZS
Business labor tax and contributions	IC.TAX.LABR.CP.ZS
Other business taxes	IC.TAX.OTHR.CP.ZS
Total business tax rate	IC.TAX.TOTL.CP.ZS

5.7 Military expenditures and arms transfers

Military expenditure, % of GDP	MS.MIL.XPND.GD.ZS
Military expenditure, % of central government expenditure	MS.MIL.XPND.ZS
Arm forces personnel	MS.MIL.TOTL.P1
Arm forces personnel, % of total labor force	MS.MIL.TOTL.TF.ZS
Arms transfers, Exports	MS.MIL.XPRT.KD
Arms transfers, Imports	MS.MIL.MPRT.KD

5.8 Fragile situations

International Development Association Resource Allocation Index	IQ.CPA.IRAI.XQ
Peacekeeping troops, police, and military observers	VC.PKP.TOTL.UN
Battle related deaths	VC.BTL.DETH
Intentional homicides	VC.IHR.PSRC.P5
Military expenditures	MS.MIL.XPND.GD.ZS
Losses due to theft, robbery, vandalism, and arson	IC.FRM.CRIM.ZS
Firms formally registered when operations started	IC.FRM.FREG.ZS
Children in employment ♀♂	SL.TLF.0714.ZS
Refugees, By country of origin	SM.POP.REFG.OR
Refugees, By country of asylum	SM.POP.REFG

Internally displaced persons	VC.IDP.TOTL.HE
Access to an improved water source	SH.H2O.SAFE.ZS
Access to improved sanitation facilities	SH.STA.ACSN
Maternal mortality ratio, National estimate	SH.STA.MMRT.NE
Maternal mortality ratio, Modeled estimate	SH.STA.MMRT
Under-five mortality rate ♀♂	SH.DYN.MORT
Depth of food deficit	SN.ITK.DFCT
Primary gross enrollment ratio ♀♂	SE.PRM.ENRR

5.9 Public policies and institutions

International Development Association Resource Allocation Index	IQ.CPA.IRAI.XQ
Macroeconomic management	IQ.CPA.MACR.XQ
Fiscal policy	IQ.CPA.FISP.XQ
Debt policy	IQ.CPA.DEBT.XQ
Economic management, Average	IQ.CPA.ECON.XQ
Trade	IQ.CPA.TRAD.XQ
Financial sector	IQ.CPA.FINS.XQ
Business regulatory environment	IQ.CPA.BREG.XQ
Structural policies, Average	IQ.CPA.STRC.XQ
Gender equality	IQ.CPA.GNDR.XQ
Equity of public resource use	IQ.CPA.PRES.XQ
Building human resources	IQ.CPA.HRES.XQ
Social protection and labor	IQ.CPA.PROT.XQ
Policies and institutions for environmental sustainability	IQ.CPA.ENVR.XQ
Policies for social inclusion and equity, Average	IQ.CPA.SOCI.XQ
Property rights and rule-based governance	IQ.CPA.PROP.XQ
Quality of budgetary and financial management	IQ.CPA.FINQ.XQ
Efficiency of revenue mobilization	IQ.CPA.REVN.XQ
Quality of public administration	IQ.CPA.PADM.XQ
Transparency, accountability, and corruption in the public sector	IQ.CPA.TRAN.XQ
Public sector management and institutions, Average	IQ.CPA.PUBS.XQ

5.10 Transport services

Total road network	IS.ROD.TOTL.KM
Paved roads	IS.ROD.PAVE.ZS
Road passengers carried	IS.ROD.PSGR.K6
Road goods hauled	IS.ROD.GOOD.MT.K6
Rail lines	IS.RRS.TOTL.KM
Railway passengers carried	IS.RRS.PASG.KM
Railway goods hauled	IS.RRS.GOOD.MT.K6
Port container traffic	IS.SHP.GOOD.TU
Registered air carrier departures worldwide	IS.AIR.DPRT
Air passengers carried	IS.AIR.PSGR
Air freight	IS.AIR.GOOD.MT.K1

5.11 Power and communications

Electric power consumption per capita	EG.USE.ELEC.KH.PC
Electric power transmission and distribution losses	EG.ELC.LOSS.ZS

Fixed telephone subscriptions	IT.MLT.MAIN.P2
Mobile cellular subscriptions	IT.CEL.SETS.P2
Fixed telephone international voice traffic	..[a]
Mobile cellular network international voice traffic	..[a]
Population covered by mobile cellular network	..[a]
Fixed telephone sub-basket	..[a]
Mobile cellular sub-basket	..[a]
Telecommunications revenue	..[a]
Mobile cellular and fixed-line subscribers per employee	..[a]

5.12 The information age

Households with television	..[a]
Households with a computer	..[a]
Individuals using the Internet	..[a]
Fixed (wired) broadband Internet subscriptions	IT.NET.BBND.P2
International Internet bandwidth	..[a]
Fixed broadband sub-basket	..[a]
Secure Internet servers	IT.NET.SECR.P6
Information and communications technology goods, Exports	TX.VAL.ICTG.ZS.UN
Information and communications technology goods, Imports	TM.VAL.ICTG.ZS.UN
Information and communications technology services, Exports	BX.GSR.CCIS.ZS

5.13 Science and technology

Research and development (R&D), Researchers	SP.POP.SCIE.RD.P6
Research and development (R&D), Technicians	SP.POP.TECH.RD.P6
Scientific and technical journal articles	IP.JRN.ARTC.SC
Expenditures for R&D	GB.XPD.RSDV.GD.ZS
High-technology exports, $	TX.VAL.TECH.CD
High-technology exports, % of manufactured exports	TX.VAL.TECH.MF.ZS
Charges for the use of intellectual property, Receipts	BX.GSR.ROYL.CD
Charges for the use of intellectual property, Payments	BM.GSR.ROYL.CD
Patent applications filed, Residents	IP.PAT.RESD
Patent applications filed, Nonresidents	IP.PAT.NRES
Trademark applications filed, Total	IP.TMK.TOTL

5.14 Statistical capacity

Overall level of statistical capacity	IQ.SCI.OVRL
Methodology assessment	IQ.SCI.MTHD
Source data assessment	IQ.SCI.SRCE
Periodicity and timeliness assessment	IQ.SCI.PRDC

♀♂ Data disaggregated by sex are available in the World Development Indicators database.

a. Available online only as part of the table, not as an individual indicator.

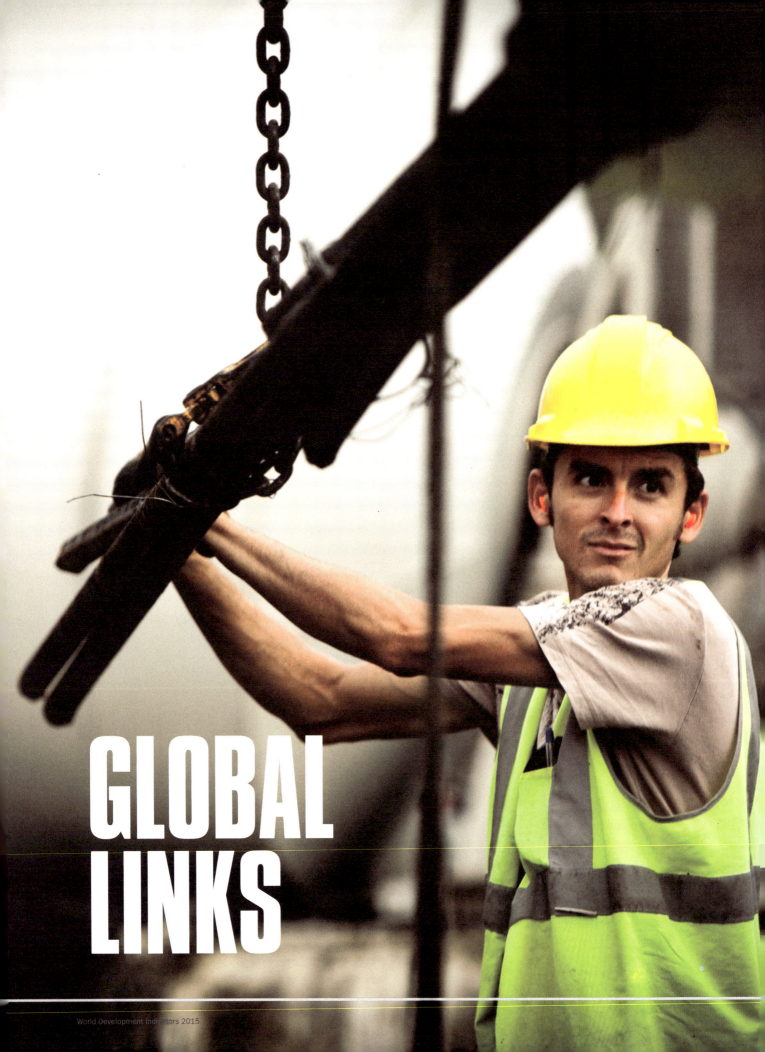

GLOBAL
LINKS

The world economy is bound together by trade in goods and services, financial flows, and movements of people. As national economies develop, their links expand and grow more complex. The indicators in *Global links* measure the size and direction of these flows and document the effects of policy interventions, such as tariffs, trade facilitation, and aid flows, on the development of the world economy.

Despite signs that international financial markets started to regain confidence in 2013, concerns in capital markets caused international investment to fluctuate, mainly in emerging market economies. Real exchange rates depreciated, causing the withdrawal of capital and making capital flows more volatile. Global portfolio equity flows declined sharply in the second and third quarters, resulting in an overall decline of 11 percent by the end of 2013 and a decline of 33 percent in middle-income economies and 8 percent in high-income economies. The value of stock markets in low-income economies grew faster than expected, resulting in equity inflows that were twice as high as in 2012.

Foreign direct investment (FDI) flows were less volatile than portfolio equity investment. Global FDI inflows increased 10.5 percent in 2013, to $1.7 trillion. FDI flows to high-income economies increased 11 percent, compared with a 22 percent decrease in 2012. FDI flows to developing economies were around $734 billion

in 2012, some 42 percent of world inflows. Although many economies receive FDI, the flows remain highly concentrated among the 10 largest recipients, with Brazil, China, and India accounting for more than half.

The important economic role of the private sector in developing countries has led to a major shift in borrowing patterns in recent years and in the composition of external debt stocks and flows. Net debt flows to developing countries increased 28 percent from 2012, to $542 billion in 2013. There has also been an evolution in the composition of these flows. Bond issuance by private sector entities has grown to account for 45 percent of medium-term debt inflows of private nonguaranteed debt since 2009. And bond issuance by public and private entities in developing countries reached a record $233 billion in 2013.

Growth in international trade showed signs of recovery after the major slowdown from the sovereign debt crisis in the euro area. While demand for goods from high-income economies remains low, annual growth in merchandise imports increased slightly, from 0.6 percent in 2012 to 1.5 percent in 2013. Growth of merchandise exports also showed improvement, from 0.4 percent to 2.3 percent, with merchandise exports to developing countries rising 3 percent from 2012 and merchandise exports to high-income countries rising 1.3 percent.

Highlights

The Middle East and North Africa's merchandise exports to high-income countries decreased

Change in merchandise exports between 2008 and 2013 (%)

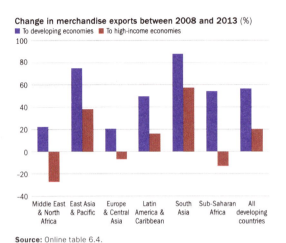

Source: Online table 6.4.

While the volume of merchandise trade continues to increase, following a fall in 2009 as a result of the 2008 financial crisis, the growth of trade has declined over the last two years. This is due mainly to merchandise exports between high-income economies falling below pre-crisis levels ($8,673 billion in 2008) for the last two years, though exports to developing economies increased. The trend is most evident in the Middle East and North Africa, where merchandise exports to high-income economies fell to $201 billion in 2013, 27 percent below their 2008 peak of $276 billion. Even though merchandise exports to developing economies have decreased since 2012, they are 22 percent higher than in 2008.

Aid to Sub-Saharan Africa is not keeping pace with economic growth

Official development assistance (% of GNI)

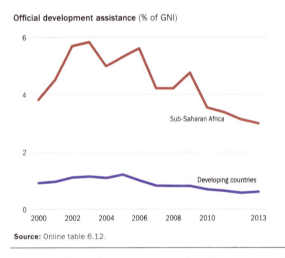

Source: Online table 6.12.

Official development assistance (ODA) increased to $150 billion in 2013, 0.62 percent of the combined gross national income (GNI) of developing countries. Donor governments increased their spending on foreign aid, after a decline in 2012. Despite the increases in total ODA, aid as a share of GNI to Sub-Saharan Africa continues to decline. The biggest drop was for Côte d'Ivoire—from 10 percent in 2012 to 4 percent in 2013, though the 2012 figure was unusually high because of increased debt relief from reaching the completion point under the Heavily Indebted Poor Countries (HIPC) initiative in June 2012. Liberia also registered close to a 6 percentage point drop, while Mauritania, Niger, Sierra Leone, and Gambia all had 3 percentage point decreases. Total bilateral aid from Development Assistance Committee donors to the region also fell 5 percent from the previous year, to $31.9 billion in 2013.

Foreign direct investment and private sector borrowing drive financial flows to Mexico

Debt and foreign direct investment inflows ($ billions)

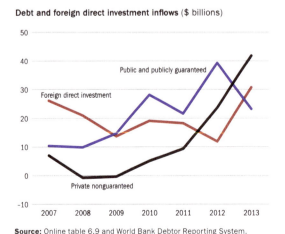

Source: Online table 6.9 and World Bank Debtor Reporting System.

Foreign direct investment (FDI) inflows in Mexico amounted to $30 billion in 2013, more than double the 2012 level, making Mexico the third largest developing country recipient behind China and Brazil. Net financial flows to private sector borrowers exceeded net debt flows to public borrowers through FDI and long-term private nonguaranteed debt inflows. The large increase in FDI inflows was due to investment in acquisitions and is usually an important indication of improved investor confidence, especially in the private sector. Further evidence can be found in the steady increase in net debt inflows to private nonguaranteed borrowers, up 77 percent in 2013, to $42 billion, and accounting for almost half of total net debt inflows. But net debt flows to public borrowers, the main component of the country's financial flows until 2012, declined 41 percent, to $23 billion in 2013.

 Front User guide World view People Environment

Bond issuance in Sub-Saharan Africa increased sharply

Total bond issuance by public and private entities in developing countries continued to increase in 2013, reaching a record $233 billion. The rapid growth was led by Sub-Saharan Africa, which registered an increase of 109 percent in 2013, to $13.5 billion, with debut issues from Mozambique, Rwanda, and Tanzania. Even though the region's international bond market remains small, bond issuance continues to increase substantially: Bond issuance by public sector borrowers increased 155 percent, to $8.4 billion in 2013, and bond issuance by private sector borrowers increased 62 percent, to $5.1 billion. The region's high return potential and considerable development needs have facilitated access to markets. Bond issuance continues to rely mainly on public and government bodies to finance development in infrastructure and manage debt, as corporate bond issuance is not fully open to international markets.

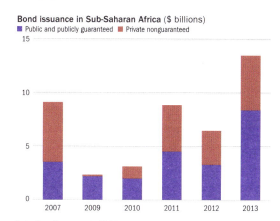

Bond issuance in Sub-Saharan Africa ($ billions)
- Public and publicly guaranteed
- Private nonguaranteed

Note: Bond issuance in 2008 was zero.
Source: Online table 6.9.

India saw a downturn in net capital flows in 2013

The depreciation of the rupee increased the vulnerability of capital inflows into India's economy. Net short-term capital flows saw an outflow of $642 million in 2013, compared with an inflow of $15.3 billion in 2012. In addition to a 13 percent decline in net portfolio equity inflows, net flows to holders of Indian bonds fell from an inflow of $4.5 billion in 2012 to an outflow of $3 billion in 2013. This was partly offset by the surge in long-term bank lending to $36.5 billion, an increase of 33 percent from 2012, directed almost entirely to the private sector. Despite the volatility of capital flows, foreign direct investment was more resilient, rising 17 percent in 2013, resulting in overall net flows of $28 billion.

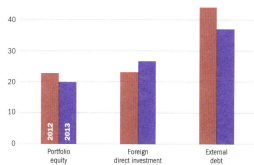

Net capital inflows to India ($ billions)

Source: Online tables 6.8 and 6.9.

Private sector borrowing has accelerated in Europe and Central Asia

In Europe and Central Asia net inflows from official creditors doubled in 2009, to $49 billion, while inflows from private creditors fell to $7.7 billion, from $130 billion in 2008. This was driven by the 2008 financial crisis, which resulted in costly cross-border borrowing from the private sector and caused official creditors, mainly multilateral organizations, to lend money to the public sector. The situation has now reversed: Net medium- and long-term borrowing from foreign private creditors has rapidly increased, from –$11.5 billion in 2010 to $80.7 billion in 2013, its highest level. More than half of those net flows came from borrowing by commercial banks and other sectors, while official creditors recorded an outflow of $19 billion. Hungary, Kazakhstan, and Turkey received 81 percent of those net inflows.

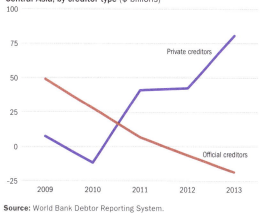

Net medium- and long-term debt inflows to Europe and Central Asia, by creditor type ($ billions)

Source: World Bank Debtor Reporting System.

Over the past decade flows of foreign direct investment (FDI) toward developing economies have increased substantially. It has long been recognized that FDI flows can carry with them benefits of knowledge and technology transfer to domestic firms and the labor force, productivity spillover, enhanced competition, and improved access for exports abroad. Moreover, they are the preferred source of capital for financing a current account deficit because FDI is non-debt-creating. Although slowed by the financial crisis, FDI inflows to developing economies recovered considerably, from $418 billion in 2009 to $739 billion in 2013, an increase of 76 percent.

Foreign direct investment

FOREIGN DIRECT INVESTMENT NET INFLOWS AS A SHARE OF GDP, 2013 (%)

- Less than 1.0
- 1.0–1.9
- 2.0–3.9
- 4.0–5.9
- 6.0 or more
- No data

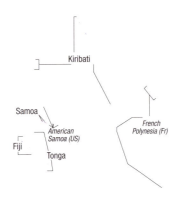

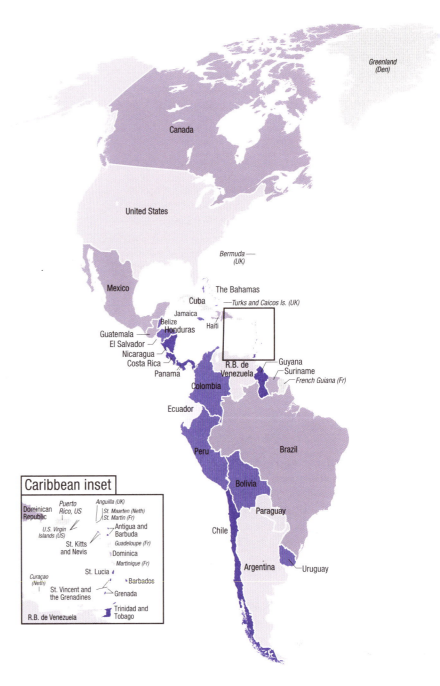

IBRD 41455

○ Front | ? User guide | ◉ World view | People | Environment

Brazil ($81 billion), Mexico ($42 billion), and Colombia ($16 billion) are the top three recipients of foreign direct investment among developing countries in Latin America and the Caribbean.

A large portion of Mozambique's GDP is from foreign direct investment inflows: 42 percent in 2013.

China received the most foreign direct investment (FDI) among all countries in East Asia and Pacific (84 percent) and commanded almost half of all FDI inflows in developing countries.

Foreign direct investment in Djibouti more than doubled in 2013, increasing from 8 percent of GDP in 2012 to 20 percent in 2013.

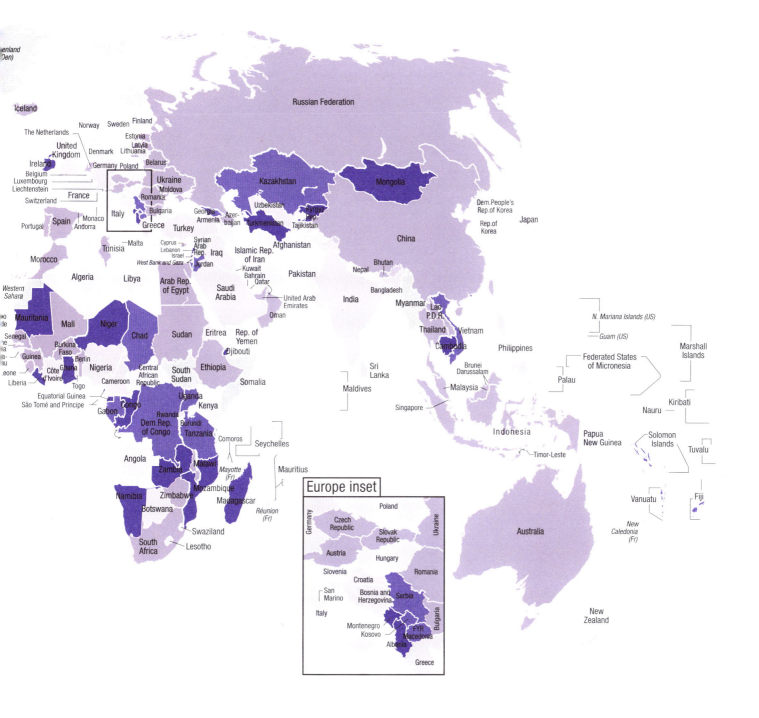

Europe inset

6 Global links

	Merchandise trade	Net barter terms of trade index	Inbound tourism expenditure	Net official development assistance	Net migration	Personal remittances, received	Foreign direct investment	Portfolio equity	Total external debt stock	Total debt service
							Net inflow	Net inflow		% of exports of goods, services, and primary income
	% of GDP	2000 = 100	% of exports	% of GNI	thousands	$ millions	$ millions	$ millions	$ millions	
	2013	2013	2013	2013	2010–15	2013	2013	2013	2013	2013
Afghanistan	45.5	136.1	2.5	25.7	−400	538	60	0	2,577	0.6
Albania	55.8	94.4	43.4	2.3	−50	1,094	1,254	2	7,776	10.2
Algeria	57.1	215.7	0.5	0.1	−50	210	1,689	..	5,231	0.7
American Samoa		138.5	..	..	..	..	..	..	..	..
Andorra	..	..	..	..	..	..	..	..	..	..
Angola	75.1	257.4	1.8	0.3	66	..	−7,120	..	24,004	6.9
Antigua and Barbuda	47.7	62.1	56.5	0.1	0	21	134	..	..	..
Argentina	25.5	131.2	5.2	0.0	−100	532	11,392	462	136,272	13.7
Armenia	57.1	114.4	17.4	2.7	−50	2,192	370	−2	8,677	50.8
Aruba	..	113.2	69.8	..	1	6	169	..	..	..
Australia	31.7	177.0	10.9	..	750	2,465	51,967	15,433	..	..
Austria	83.3	86.7	9.9	..	150	2,810	15,608	2,348	..	..
Azerbaijan	58.4	194.8	7.3	−0.1	0	1,733	2,619	30	9,219	6.8
Bahamas, The	48.3	90.3	63.5	..	10	..	382	..	..	..
Bahrain	107.3	122.0	7.7	..	22	..	989	1,386	..	..
Bangladesh	43.7	57.4	0.4	1.6	−2,041	13,857	1,502	270	27,804	5.2
Barbados	..	113.5	..	..	2	..	376	..	..	..
Belarus	111.9	104.4	2.6	0.2	−10	1,214	2,246	2	39,108	10.3
Belgium	175.3	94.4	3.4	..	150	11,126	−3,269	12,633	..	..
Belize	94.6	99.5	33.2	3.3	8	74	89	..	1,249	12.7
Benin	46.9	117.0	..	7.9	−10	..	320	..	2,367	..
Bermuda	..	96.9	32.1	..	..	1,225	55	−10	..	..
Bhutan	87.0	122.8	17.6	8.1	10	12	50	..	1,480	11.0
Bolivia	68.1	174.2	5.0	2.4	−125	1,201	1,750	..	7,895	4.3
Bosnia and Herzegovina	89.5	97.6	13.2	3.0	−5	1,929	315	..	11,078	17.8
Botswana	102.5	82.3	1.4	0.7	20	36	189	2	2,430	2.2
Brazil	21.9	126.2	2.5	0.1	−190	2,537	80,843	11,636	482,470	28.6
Brunei Darussalam	93.5	216.9	..	..	2	..	895	..	..	..
Bulgaria	117.2	107.0	12.5	..	−50	1,667	1,888	−19	52,995	13.0
Burkina Faso	44.7	118.0	..	8.1	−125	..	374	..	2,564	..
Burundi	33.5	130.7	1.4	20.1	−20	49	7	..	683	14.1
Cabo Verde	..	100.2	59.9	13.4	−17	176	41	..	1,484	4.6
Cambodia	146.3	69.6	28.9	5.6	−175	176	1,345	..	6,427	1.5
Cameroon	37.9	154.8	7.6	2.5	−50	244	325	..	4,922	2.6
Canada	51.1	124.7	3.2	..	1,100	1,199	70,753	17,902	..	..
Cayman Islands	..	69.6	..	..	..	..	10,577	..	..	..
Central African Republic	26.0	68.1	..	12.3	10	..	1	..	574	..
Chad	51.8	213.7	..	3.1	−120	..	538	..	2,216	..
Channel Islands	..	..	..	..	4	..	..	..	..	..
Chile	56.2	187.5	3.6	0.0	30	0	20,258	6,027	..	..
China	45.0	74.8	2.4	0.0	−1,500	38,819	347,849	32,595	874,463	1.5
Hong Kong SAR, China	422.5	96.4	6.9	..	150	360	76,639	11,916	..	..
Macao SAR, China	22.0	85.0	94.7	..	35	49	3,708	..	..	..
Colombia	31.2	144.1	7.1	0.2	−120	4,119	16,198	1,926	91,978	14.1
Comoros	50.8	83.2	..	13.3	−10	..	14	..	146	..
Congo, Dem. Rep.	38.5	128.9	0.0	8.6	−75	33	1,698	..	6,082	3.0
Congo, Rep.	108.6	226.8	..	1.4	−45	..	2,038	..	3,452	..

 Front | User guide |  World view   People | Environment

	Merchandise trade	Net barter terms of trade index	Inbound tourism expenditure	Net official development assistance	Net migration	Personal remittances, received	Foreign direct investment	Portfolio equity	Total external debt stock	Total debt service % of exports of goods, services, and primary income
	% of GDP 2013	2000 = 100 2013	% of exports 2013	% of GNI 2013	thousands 2010–15	$ millions 2013	Net inflow $ millions 2013	Net inflow $ millions 2013	$ millions 2013	2013
Costa Rica	59.7	77.8	21.2	0.1	64	596	3,234	..	17,443	22.3
Côte d'Ivoire	83.6	141.9	..	4.2	50	..	371	..	11,288	..
Croatia	56.6	97.7	39.1	..	−20	1,497	588	−98	..	..
Cuba	..	140.1	..	..	−140	..	..	..	..	..
Curaçao	..	..	..	..	14	33	17	..	..	..
Cyprus	38.0	92.2	31.2	..	35	83	607	−2	..	..
Czech Republic	146.1	101.6	5.1	..	200	2,270	5,007	110	..	..
Denmark	61.6	100.0	3.6	..	75	1,459	1,597	5,800	..	..
Djibouti	57.6	85.7	4.6	..	−16	36	286	..	833	8.2
Dominica	46.6	100.6	48.3	4.0	..	24	18	..	293	10.7
Dominican Republic	43.4	93.2	31.6	0.3	−140	4,486	1,600	..	23,831	16.8
Ecuador	55.3	134.5	4.5	0.2	−30	2,459	725	2	20,280	11.2
Egypt, Arab Rep.	31.9	153.0	..	2.1	−216	..	5,553	..	44,430	..
El Salvador	67.0	87.6	16.5	0.7	−225	3,971	197	..	13,372	17.1
Equatorial Guinea	138.0	230.6	..	0.1	20	..	1,914	..	..	..
Eritrea	39.5	84.8	..	2.5	55	..	44	..	946	..
Estonia	138.5	94.1	8.4	..	0	429	965	53	..	..
Ethiopia	31.4	124.4	..	8.1	−60	..	953	..	12,557	..
Faeroe Islands	..	95.6	..	..	..	..	..	..	..	..
Fiji	102.7	108.2	42.8	2.4	−29	204	158	..	797	1.9
Finland	56.8	87.9	5.5	..	50	1,066	−5,297	2,447	..	..
France	44.9	88.3	7.9	..	650	23,336	6,480	35,019	..	..
French Polynesia	..	78.6	..	..	−1	..	119	..	..	..
Gabon	69.3	226.3	..	0.5	5	..	856	..	4,316	..
Gambia, The	48.7	96.5	..	12.7	−13	..	25	..	523	..
Georgia	66.8	132.6	26.7	4.1	−125	1,945	956	1	13,694	22.0
Germany	70.8	96.3	3.2	..	550	15,792	51,267	15,345	..	..
Ghana	65.1	178.1	6.2	2.8	−100	119	3,227	..	15,832	5.6
Greece	40.8	88.3	24.2	..	50	805	2,945	3,135	..	..
Greenland	..	76.2	..	..	..	..	..	..	..	..
Grenada	48.6	85.3	57.2	1.2	−4	30	75	..	586	16.5
Guam	..	76.8	..	..	0	..	..	..	..	..
Guatemala	51.2	83.8	11.6	0.9	−75	5,371	1,350	..	16,823	9.5
Guinea	55.3	98.1	..	8.8	−10	93	135	..	1,198	3.0
Guinea-Bissau	44.8	79.8	..	10.8	−10	..	15	..	277	..
Guyana	104.8	114.4	5.0	3.4	−33	328	201	..	2,303	4.9
Haiti	54.4	71.7	37.0	13.7	−175	1,781	186	..	1,271	0.6
Honduras	101.7	72.4	11.1	3.6	−50	3,136	1,069	..	6,831	14.4
Hungary	156.0	95.2	5.5	..	75	4,325	−4,302	25	196,739	95.5
Iceland	63.8	84.6	13.1	..	5	176	469	−19	..	..
India	41.5	131.1	4.1	0.1	−2,294	69,970	28,153	19,892	427,562	8.6
Indonesia	42.7	121.8	5.0	0.0	−700	7,614	23,344	−1,827	259,069	19.4
Iran, Islamic Rep.	35.5	190.3	..	0.0	−300	..	3,050	..	7,647	0.4
Iraq	65.6	222.0	..	0.7	450	..	2,852	..	..	..
Ireland	77.4	94.8	4.1	..	50	718	49,960	109,126	..	..
Isle of Man	..	..	..	..	..	..	..	..	..	..
Israel	48.8	100.6	6.7	..	−76	765	11,804	2,712	..	..

6 Global links

	Merchandise trade	Net barter terms of trade index	Inbound tourism expenditure	Net official development assistance	Net migration	Personal remittances, received	Foreign direct investment	Portfolio equity	Total external debt stock	Total debt service % of exports of goods, services, and primary income
	% of GDP 2013	2000 = 100 2013	% of exports 2013	% of GNI 2013	thousands 2010–15	$ millions 2013	Net inflow $ millions 2013	Net inflow $ millions 2013	$ millions 2013	2013
Italy	46.3	97.7	7.5	..	900	7,471	13,126	17,454	..	..
Jamaica	54.4	81.8	48.2	0.5	−80	2,161	666	103	13,790	25.9
Japan	31.5	59.0	2.0	..	350	2,364	3,715	169,753	..	..
Jordan	88.4	75.9	36.1	4.2	400	3,643	1,798	158	23,970	6.7
Kazakhstan	56.7	229.6	1.9	0.0	0	207	9,739	65	148,456	34.0
Kenya	40.2	88.3	..	5.9	−50	..	514	..	13,471	5.7
Kiribati	70.7	84.8	..	25.5	−1	..	9	..	..	..
Korea, Dem. People's Rep.	..	71.2	..	..	0	..	227	..	..	..
Korea, Rep.	82.4	61.4	2.7	..	300	6,425	12,221	4,243	..	..
Kosovo	..	..	..	7.4	..	1,122	343	−1	2,199	3.7
Kuwait	82.1	222.8	0.5	..	300	4	1,843	509	..	..
Kyrgyz Republic	108.8	108.8	18.9	7.7	−175	2,278	758	−2	6,804	12.4
Lao PDR	47.0	107.4	20.1	4.0	−75	60	427	7	8,615	9.7
Latvia	104.4	104.2	6.6	..	−10	762	881	41	..	..
Lebanon	..	98.1	33.6	1.4	500	7,864	3,029	−134	30,947	16.7
Lesotho	130.5	72.2	4.3	11.2	−20	462	45	..	885	2.8
Liberia	..	149.1	..	30.5	−20	383	700	..	542	0.7
Libya	95.0	199.5	..	..	−239	..	702	..	..	..
Liechtenstein	..	..	..	..	..	..	..	..	..	..
Lithuania	147.6	93.4	4.1	..	−28	2,060	712	−18	..	..
Luxembourg	75.0	77.7	5.0	..	26	1,818	30,075	225,929	..	..
Macedonia, FYR	106.6	89.0	5.8	2.5	−5	376	413	−1	6,934	18.9
Madagascar	48.1	81.0	..	4.9	−5	..	838	..	2,849	..
Malawi	109.4	97.6	..	31.5	0	..	118	..	1,558	..
Malaysia	138.7	100.5	8.1	0.0	450	1,396	11,583	..	213,129	3.5
Maldives	89.8	88.9	82.3	1.2	0	3	361	..	821	2.5
Mali	57.0	148.9	..	13.5	−302	..	410	..	3,423	..
Malta	96.8	124.8	18.1	..	5	34	−1,869	0	..	..
Marshall Islands	104.8	98.4	..	41.4	..	..	23	..	..	..
Mauritania	142.5	156.1	1.8	7.5	−20	..	1,126	..	3,570	5.6
Mauritius	69.3	67.5	25.4	1.2	0	1	259	706	10,919	42.0
Mexico	61.2	104.4	3.6	0.0	−1,200	23,022	42,093	−943	443,012	10.3
Micronesia, Fed. Sts.	72.7	85.4	..	41.7	−8	22	2	..	..	..
Moldova	99.0	102.0	10.5	4.2	−103	1,985	249	10	6,613	16.1
Monaco	..	..	..	..	..	..	..	..	..	..
Mongolia	92.3	190.3	4.6	4.0	−15	256	2,151	3	18,921	27.9
Montenegro	64.4	..	50.3	2.8	−3	423	446	14	2,956	17.2
Morocco	64.4	112.8	25.1	1.9	−450	6,882	3,361	43	39,261	15.3
Mozambique	83.8	94.8	5.2	14.9	−25	217	6,697	0	6,890	2.6
Myanmar	..	112.5	8.3	..	−100	229	2,255	..	7,367	8.2
Namibia	93.0	119.9	9.5	2.0	−3	11	904	12	..	..
Nepal	38.8	74.8	21.0	4.5	−401	5,552	74	..	3,833	8.7
Netherlands	147.8	92.7	3.4	..	50	1,565	32,110	14,174	..	..
New Caledonia	..	174.7	..	..	6	..	2,065	..	..	..
New Zealand	42.6	123.9	14.1	..	75	459	−510	3,506	..	..
Nicaragua	71.5	80.9	8.3	4.5	−120	1,081	845	..	9,601	12.6
Niger	49.3	172.7	..	10.7	−28	..	631	..	2,656	..

	Merchandise trade	Net barter terms of trade index	Inbound tourism expenditure	Net official development assistance	Net migration	Personal remittances, received	Foreign direct investment	Portfolio equity	Total external debt stock	Total debt service % of exports of goods, services, and primary income
	% of GDP 2013	2000 = 100 2013	% of exports 2013	% of GNI 2013	thousands 2010–15	$ millions 2013	Net inflow $ millions 2013	Net inflow $ millions 2013	$ millions 2013	2013
Nigeria	30.5	222.1	..	0.5	−300	..	5,609	..	13,792	0.5
Northern Mariana Islands	..	73.4	..	..	..	..	6	..	..	..
Norway	47.6	159.7	3.2	..	150	791	2,627	2,678	..	..
Oman	114.7	240.4	3.2	..	1,030	39	1,626	1,361	..	..
Pakistan	30.1	59.1	3.1	0.9	−1,634	14,626	1,307	118	56,461	26.3
Palau	63.6	92.0	..	14.8	..	..	6	..	..	..
Panama	86.6	88.9	19.0	0.0	29	452	5,053	..	16,471	5.7
Papua New Guinea	74.2	191.1	..	4.5	0	..	18	..	21,733	..
Paraguay	74.4	105.2	2.1	0.5	−40	591	346	..	13,430	12.9
Peru	42.4	153.8	8.3	0.2	−300	2,707	9,298	585	56,661	14.0
Philippines	44.8	62.4	8.3	0.1	−700	26,700	3,664	−34	60,609	7.7
Poland	77.4	97.9	5.0	..	−38	6,984	−4,586	2,602	..	..
Portugal	60.8	92.6	17.9	..	100	4,372	7,882	584	..	..
Puerto Rico	..	..	..	..	−104	..	..	..	..	..
Qatar	84.5	219.7	5.7	..	500	574	−840	616	..	..
Romania	73.4	109.7	2.5	..	−45	3,518	4,108	1,053	133,996	39.7
Russian Federation	41.3	244.8	3.4	..	1,100	6,751	70,654	−7,625	..	..
Rwanda	39.9	200.6	29.1	14.6	−45	170	111	0	1,690	3.5
Samoa	53.5	79.9	60.9	15.3	−13	158	24	..	447	6.1
San Marino	..	..	..	..	..	..	..	..	..	..
São Tomé and Príncipe	54.1	111.9	62.7	16.8	−2	27	11	0	214	11.0
Saudi Arabia	72.7	214.7	2.2	..	300	269	9,298	..	..	..
Senegal	63.3	109.1	..	6.7	−100	..	298	..	5,223	..
Serbia	77.2	103.1	6.6	1.8	−100	4,023	1,974	−41	36,397	43.6
Seychelles	115.1	88.1	37.1	1.8	−2	13	178	..	2,714	5.7
Sierra Leone	89.4	60.2	3.0	9.8	−21	68	144	9	1,395	1.2
Singapore	262.9	80.6	3.4	..	400	..	63,772	−90	..	..
Sint Maarten	..	..	..	..	..	23	34	..	..	..
Slovak Republic	171.8	91.6	2.8	..	15	2,072	2,148	86	..	..
Slovenia	140.9	94.6	8.2	..	22	686	−419	154	..	..
Solomon Islands	87.5	90.1	12.1	30.0	−12	17	45	..	204	7.4
Somalia	..	115.7	..	..	−150	..	107	..	3,054	..
South Africa	60.7	96.5	9.6	0.4	−100	971	8,118	1,011	139,845	8.3
South Sudan	..	..	..	13.4	865	..	..	..	..	..
Spain	47.1	89.3	14.8	..	600	9,584	44,917	9,649	..	..
Sri Lanka	41.6	68.8	16.6	0.6	−317	6,422	916	263	25,168	11.9
St. Kitts and Nevis	38.0	68.2	34.3	3.9	..	52	111	..	..	..
St. Lucia	55.2	91.4	57.6	1.9	0	30	84	..	486	5.9
St. Martin	..	..	..	..	..	..	..	..	..	..
St. Vincent & the Grenadines	60.1	94.5	47.4	1.1	−5	32	127	..	293	13.5
Sudan	25.5ᵃ	..	9.3ᵃ	1.8	−800	424ᵃ	2,179ᵃ	0ᵃ	22,416ᵃ	3.5ᵃ
Suriname	86.2	127.1	3.6	0.6	−5	7	137	..	..	..
Swaziland	97.9	108.9	0.6	3.4	−6	30	24	..	464	1.3
Sweden	56.5	92.9	5.6	..	200	1,167	−5,119	5,100	..	..
Switzerland	62.7	78.8	4.4	..	320	3,149	−8,179	3,026	..	..
Syrian Arab Republic	..	148.4	..	..	−1,500	..	..	..	4,753	..
Tajikistan	62.3	92.4	..	4.5	−100	..	108	..	3,538	..

6 Global links

	Merchandise trade	Net barter terms of trade index	Inbound tourism expenditure	Net official development assistance	Net migration	Personal remittances, received	Foreign direct investment	Portfolio equity	Total external debt stock	Total debt service
							Net inflow	Net inflow		% of exports of goods, services, and primary income
	% of GDP	2000 = 100	% of exports	% of GNI	thousands	$ millions	$ millions	$ millions	$ millions	
	2013	2013	2013	2013	2010–15	2013	2013	2013	2013	2013
Tanzania	51.7	135.9	22.9	10.4	−150	59	1,872	4	13,024	1.9
Thailand	123.8	91.6	16.2	0.0	100	5,690	12,650	−6,487	135,379	4.4
Timor-Leste	..	..	33.0	..	−75	34	52	2	..	..
Togo	84.1	28.9	..	6.0	−10	..	84	..	903	..
Tonga	48.3	83.1	..	16.8	−8	..	12	..	199	..
Trinidad and Tobago	87.8	147.7	..	..	−15	..	1,713	..	..	..
Tunisia	87.9	96.3	13.0	1.6	−33	2,291	1,059	80	25,827	11.8
Turkey	49.1	90.4	16.6	0.3	350	1,135	12,823	841	388,243	28.9
Turkmenistan	66.9	231.0	..	0.1	−25	..	3,061	..	502	..
Turks and Caicos Islands	..	71.1	..	..	..	..	..	..	..	..
Tuvalu	42.5	..	..	48.3	..	4	0	..	..	..
Uganda	33.3	106.1	23.4	7.0	−150	932	1,194	95	4,361	1.6
Ukraine	79.1	116.8	7.3	0.4	−40	9,667	4,509	1,180	147,712	42.3
United Arab Emirates	156.6	185.4	..	..	514	..	10,488	..	..	..
United Kingdom	44.7	102.2	6.4	..	900	1,712	48,314	27,517	..	..
United States	23.3	95.3	9.4	..	5,000	6,695	294,971	−85,407	..	..
Uruguay	37.2	107.8	14.8	0.1	−30	123	2,789	0	..	..
Uzbekistan	45.1	171.1	..	0.5	−200	..	1,077	..	10,605	..
Vanuatu	42.5	89.9	77.9	11.4	0	24	33	..	132	1.9
Venezuela, RB	32.5	254.6	..	0.0	40	..	7,040	..	118,758	..
Vietnam	154.1	98.6	5.3	2.5	−200	..	8,900	1,389	65,461	3.5
Virgin Islands (U.S.)	..	..	..	..	−4	..	..	..	..	..
West Bank and Gaza	..	74.2	17.3	19.1	−44	1,748	177	−14	..	..
Yemen, Rep.	60.4	165.5	9.8	2.9	−135	3,343	−134	..	7,671	2.8
Zambia	77.4	177.1	2.0	4.4	−40	54	1,811	5	5,596	2.8
Zimbabwe	57.9	104.7	..	6.5	400	..	400	..	8,193	..
World	**49.4 w**	**..**	**6.1[b] w**	**0.2[c] w**	**0 s**	**460,224 s**	**1,756,575 s**	**702,202 s**	**.. s**	**.. w**
Low income	48.6	..	9.5	7.1	−4,337	24,136	23,702	378	146,957	5.8
Middle income	48.6	..	5.6	0.3	−12,655	300,393	714,923	64,721	5,359,415	10.6
Lower middle income	47.7	..	6.2	0.9	−10,340	174,327	109,463	21,034	1,398,505	11.8
Upper middle income	48.9	..	5.5	0.1	−2,314	126,066	605,460	43,687	3,960,910	10.3
Low & middle income	48.6	..	5.7	0.6	−16,991	324,529	738,625	65,099	5,506,372	10.5
East Asia & Pacific	52.0	..	4.6	0.1	−3,061	81,401	414,775	25,648	1,672,953	3.3
Europe & Central Asia	68.9	..	9.1	0.5	−661	40,833	44,955	3,158	1,234,241	39.5
Latin America & Carib.	36.6	..	5.5	0.2	−3,017	60,729	184,616	13,771	1,495,399	16.5
Middle East & N. Africa	52.3	..	14.4	..	−1,632	26,015	23,423	134	190,569	4.9
South Asia	40.6	..	4.6	0.6	−7,076	110,980	32,421	20,543	545,704	9.4
Sub-Saharan Africa	50.1	..	7.6	3.0	−1,545	4,572	38,435	1,845	367,507	6.2
High income	49.8	..	6.2	0.0	16,941	135,695	1,017,950	637,104	..	..
Euro area	68.9	..	6.3	0.0	3,364	86,590	248,832	448,156	..	..

a. Includes South Sudan. b. Calculated using the World Bank's weighted aggregation methodology (see *Statistical methods*) and thus may differ from data reported by the World Tourism Organization. c. Based on the World Bank classification of economies and thus may differ from data reported by the Organisation for Economic Co-operation and Development.

 Front   User guide   World view   People   Environment

Starting with *World Development Indicators 2013,* the World Bank changed its presentation of balance of payments data to conform to the International Monetary Fund's (IMF) Balance of Payments Manual, 6th edition (BPM6). The historical data series based on BPM5 ends with data for 2005. Balance of payments data from 2005 forward have been presented in accord with the BPM6 methodology, which can be accessed at www.imf.org/external/np/sta /bop/bop.htm.

Trade in goods

Data on merchandise trade are from customs reports of goods moving into or out of an economy or from reports of financial transactions related to merchandise trade recorded in the balance of payments. Because of differences in timing and definitions, trade flow estimates from customs reports and balance of payments may differ. Several international agencies process trade data, each correcting unreported or misreported data, leading to other differences. The most detailed source of data on international trade in goods is the United Nations Statistics Division's Commodity Trade Statistics (Comtrade) database. The IMF and the World Trade Organization also collect customs-based data on trade in goods.

The "terms of trade" index measures the relative prices of a country's exports and imports. The most common way to calculate terms of trade is the net barter (or commodity) terms of trade index, or the ratio of the export price index to the import price index. When a country's net barter terms of trade index increases, its exports have become more expensive or its imports cheaper.

Tourism

Tourism is defined as the activity of people traveling to and staying in places outside their usual environment for no more than one year for leisure, business, and other purposes not related to an activity remunerated from within the place visited. Data on inbound and outbound tourists refer to the number of arrivals and departures, not to the number of unique individuals. Thus a person who makes several trips to a country during a given period is counted each time as a new arrival. Data on inbound tourism show the arrivals of nonresident tourists (overnight visitors) at national borders. When data on international tourists are unavailable or incomplete, the table shows the arrivals of international visitors, which include tourists, same-day visitors, cruise passengers, and crew members. The aggregates are calculated using the World Bank's weighted aggregation methodology (see *Statistical methods*) and differ from the World Tourism Organization's aggregates.

For tourism expenditure, the World Tourism Organization uses balance of payments data from the IMF supplemented by data from individual countries. These data, shown in the table, include travel and passenger transport items as defined by the BPM6. When the IMF does not report data on passenger transport items, expenditure data for travel items are shown.

Official development assistance

Data on official development assistance received refer to aid to eligible countries from members of the Organisation of Economic Co-operation and Development's (OECD) Development Assistance Committee (DAC), multilateral organizations, and non-DAC donors. Data do not reflect aid given by recipient countries to other developing countries or distinguish among types of aid (program, project, or food aid; emergency assistance; or postconflict peacekeeping assistance), which may have different effects on the economy.

Ratios of aid to gross national income (GNI), gross capital formation, imports, and government spending measure a country's dependency on aid. Care must be taken in drawing policy conclusions. For foreign policy reasons some countries have traditionally received large amounts of aid. Thus aid dependency ratios may reveal as much about a donor's interests as about a recipient's needs. Increases in aid dependency ratios can reflect events affecting both the numerator (aid) and the denominator (GNI).

Data are based on information from donors and may not be consistent with information recorded by recipients in the balance of payments, which often excludes all or some technical assistance— particularly payments to expatriates made directly by the donor. Similarly, grant commodity aid may not always be recorded in trade data or in the balance of payments. DAC statistics exclude aid for military and antiterrorism purposes. The aggregates refer to World Bank classifications of economies and therefore may differ from those reported by the OECD.

Migration and personal remittances

The movement of people, most often through migration, is a significant part of global integration. Migrants contribute to the economies of both their host country and their country of origin. Yet reliable statistics on migration are difficult to collect and are often incomplete, making international comparisons a challenge.

Since data on emigrant stock is difficult for countries to collect, the United Nations Population Division provides data on net migration, taking into account the past migration history of a country or area, the migration policy of a country, and the influx of refugees in recent periods to derive estimates of net migration. The data to calculate these estimates come from various sources, including border statistics, administrative records, surveys, and censuses. When there are insufficient data, net migration is derived through the difference between the growth rate of a country's population over a certain period and the rate of natural increase of that population (itself being the difference between the birth rate and the death rate).

Migrants often send funds back to their home countries, which are recorded as personal transfers in the balance of payments. Personal transfers thus include all current transfers between resident and nonresident individuals, independent of the source of income of the sender (irrespective of whether the sender receives income from labor, entrepreneurial or property income, social benefits, or any

other types of transfers or disposes of assets) and the relationship between the households (irrespective of whether they are related or unrelated individuals).

Compensation of employees refers to the income of border, seasonal, and other short-term workers who are employed in an economy where they are not resident and of residents employed by nonresident entities. Compensation of employees has three main components: wages and salaries in cash, wages and salaries in kind, and employers' social contributions. Personal remittances are the sum of personal transfers and compensation of employees.

Equity flows

Equity flows comprise foreign direct investment (FDI) and portfolio equity. The internationally accepted definition of FDI (from BPM6) includes the following components: equity investment, including investment associated with equity that gives rise to control or influence; investment in indirectly influenced or controlled enterprises; investment in fellow enterprises; debt (except selected debt); and reverse investment. The Framework for Direct Investment Relationships provides criteria for determining whether cross-border ownership results in a direct investment relationship, based on control and influence.

Direct investments may take the form of greenfield investment, where the investor starts a new venture in a foreign country by constructing new operational facilities; joint venture, where the investor enters into a partnership agreement with a company abroad to establish a new enterprise; or merger and acquisition, where the investor acquires an existing enterprise abroad. The IMF suggests that investments should account for at least 10 percent of voting stock to be counted as FDI. In practice many countries set a higher threshold. Many countries fail to report reinvested earnings, and the definition of long-term loans differs among countries.

Portfolio equity investment is defined as cross-border transactions and positions involving equity securities, other than those included in direct investment or reserve assets. Equity securities are equity instruments that are negotiable and designed to be traded, usually on organized exchanges or "over the counter." The negotiability of securities facilitates trading, allowing securities to be held by different parties during their lives. Negotiability allows investors to diversify their portfolios and to withdraw their investment readily. Included in portfolio investment are investment fund shares or units (that is, those issued by investment funds) that are evidenced by securities and that are not reserve assets or direct investment. Although they are negotiable instruments, exchange-traded financial derivatives are not included in portfolio investment because they are in their own category.

External debt

External indebtedness affects a country's creditworthiness and investor perceptions. Data on external debt are gathered through the World Bank's Debtor Reporting System (DRS). Indebtedness is calculated using loan-by-loan reports submitted by countries on long-term public and publicly guaranteed borrowing and using information on short-term debt collected by the countries, from creditors through the reporting systems of the Bank for International Settlements, or based on national data from the World Bank's *Quarterly External Debt Statistics*. These data are supplemented by information from major multilateral banks and official lending agencies in major creditor countries. Currently, 124 developing countries report to the DRS. Debt data are reported in the currency of repayment and compiled and published in U.S. dollars. End-of-period exchange rates are used for the compilation of stock figures (amount of debt outstanding), and projected debt service and annual average exchange rates are used for the flows. Exchange rates are taken from the IMF's *International Financial Statistics*. Debt repayable in multiple currencies, goods, or services and debt with a provision for maintenance of the value of the currency of repayment are shown at book value.

While data related to public and publicly guaranteed debt are reported to the DRS on a loan-by-loan basis, data on long-term private nonguaranteed debt are reported annually in aggregate by the country or estimated by World Bank staff for countries. Private nonguaranteed debt is estimated based on national data from the World Bank's *Quarterly External Debt Statistics*.

Total debt service as a share of exports of goods, services, and primary income provides a measure of a country's ability to service its debt out of export earnings.

 Front User guide World view People Environment

Definitions

• **Merchandise trade** includes all trade in goods and excludes trade in services. • **Net barter terms of trade index** is the percentage ratio of the export unit value indexes to the import unit value indexes, measured relative to the base year 2000. • **Inbound tourism expenditure** is expenditures by international inbound visitors, including payments to national carriers for international transport and any other prepayment made for goods or services received in the destination country. They may include receipts from same-day visitors, except when these are important enough to justify separate classification. Data include travel and passenger transport items as defined by BPM6. When passenger transport items are not reported, expenditure data for travel items are shown. Exports refer to all transactions between residents of a country and the rest of the world involving a change of ownership from residents to nonresidents of general merchandise, goods sent for processing and repairs, nonmonetary gold, and services. • **Net official development assistance** is flows (net of repayment of principal) that meet the DAC definition of official development assistance and are made to countries and territories on the DAC list of aid recipients, divided by World Bank estimates of GNI. • **Net migration** is the net total of migrants (immigrants less emigrants, including both citizens and noncitizens) during the period. Data are five-year estimates. • **Personal remittances, received,** are the sum of personal transfers (current transfers in cash or in kind made or received by resident households to or from nonresident households) and compensation of employees (remuneration for the labor input to the production process contributed by an individual in an employer-employee relationship with the enterprise). • **Foreign direct investment** is cross-border investment associated with a resident in one economy having control or a significant degree of influence on the management of an enterprise that is resident in another economy. • **Portfolio equity** is net inflows from equity securities other than those recorded as direct investment or reserve assets, including shares, stocks, depository receipts, and direct purchases of shares in local stock markets by foreign investors • **Total external debt stock** is debt owed to nonresident creditors and repayable in foreign currency, goods, or services by public and private entities in the country. It is the sum of long-term external debt, short-term debt, and use of IMF credit. • **Total debt service** is the sum of principal repayments and interest actually paid in foreign currency, goods, or services on long-term debt; interest paid on short-term debt; and repayments (repurchases and charges) to the IMF. Exports of goods and services and primary income are the total value of exports of goods and services, receipts of compensation of nonresident workers, and primary investment income from abroad.

Data sources

Data on merchandise trade are from the World Trade Organization. Data on trade indexes are from the United Nations Conference on Trade and Development's (UNCTAD) annual *Handbook of Statistics*. Data on tourism expenditure are from the World Tourism Organization's *Yearbook of Tourism Statistics* and World Tourism Organization (2015) and updated from its electronic files. Data on net official development assistance are compiled by the OECD (http://stats .oecd.org). Data on net migration are from United Nations Population Division (2013). Data on personal remittances are from the IMF's *Balance of Payments Statistics Yearbook* supplemented by World Bank staff estimates. Data on FDI are World Bank staff estimates based on IMF balance of payments statistics and UNCTAD data (http://unctadstat.unctad.org/ReportFolders/reportFolders.aspx). Data on portfolio equity are from the IMF's *Balance of Payments Statistics Yearbook*. Data on external debt are mainly from reports to the World Bank through its DRS from member countries that have received International Bank for Reconstruction and Development loans or International Development Assistance credits, with additional information from the files of the World Bank, the IMF, the African Development Bank and African Development Fund, the Asian Development Bank and Asian Development Fund, and the Inter-American Development Bank. Summary tables of the external debt of developing countries are published annually in the World Bank's *International Debt Statistics* and International Debt Statistics database.

References

IMF (International Monetary Fund). Various issues. *International Financial Statistics.* Washington, DC.

———. Various years. *Balance of Payments Statistics Yearbook. Parts 1 and 2.* Washington, DC.

UNCTAD (United Nations Conference on Trade and Development). Various years. *Handbook of Statistics.* New York and Geneva.

United Nations Population Division. 2013. *World Population Prospects: The 2012 Revision.* New York: United Nations, Department of Economic and Social Affairs.

World Bank. Various years. *International Debt Statistics.* Washington, DC.

World Tourism Organization. 2015. *Compendium of Tourism Statistics 2015.* Madrid.

———. Various years. *Yearbook of Tourism Statistics. Vols. 1 and 2.* Madrid.

6 Global links

To access the World Development Indicators online tables, use the URL http://wdi.worldbank.org/table/ and the table number (for example, http://wdi.worldbank.org/table/6.1). To view a specific indicator online, use the URL http://data.worldbank.org/indicator/ and the indicator code (for example, http://data.worldbank.org /indicator/TX.QTY.MRCH.XD.WD).

6.1 Growth of merchandise trade

Export volume	TX.QTY.MRCH.XD.WD
Import volume	TM.QTY.MRCH.XD.WD
Export value	TX.VAL.MRCH.XD.WD
Import value	TM.VAL.MRCH.XD.WD
Net barter terms of trade index	TT.PRI.MRCH.XD.WD

6.2 Direction and growth of merchandise trade

This table provides estimates of the flow of trade in goods between groups of economies. ..[a]

6.3 High-income economy trade with low- and middle-income economies

This table illustrates the importance of developing economies in the global trading system. ..[a]

6.4 Direction of trade of developing economies

Exports to developing economies within region	TX.VAL.MRCH.WR.ZS
Exports to developing economies outside region	TX.VAL.MRCH.OR.ZS
Exports to high-income economies	TX.VAL.MRCH.HI.ZS
Imports from developing economies within region	TM.VAL.MRCH.WR.ZS
Imports from developing economies outside region	TM.VAL.MRCH.OR.ZS
Imports from high-income economies	TM.VAL.MRCH.HI.ZS

6.5 Primary commodity prices

This table provides historical commodity price data. ..[a]

6.6 Tariff barriers

All products, Binding coverage	TM.TAX.MRCH.BC.ZS
Simple mean bound rate	TM.TAX.MRCH.BR.ZS
Simple mean tariff	TM.TAX.MRCH.SM.AR.ZS
Weighted mean tariff	TM.TAX.MRCH.WM.AR.ZS
Share of tariff lines with international peaks	TM.TAX.MRCH.IP.ZS
Share of tariff lines with specific rates	TM.TAX.MRCH.SR.ZS
Primary products, Simple mean tariff	TM.TAX.TCOM.SM.AR.ZS
Primary products, Weighted mean tariff	TM.TAX.TCOM.WM.AR.ZS
Manufactured products, Simple mean tariff	TM.TAX.MANF.SM.AR.ZS
Manufactured products, Weighted mean tariff	TM.TAX.MANF.WM.AR.ZS

6.7 Trade facilitation

Logistics performance index	LP.LPI.OVRL.XQ
Burden of customs procedures	IQ.WEF.CUST.XQ
Lead time to export	LP.EXP.DURS.MD
Lead time to import	LP.IMP.DURS.MD
Documents to export	IC.EXP.DOCS
Documents to import	IC.IMP.DOCS
Liner shipping connectivity index	IS.SHP.GCNW.XQ
Quality of port infrastructure	IQ.WEF.PORT.XQ

6.8 External debt

Total external debt, $	DT.DOD.DECT.CD
Total external debt, % of GNI	DT.DOD.DECT.GN.ZS
Long-term debt, Public and publicly guaranteed	DT.DOD.DPPG.CD
Long-term debt, Private nonguaranteed	DT.DOD.DPNG.CD
Short-term debt, $	DT.DOD.DSTC.CD
Short-term debt, % of total debt	DT.DOD.DSTC.ZS
Short-term debt, % of total reserves	DT.DOD.DSTC.IR.ZS
Total debt service	DT.TDS.DECT.EX.ZS
Present value of debt, % of GNI	DT.DOD.PVLX.GN.ZS
Present value of debt, % of exports of goods, services and primary income	DT.DOD.PVLX.EX.ZS

6.9 Global private financial flows

Foreign direct investment net inflows, $	BX.KLT.DINV.CD.WD
Foreign direct investment net inflows, % of GDP	BX.KLT.DINV.WD.GD.ZS
Portfolio equity	BX.PEF.TOTL.CD.WD
Bonds	DT.NFL.BOND.CD
Commercial banks and other lendings	DT.NFL.PCBO.CD

6.10 Net official financial flows

Net financial flows from bilateral sources	DT.NFL.BLAT.CD
Net financial flows from multilateral sources	DT.NFL.MLAT.CD
World Bank, IDA	DT.NFL.MIDA.CD
World Bank, IBRD	DT.NFL.MIBR.CD
IMF, Concessional	DT.NFL.IMFC.CD
IMF, Nonconcessional	DT.NFL.IMFN.CD
Regional development banks, Concessional	DT.NFL.RDBC.CD
Regional development banks, Nonconcessional	DT.NFL.RDBN.CD
Regional development banks, Other institutions	DT.NFL.MOTH.CD

6.11 Aid dependency

Net official development assistance (ODA)	DT.ODA.ODAT.CD
Net ODA per capita	DT.ODA.ODAT.PC.ZS

 Front | User guide | World view | People | Environment

Grants, excluding technical cooperation	BX.GRT.EXTA.CD.WD
Technical cooperation grants	BX.GRT.TECH.CD.WD
Net ODA, % of GNI	DT.ODA.ODAT.GN.ZS
Net ODA, % of gross capital formation	DT.ODA.ODAT.GI.ZS
Net ODA, % of imports of goods and services and income	DT.ODA.ODAT.MP.ZS
Net ODA, % of central government expenditure	DT.ODA.ODAT.XP.ZS

6.12 Distribution of net aid by Development Assistance Committee members

Net bilateral aid flows from DAC donors	DC.DAC.TOTL.CD
United States	DC.DAC.USAL.CD
EU institutions	DC.DAC.CECL.CD
Germany	DC.DAC.DEUL.CD
France	DC.DAC.FRAL.CD
United Kingdom	DC.DAC.GBRL.CD
Japan	DC.DAC.JPNL.CD
Netherlands	DC.DAC.NLDL.CD
Australia	DC.DAC.AUSL.CD
Norway	DC.DAC.NORL.CD
Sweden	DC.DAC.SWEL.CD
Other DAC donors	.. [a,b]

6.13 Movement of people

Net migration	SM.POP.NETM
International migrant stock	SM.POP.TOTL
Emigration rate of tertiary educated to OECD countries	SM.EMI.TERT.ZS
Refugees by country of origin	SM.POP.REFG.OR
Refugees by country of asylum	SM.POP.REFG
Personal remittances, Received	BX.TRF.PWKR.CD.DT
Personal remittances, Paid	BM.TRF.PWKR.CD.DT

6.14 Travel and tourism

International inbound tourists	ST.INT.ARVL
International outbound tourists	ST.INT.DPRT
Inbound tourism expenditure, $	ST.INT.RCPT.CD
Inbound tourism expenditure, % of exports	ST.INT.RCPT.XP.ZS
Outbound tourism expenditure, $	ST.INT.XPND.CD
Outbound tourism expenditure, % of imports	ST.INT.XPND.MP.ZS

a. Available online only as part of the table, not as an individual indicator.
b. Derived from data elsewhere in the World Development Indicators database.

Front | User guide | World view | People | Environment

Primary data documentation

As a major user of development data, the World Bank recognizes the importance of data documentation to inform users of the methods and conventions used by primary data collectors—usually national statistical agencies, central banks, and customs services—and by international organizations, which compile the statistics that appear in the World Development Indicators database.

This section provides information on sources, methods, and reporting standards of the principal demographic, economic, and environmental indicators in *World Development Indicators.* Additional documentation is available in the World Development Indicators database and from the World Bank's Bulletin Board on Statistical Capacity at http://data.worldbank.org.

The demand for good-quality statistical data is ever increasing. Statistics provide the evidence needed to improve decisionmaking, document results, and heighten public accountability. However, differences among data collectors may give rise to large discrepancies over time, both within and across countries. Data relevant at the national level may not be suitable for standardized international use due to methodological concerns or the lack of clear documentation. Delays in reporting data and the use of old surveys as the base for current estimates may further compromise the quality of data reported.

To meet these challenges and improve the quality of data disseminated, the World Bank works closely with other international agencies, regional development banks, donors, and other partners to:

- Develop appropriate frameworks, guidance, and standards of good practice for statistics.
- Build consensus and define internationally agreed indicators, such as those for the Millennium Development Goals and the post-2015 development agenda.
- Establish data exchange processes and methods.
- Help countries improve their statistical capacity.

More information on these activities and other data programs is available at http://data.worldbank.org.

Primary data documentation

	Currency	National accounts						Balance of payments and trade			Government finance	IMF data dissemination standard
		Base year	Reference year	System of National Accounts	SNA price valuation	Alternative conversion factor	PPP survey year	Balance of Payments Manual in use	External debt	System of trade	Accounting concept	
Afghanistan	Afghan afghani	2002/03		1993	B				A	G	C	G
Albania	Albanian lek	ᵃ	1996	1993	B		Rolling	6	A	G	B	G
Algeria	Algerian dinar	1980		1968	B		2011	6	A	S	B	G
American Samoa	U.S. dollar			1968			2011ᵇ			S		
Andorra	Euro	1990		1968						S		
Angola	Angolan kwanza	2002		1993	P	1991–96	2011	6	A	S	B	G
Antigua and Barbuda	East Caribbean dollar	2006		1968	B		2011	6		G	B	G
Argentina	Argentine peso	2004		2008	B	1971–84		6	A	S	C	S
Armenia	Armenian dram	ᵃ	1996	1993	B	1990–95	2011	6	A	S	C	S
Aruba	Aruban florin	2000		1993	B		2011	6		S		
Australia	Australian dollar	ᵃ	2012/13	2008	B		2011	6		G	C	S
Austria	Euro	2005		2008	B		Rolling	6		S	C	S
Azerbaijan	New Azeri manat	2000		1993	B	1992–95	2011	6	A	G	C	G
Bahamas, The	Bahamian dollar	2006		1993	B		2011	6		G	B	G
Bahrain	Bahraini dinar	2010		1968	P		2011	6		G	B	G
Bangladesh	Bangladeshi taka	2005/06		1993	B		2011	6	E	G	C	G
Barbados	Barbados dollar	1974		1968	B		2011	6		G	B	G
Belarus	Belarusian rubel	ᵃ	2000	1993	B	1990–95	2011	6	A	G	C	S
Belgium	Euro	2005		2008	B		Rolling	6		S	C	S
Belize	Belize dollar	2000		1993	B		2011	6	A	G	B	G
Benin	CFA franc	1985		1968	P	1992	2011	6	A	S	B	G
Bermuda	Bermuda dollar	2006		1993	B		2011	6		G		
Bhutan	Bhutanese ngultrum	2000		1993	B		2011	6	A	G	C	G
Bolivia	Bolivian Boliviano	1990		1968	B	1960–85	2011	6	A	G	C	G
Bosnia and Herzegovina	Bosnia and Herzegovina convertible mark	ᵃ	2010	1993	B		Rolling	6	A	S	C	G
Botswana	Botswana pula	2006		1993	B		2011	6	A	G	B	G
Brazil	Brazilian real	2000		1993	B		2011	6	A	G	C	S
Brunei Darussalam	Brunei dollar	2000		1993	P		2011			S		G
Bulgaria	Bulgarian lev	ᵃ	2010	1993	B	1978–89, 1991–92	Rolling	6	A	S	C	S
Burkina Faso	CFA franc	1999		1993	B	1992–93	2011	6	A	G	B	G
Burundi	Burundi franc	2005		1993	B		2011	6	A	S	C	G
Cabo Verde	Cabo Verde escudo	2007		1993	P		2011	6	A	G	B	G
Cambodia	Cambodian riel	2000		1993	B		2011	6	A	S	B	G
Cameroon	CFA franc	2000		1993	B		2011	6	A	S	B	G
Canada	Canadian dollar	2005		2008	B		2011	6		G	C	S
Cayman Islands	Cayman Islands dollar	2007		1993			2011			G		
Central African Republic	CFA franc	2000		1968	B		2011	6	A	S	B	G
Chad	CFA franc	2005		1993	B		2011	6	P	S		G
Channel Islands	Pound sterling	2003	2007	1968	B							
Chile	Chilean peso	2008		1993	B		2011	6		S	C	S
China	Chinese yuan	2000		1993	P	1978–93	2011	6	P	S	C	G
Hong Kong SAR, China	Hong Kong dollar	ᵃ	2012	2008	B		2011	6		G	C	S
Macao SAR, China	Macao pataca	2012		1993	B		2011	6		G	C	G
Colombia	Colombian peso	2005		1993	B	1992–94	2011	6	A	G	C	S
Comoros	Comorian franc	1990		1968	P		2011		A	S		G
Congo, Dem. Rep.	Congolese franc	2005		1968	B	1999–2001	2011	6	P	S	C	G
Congo, Rep.	CFA franc	1990		1968	P	1993	2011	6	A	S	C	G
Costa Rica	Costa Rican colon	1991		1993	B		2011	6	A	S	C	S
Côte d'Ivoire	CFA franc	2009		1968	P		2011	6	A	S	B	G
Croatia	Croatian kuna	ᵃ	2010	1993	B		Rolling	6		G	C	S
Cuba	Cuban peso	2005		1993	B		2011			S		
Curaçao	Netherlands Antillean guilder			1993			2011					
Cyprus	Euro	ᵃ	2000	1993	B		Rolling	6		G	C	S

 Front User guide World view People ⚒ Environment

	Latest population census	Latest demographic, education, or health household survey	Source of most recent income and expenditure data	Vital registration complete	Latest agricultural census	Latest industrial data	Latest trade data	Latest water withdrawal data
Afghanistan	1979	MICS, 2010/11	IHS, 2008		2013/14		2013	2000
Albania	2011	DHS, 2008/09	LSMS, 2011/12	Yes	2012	2011	2013	2006
Algeria	2008	MICS, 2012	IHS, 1995			2010	2013	2001
American Samoa	2010			Yes	2007			
Andorra	2011c			Yes			2006	
Angola	2014	MIS, 2011	IHS, 2008/09		2015			2005
Antigua and Barbuda	2011			Yes	2007		2013	2005
Argentina	2010	MICS, 2011/12	IHS, 2012	Yes	2013	2002	2013	2011
Armenia	2011	DHS, 2010	IHS, 2012	Yes	2013/14	2008	2013	2012
Aruba	2010			Yes			2012	
Australia	2011		ES/BS, 2003	Yes	2011	2011	2013	2000
Austria	2011c		IHS, 2004	Yes	2010	2010	2013	2002
Azerbaijan	2009	DHS, 2006	LSMS, 2011/12	Yes	2015	2011	2013	2012
Bahamas, The	2010						2013	
Bahrain	2010			Yes		2010	2011	2003
Bangladesh	2011	DHS, 2014; HIV/MCH SPA, 2014	IHS, 2010		2008		2007	2008
Barbados	2010	MICS, 2012		Yes	2010d		2013	2005
Belarus	2009	MICS, 2012	IHS, 2013	Yes		2011	2013	2000
Belgium	2011		IHS, 2000	Yes	2010	2010	2013	2007
Belize	2010	MICS, 2011	LFS, 1999				2013	2000
Benin	2013	MICS, 2014	CWIQ, 2011/12		2011/12		2013	2001
Bermuda	2010			Yes			2013	
Bhutan	2005	MICS, 2010	IHS, 2012		2009		2011	2008
Bolivia	2012	DHS, 2008	IHS, 2012		2013		2013	2000
Bosnia and Herzegovina	2013	MICS, 2011/12	LSMS, 2007	Yes			2013	2012
Botswana	2011	MICS, 2000	ES/BS, 2009/10		2011d	2011	2013	2000
Brazil	2010	WHS, 2003	IHS, 2012		2006	2011	2013	2010
Brunei Darussalam	2011			Yes			2013	1994
Bulgaria	2011	LSMS, 2007	ES/BS, 2012	Yes	2010	2011	2013	2009
Burkina Faso	2006	MIS, 2014	CWIQ, 2009		2010		2013	2005
Burundi	2008	MIS, 2012	CWIQ, 2006			2010	2012	2000
Cabo Verde	2010	DHS, 2005	CWIQ, 2007	Yes	2014		2013	2001
Cambodia	2008	DHS, 2014	IHS, 2011		2013		2013	2006
Cameroon	2005	MICS, 2014	PS, 2007				2012	2000
Canada	2011		LFS, 2010	Yes	2011	2011	2013	1986
Cayman Islands	2010			Yes				
Central African Republic	2003	MICS, 2010	PS, 2008				2011	2005
Chad	2009	DHS, 2014	PS, 2011		2010/11		1995	2005
Channel Islands	2009/11e			Yesf				
Chile	2012		IHS, 2011	Yes	2007		2013	2006
China	2010	NSS, 2013	IHS, 2013		2007	2007	2013	2005
Hong Kong SAR, China	2011			Yes		2011	2012	
Macao SAR, China	2011			Yes		2011	2012	
Colombia	2006	DHS, 2010	IHS, 2012		2013	2011	2013	2008
Comoros	2003	DHS, 2012	IHS, 2004				2009	1999
Congo, Dem. Rep.	1984	DHS, 2013/14	1-2-3, 2005/06					2005
Congo, Rep.	2007	DHS, 2011/12	CWIQ/PS, 2011		2013	2009	2013	2002
Costa Rica	2011	MICS, 2011	IHS, 2012	Yes	2014	2011	2013	2013
Côte d'Ivoire	2014	DHS, 2011/12	IHS, 2008		2014		2013	2005
Croatia	2011	WHS, 2003	IHS, 2012	Yes	2010		2013	2010
Cuba	2012	MICS, 2014		Yes			2006	2007
Curaçao	2011			Yes		2010		
Cyprus	2011			Yes	2010	2011	2013	2009

Primary data documentation

	Currency	National accounts						Balance of payments and trade			Government finance	IMF data dissemination standard
		Base year	Reference year	System of National Accounts	SNA price valuation	Alternative conversion factor	PPP survey year	Balance of Payments Manual in use	External debt	System of trade	Accounting concept	
Czech Republic	Czech koruna	2005		2008	B		Rolling	6		S	C	S
Denmark	Danish krone	2005		2008	B		Rolling	6		S	C	S
Djibouti	Djibouti franc	1990		1968	B		2011	6	A	G		G
Dominica	East Caribbean dollar	2006		1993	B		2011	6	A	S	B	G
Dominican Republic	Dominican peso	1991		1993	B		2011	6	A	G	C	G
Ecuador	U.S. dollar	2007		2008	B		2011	6	A	G	B	S
Egypt, Arab Rep.	Egyptian pound	2001/02		1993	B		2011	6	A	G	C	S
El Salvador	U.S. dollar	1990		1968	B		2011	6	A	S	C	S
Equatorial Guinea	CFA franc	2006		1968	B	1965–84	2011			G	B	
Eritrea	Eritrean nakfa	2000		1968	B			6	E			
Estonia	Euro	2005		2008	B	1987–95	Rolling	6		S	C	S
Ethiopia	Ethiopian birr	2010/11		1993	B		2011	6	A	G	B	G
Faeroe Islands	Danish krone			1993	B			6		G		
Fiji	Fijian dollar	2005		1993	B		2011	6	A	G	B	S
Finland	Euro	2005		2008	B		Rolling	6		G	C	S
France	Euro	a	2005	2008	B		Rolling	6		S	C	S
French Polynesia	CFP franc	1990		1993			2011[b]			S		
Gabon	CFA franc	2001		1993	P	1993	2011	6	A	S		G
Gambia, The	Gambian dalasi	2004		1993	P		2011	6	A	G	B	G
Georgia	Georgian lari	a	1996	1993	B	1990–95	2011	6	A	G	C	S
Germany	Euro	2005		2008	B		Rolling	6		S	C	S
Ghana	New Ghanaian cedi	2006		1993	B	1973–87	2011	6	A	G	B	G
Greece	Euro	a	2005	2008	B		Rolling	6		S	C	S
Greenland	Danish krone	1990		1993						G		
Grenada	East Caribbean dollar	2006		1968	B		2011	6	A	S	B	G
Guam	U.S. dollar			1993			2011[b]			G		
Guatemala	Guatemalan quetzal	2001		1993	B		2011	6	A	S	B	G
Guinea	Guinean franc	2003		1993	B		2011	6	E	S	B	G
Guinea-Bissau	CFA franc	2005		1993	B		2011	6	E	G		G
Guyana	Guyana dollar	2006		1993	B			6	A	S		G
Haiti	Haitian gourde	1986/87		1968	B	1991	2011	6	A	G		G
Honduras	Honduran lempira	2000		1993	B	1988–89	2011	6	A	S	C	G
Hungary	Hungarian forint	a	2005	2008	B		Rolling	6	A	S	C	S
Iceland	Iceland krona	2005		2008	B		Rolling	6		G	C	S
India	Indian rupee	2011/12		2008	B		2011	6	A	G	C	S
Indonesia	Indonesian rupiah	2000		1993	P		2011	6	A	S	B	S
Iran, Islamic Rep.	Iranian rial	1997/98		1993	B	1980–2002	2011	6	A	S	C	G
Iraq	Iraqi dinar	1988		1968	P	1997, 2004	2011	6				G
Ireland	Euro	2005		2008	B		Rolling	6		G	C	S
Isle of Man	Pound sterling	2003		1968								
Israel	Israeli new shekel	a	2010	1993	P		2011	6		S	C	S
Italy	Euro	2005		2008	B		Rolling	6		S	C	S
Jamaica	Jamaican dollar	2007		1993	B		2011	6	A	G	C	G
Japan	Japanese yen	2005		1993	B		2011	6		G	C	S
Jordan	Jordanian dinar	1994		1968	B		2011	6	A	G		
Kazakhstan	Kazakh tenge	a	2005	1993	B	1987–95	2011	6	A	G	C	S
Kenya	Kenyan shilling	2009		1993	B		2011	6	A	G	B	G
Kiribati	Australian dollar	2006		1993	B		2011[b]	6		G	B	G
Korea, Dem. People's Rep.	Democratic People's Republic of Korean won			1968				6				
Korea, Rep.	Korean won	2010		2008	B		2011	6		G	C	S
Kosovo	Euro	2008		1993	B				A			G
Kuwait	Kuwaiti dinar	2010		1968	P		2011	6		S	B	G
Kyrgyz Republic	Kyrgyz som	a	1995	1993	B	1990–95	2011	6	A	S	B	S
Lao PDR	Lao kip	2002		1993	B		2011	6	A	S	B	
Latvia	Latvian lats	2000		1993	B	1987–95	Rolling	6		S	C	S
Lebanon	Lebanese pound	1997		1993	B		2011	6	A	G	B	G

Front | User guide | World view | People | Environment

	Latest population census	Latest demographic, education, or health household survey	Source of most recent income and expenditure data	Vital registration complete	Latest agricultural census	Latest industrial data	Latest trade data	Latest water withdrawal data
Czech Republic	2011	WHS, 2003	IHS, 2012	Yes	2010	2010	2013	2007
Denmark	2011		ITR, 2010	Yes	2010		2013	2009
Djibouti	2009	MICS, 2006	PS, 2002				2009	2000
Dominica	2011			Yes			2012	2004
Dominican Republic	2010	MICS, 2014	IHS, 2012		2012/13	2008	2012	2005
Ecuador	2010	RHS, 2004	IHS, 2013		2013/15		2013	2005
Egypt, Arab Rep.	2006	DHS, 2014	ES/BS, 2011	Yes	2009/10	2010	2013	2000
El Salvador	2007	MICS, 2014	IHS, 2012	Yes	2007/08		2013	2005
Equatorial Guinea	2002	DHS, 2011	PS, 2006					2000
Eritrea	1984	DHS, 2002	PS, 1993			2011	2003	2004
Estonia	2012	WHS, 2003	IHS, 2011	Yes	2010	2011	2013	2007
Ethiopia	2007	HIV/MCH SPA, 2014	ES/BS, 2010/11			2009	2013	2002
Faeroe Islands	2011			Yes			2009	
Fiji	2007		ES/BS, 2008/09	Yes	2009	2010	2013	2000
Finland	2010		IHS, 2010	Yes	2010	2010	2013	2005
France	2006[g]		ES/BS, 2005	Yes	2010	2010	2013	2007
French Polynesia	2007			Yes			2013	
Gabon	2013	DHS, 2012	CWIQ/IHS, 2005				2009	2005
Gambia, The	2013	DHS, 2013	IHS, 2010			2004	2013	2000
Georgia	2002	MICS, 2005; RHS, 2005	IHS, 2012	Yes		2011	2013	2008
Germany	2011		IHS, 2010	Yes	2010	2010	2013	2007
Ghana	2010	DHS, 2014	LSMS, 2012		2013/14	2003	2013	2000
Greece	2011		IHS, 2010	Yes	2009	2007	2013	2007
Greenland	2010			Yes			2013	
Grenada	2011	RHS, 1985		Yes	2012		2009	2005
Guam	2010			Yes	2007			
Guatemala	2002	RHS, 2008/09	LSMS, 2011	Yes	2013		2013	2006
Guinea	2014	DHS, 2012	CWIQ, 2012				2008	2001
Guinea-Bissau	2009	MICS, 2014	CWIQ, 2010				2005	2000
Guyana	2012	MICS, 2014	IHS, 1998				2013	2010
Haiti	2003	HIV/MCH SPA, 2013	IHS, 2012		2008/09		1997	2000
Honduras	2013	DHS, 2011/12	IHS, 2013		2013		2012	2003
Hungary	2011	WHS, 2003	IHS, 2012	Yes	2010	2010	2013	2007
Iceland	2011		IHS, 2010	Yes	2010	2005	2013	2005
India	2011	DHS, 2005/06	IHS, 2011/12		2011	2010	2013	2010
Indonesia	2010	DHS, 2012	IHS, 2013		2013	2011	2013	2000
Iran, Islamic Rep.	2011	IrMIDHS, 2010	ES/BS, 2005	Yes	2013	2010	2011	2004
Iraq	1997	MICS, 2011	IHS, 2012		2011/12	2011		2000
Ireland	2011		IHS, 2010	Yes	2010	2010	2013	1979
Isle of Man	2011			Yes				
Israel	2009		ES/BS, 2010	Yes		2010	2013	2004
Italy	2012		IS, 2010	Yes	2010	2010	2013	2000
Jamaica	2011	MICS, 2011	LSMS, 2010		2007		2013	1993
Japan	2010		IHS, 2008	Yes	2010	2010	2013	2001
Jordan	2004	DHS, 2012	ES/BS, 2010		2007	2011	2013	2005
Kazakhstan	2009	MICS, 2010/11	ES/BS, 2013	Yes			2013	2010
Kenya	2009	DHS, 2014	IHS, 2005/06		2009[d]	2011	2010	2003
Kiribati	2010	KDHS, 2009					2012	
Korea, Dem. People's Rep.	2008	MICS, 2009						2005
Korea, Rep.	2010		ES/BS, 1998	Yes	2010	2009	2013	2002
Kosovo	2011	MICS, 2013/14	IHS, 2011					
Kuwait	2011	FHS, 1996		Yes		2011	2013	2002
Kyrgyz Republic	2009	MICS, 2014	ES/BS, 2013	Yes	2014	2010	2013	2006
Lao PDR	2005	MICS, 2011/12	ES/BS, 2012		2010/11			2005
Latvia	2011	WHS, 2003	IHS, 2012	Yes	2010	2011	2013	2002
Lebanon	1970	FHS, 2004		Yes	2011	2007	2013	2005

Primary data documentation

	Currency	National accounts					Balance of payments and trade			Government finance	IMF data dissemination standard
		Base year	Reference year	System of National Accounts	SNA price valuation	Alternative conversion factor	PPP survey year	Balance of Payments Manual in use	External debt	System of trade	Accounting concept	
Lesotho	Lesotho loti	2004		1993	B		2011	6	A	G	C	G
Liberia	Liberian dollar	2000		1968	P		2011	6	A	S	B	G
Libya	Libyan dinar	1999		1993	B	1986		6		G		G
Liechtenstein	Swiss franc	1990		1993	B					S		
Lithuania	Lithuanian litas	2000		1993	B	1990–95	Rolling	6		G	C	S
Luxembourg	Euro	a	2005	2008	B		Rolling	6		S	C	S
Macedonia, FYR	Macedonian denar	1995		1993	B		Rolling	6	A	S	C	S
Madagascar	Malagasy ariary	1984		1968	B		2011	6	A	S	C	G
Malawi	Malawi kwacha	2009		1993	B		2011	6	A	G		G
Malaysia	Malaysian ringgit	2005		1993	P		2011	6	E	G	B	S
Maldives	Maldivian rufiyaa	2003		1993	B		2011	6	A	G	C	G
Mali	CFA franc	1987		1968	B		2011	6	A	S	B	G
Malta	Euro	2005		1993	B		Rolling	6		G	C	S
Marshall Islands	U.S. dollar	2003/04		1968	B		2011[b]			G		G
Mauritania	Mauritanian ouguiya	1998		1993	B		2011	6	A	S		G
Mauritius	Mauritian rupee	2006		1993	B		2011	6	A	G		S
Mexico	Mexican peso	2008		2008	B		2011	6	A	G	C	G
Micronesia, Fed. Sts.	U.S. dollar	2003/04		1993	B		2011[b]					G
Moldova	Moldovan leu	a	1996	1993	B	1990–95	2011	6	A	G	C	S
Monaco	Euro	1990		1993						S		
Mongolia	Mongolian tugrik	2005		1993	B		2011	6	A	G	C	G
Montenegro	Euro	2000		1993	B		Rolling	6	A	S		G
Morocco	Moroccan dirham	1998		1993	B		2011	6	A	S	C	S
Mozambique	New Mozambican metical	2009		1993	B	1992–95	2011	6	A	S	B	G
Myanmar	Myanmar kyat	2005/06		1968	P		2011	6	E	G	C	G
Namibia	Namibian dollar	2010		1993	B		2011	6		G	B	G
Nepal	Nepalese rupee	2000/01		1993	B		2011	6	A	G	B	G
Netherlands	Euro	a	2005	2008	B		Rolling	6		S	C	S
New Caledonia	CFP franc	1990		1993			2011[b]			S		
New Zealand	New Zealand dollar	2005/06		1993	B		2011	6		G	C	
Nicaragua	Nicaraguan gold cordoba	2006		1993	B	1965–95	2011	6	A	G	B	G
Niger	CFA franc	2006		1993	P	1993	2011	6	A	S	B	G
Nigeria	Nigerian naira	2010		2008	B	1971–98	2011	6	A	G	B	G
Northern Mariana Islands	U.S. dollar			1968			2011[b]					
Norway	Norwegian krone	a	2005	1993	B		Rolling	6		G	C	S
Oman	Rial Omani	2010		1993	P		2011	6		G	B	G
Pakistan	Pakistani rupee	2005/06		1993	B		2011	6	A	G	B	G
Palau	U.S. dollar	2004/05		1993	B		2011[b]			S		G
Panama	Panamanian balboa	2007		1993	B		2011	6	A	S	C	G
Papua New Guinea	Papua New Guinea kina	1998		1993	B	1989	2011[b]	6	A	G	B	G
Paraguay	Paraguayan guarani	1994		1993	B		2011	6	A	S	C	G
Peru	Peruvian new sol	2007		1993	B	1985–90	2011	6	A	S	C	S
Philippines	Philippine peso	2000		1993	P		2011	6	A	G	B	S
Poland	Polish zloty	a	2005	2008	B		Rolling	6		S	C	S
Portugal	Euro	2005		2008	B		Rolling	6		S	C	S
Puerto Rico	U.S. dollar	1953/54		1968	P					G		
Qatar	Qatari riyal	2001		1993	P		2011			S	B	G
Romania	New Romanian leu	2000		1993	B	1987–89, 1992	Rolling	6	A	S	C	S
Russian Federation	Russian ruble	2000		1993	B	1987–95	2011	6		G	C	S
Rwanda	Rwandan franc	2011		2008	P	1994	2011	6	A	G	B	G
Samoa	Samoan tala	2008/09		1993	B		2011[b]	6	A	S	B	G
San Marino	Euro	1995	2000	1993	B						C	G
São Tomé and Príncipe	São Tomé and Príncipe dobra	2000		1993	P		2011	6	A	S	B	G
Saudi Arabia	Saudi Arabian riyal	1999		1993	P		2011	6		S		G
Senegal	CFA franc	1999		1993	B		2011	6	A	G	B	G

 Front | User guide | World view | People | Environment

	Latest population census	Latest demographic, education, or health household survey	Source of most recent income and expenditure data	Vital registration complete	Latest agricultural census	Latest industrial data	Latest trade data	Latest water withdrawal data
Lesotho	2006	DHS, 2014	ES/BS, 2010		2010		2009	2000
Liberia	2008	DHS, 2013	CWIQ, 2007		2008^d			2000
Libya	2006	FHS, 2007			2013/14		2010	2000
Liechtenstein	2010			Yes				
Lithuania	2011		ES/BS, 2012	Yes	2010	2011	2013	2007
Luxembourg	2011			Yes	2010	2010	2013	1999
Macedonia, FYR	2002	MICS, 2011	ES/BS, 2010	Yes	2007	2010	2013	2007
Madagascar	1993	MIS, 2013	PS, 2010			2006	2013	2000
Malawi	2008	MIS, 2014	IHS, 2010/11		2006/07	2010	2013	2005
Malaysia	2010	WHS, 2003	IS, 2012	Yes	2015	2010	2013	2005
Maldives	2014	DHS, 2009	IHS, 2010	Yes			2013	2008
Mali	2009	DHS, 2012/13	IHS, 2009/10				2012	2006
Malta	2011			Yes	2010	2009	2013	2002
Marshall Islands	2011	RMIDHS, 2007	IHS, 1999		2011^d			
Mauritania	2013	MICS, 2011	IHS, 2008				2013	2005
Mauritius	2011	WHS, 2003	IHS, 2012	Yes	2013/14	2011	2013	2003
Mexico	2010	ENADID, 2009	IHS, 2012		2007	2010	2013	2011
Micronesia, Fed. Sts.	2010		IHS, 2000					
Moldova	2014	MICS, 2012	ES/BS, 2012	Yes	2011	2011	2013	2007
Monaco	2008			Yes				2009
Mongolia	2010	MICS, 2013	LSMS, 2012	Yes	2012	2011	2013	2009
Montenegro	2011	MICS, 2013	ES/BS, 2013	Yes	2010		2013	2010
Morocco	2014	MICS/PAPFAM, 2006	ES/BS, 2007		2012	2010	2012	2000
Mozambique	2007	DHS, 2011	ES/BS, 2008/09		2009/10		2013	2001
Myanmar	2014	MICS, 2009/10			2010		2010	2000
Namibia	2011	DHS, 2013	ES/BS, 2009/10		2014		2013	2002
Nepal	2011	MICS, 2014	LSMS, 2010/11		2011/12	2008	2013	2006
Netherlands	2011		IHS, 2010	Yes	2010	2010	2013	2008
New Caledonia	2009			Yes			2012	
New Zealand	2013			Yes	2012	2010	2013	2002
Nicaragua	2005	RHS, 2006/07	LSMS, 2009		2011		2013	2011
Niger	2012	DHS, 2012	CWIQ/PS, 2011		2004-08	2002	2013	2005
Nigeria	2006	DHS, 2013	IHS, 2009/10		2013		2013	2005
Northern Mariana Islands	2010				2007			
Norway	2011		IS, 2010	Yes	2010	2010	2013	2006
Oman	2010	MICS, 2014			2012/13	2010	2013	2003
Pakistan	1998	DHS, 2012/13	IHS, 2010/11		2010	2006	2013	2008
Palau	2010			Yes			2012	
Panama	2010	MICS, 2013	IHS, 2012		2011	2001	2013	2010
Papua New Guinea	2011	LSMS, 1996	IHS, 2009/10			2001	2012	2005
Paraguay	2012	RHS, 2008	IHS, 2013		2008	2002	2013	2012
Peru	2007	Continuous DHS, 2013	IHS, 2013		2012	2011	2013	2008
Philippines	2010	DHS, 2013	ES/BS, 2012	Yes	2012	2008	2013	2009
Poland	2011		ES/BS, 2012	Yes	2010	2011	2013	2009
Portugal	2011			Yes	2009	2010	2013	2002
Puerto Rico	2010	RHS, 1995/96		Yes	2007	2006		2005
Qatar	2010	MICS, 2012		Yes		2010	2013	2005
Romania	2011	RHS, 2004	ES/BS, 2012	Yes	2010	2011	2013	2009
Russian Federation	2010	WHS, 2003	IHS, 2013	Yes	2014	2011	2013	2001
Rwanda	2012	MIS, 2013	IHS, 2010/11		2008		2013	2000
Samoa	2011	DHS, 2009			2009		2013	
San Marino	2010			Yes				
São Tomé and Príncipe	2012	MICS, 2014	PS, 2010		2011/12		2013	1993
Saudi Arabia	2010	Demographic survey, 2007			2010	2006	2013	2006
Senegal	2013	HIV/MCH SPA, 2014	PS, 2011		2013	2010	2012	2002

Primary data documentation

	Currency	Base year	Reference year	System of National Accounts	SNA price valuation	Alternative conversion factor	PPP survey year	Balance of Payments Manual in use	External debt	System of trade	Accounting concept	IMF data dissemination standard
Serbia	New Serbian dinar	[a]	2010	1993	B		Rolling	6	A	S	C	G
Seychelles	Seychelles rupee	2006		1993	P		2011	6	A	G	C	G
Sierra Leone	Sierra Leonean leone	2006		1993	B		2011	6	A	S	B	G
Singapore	Singapore dollar	2010		2008	B		2011	6		G	C	S
Sint Maarten	Netherlands Antillean guilder			1993			2011					
Slovak Republic	Euro	2005		2008	B		Rolling	6		S	C	S
Slovenia	Euro	[a]	2005	2008	B		Rolling	6		S	C	S
Solomon Islands	Solomon Islands dollar	2004		1993	B		2011[b]	6	A	S		G
Somalia	Somali shilling	1985		1968	B	1977–90			E			
South Africa	South African rand	2010		2008	B		2011	6	P	G	C	S
South Sudan	South Sudanese pound	2009		1993								
Spain	Euro	2005		2008	B		Rolling	6		S	C	S
Sri Lanka	Sri Lankan rupee	2002		1993	P		2011	6	A	G	B	G
St. Kitts and Nevis	East Caribbean dollar	2006		1993	B		2011	6		S	B	G
St. Lucia	East Caribbean dollar	2006		1968	B		2011	6		S	B	G
St. Martin	Euro			1993								
St. Vincent and the Grenadines	East Caribbean dollar	2006		1993	B		2011	6	A	S	B	G
Sudan	Sudanese pound	1981/82[h]	1996	1968	B		2011	6	P	G	B	G
Suriname	Suriname dollar	2007		1993	B		2011	6		G	B	G
Swaziland	Swaziland lilangeni	2000		1993	B		2011	6	A	G	C	G
Sweden	Swedish krona	[a]	2005	2008	B		Rolling	6		G	C	S
Switzerland	Swiss franc	2005		2008	B		Rolling	6		S	C	S
Syrian Arab Republic	Syrian pound	2000		1968	B	1970–2010	2011	6	E	S	B	G
Tajikistan	Tajik somoni	[a]	2000	1993	B	1990–95	2011	6	A	G	C	G
Tanzania	Tanzanian shilling	2007		2008	B		2011	6	A	G	B	G
Thailand	Thai baht	1988		1993	P		2011	6	A	S	C	S
Timor-Leste	U.S. dollar	2010		2008	B					S		G
Togo	CFA franc	2000		1968	P		2011	6	A	S	B	G
Tonga	Tongan pa'anga	2010/11		1993	B		2011[b]	6	A	G		G
Trinidad and Tobago	Trinidad and Tobago dollar	2000		1993	B		2011	6		S	C	G
Tunisia	Tunisian dinar	2005		1993	B		2011	6	A	G	C	S
Turkey	New Turkish lira	1998		1993	B		Rolling	6	A	S	C	S
Turkmenistan	New Turkmen manat	2005		1993	B	1987–95, 1997–2007		6	E	G		
Turks and Caicos Islands	U.S. dollar			1993			2011			G		
Tuvalu	Australian dollar	2005		1968	B		2011[b]			G		G
Uganda	Ugandan shilling	2009/10		2008	P		2011	6	A	G	B	G
Ukraine	Ukrainian hryvnia	[a]	2003	1993	B	1987–95	2011	6	A	G	C	S
United Arab Emirates	U.A.E. dirham	2007		1993	P		2011	6		G	C	G
United Kingdom	Pound sterling	2005		1993	B		Rolling	6		G	C	S
United States	U.S. dollar	[a]	2005	2008	B		2011	6		G	C	S
Uruguay	Uruguayan peso	2005		1993	B		2011	6		G	C	S
Uzbekistan	Uzbek sum	[a]	1997	1993	B	1990–95		6	A	G		
Vanuatu	Vanuatu vatu	2006		1993	B		2011[b]	6	E	G	B	G
Venezuela, RB	Venezuelan bolivar fuerte	1997		1993	B		2011	6	A	G	C	G
Vietnam	Vietnamese dong	2010		1993	P	1991	2011	6	A	G		G
Virgin Islands (U.S.)	U.S. dollar	1982		1968						G		
West Bank and Gaza	Israeli new shekel	2004		1968			2011	6		S	B	S
Yemen, Rep.	Yemeni rial	2007		1993	P	1990–96	2011	6	A	S	B	G
Zambia	New Zambian kwacha	2010		2008	B	1990–92	2011	6	A	S	B	G
Zimbabwe	U.S. dollar	2009		1993	B	1991, 1998	2011	6	A	G	C	G

 Front User guide World view People | Environment

	Latest population census	Latest demographic, education, or health household survey	Source of most recent income and expenditure data	Vital registration complete	Latest agricultural census	Latest industrial data	Latest trade data	Latest water withdrawal data
Serbia	2011	MICS, 2014	IHS, 2011	Yes	2012	2011		2009
Seychelles	2010		BS, 2006/07	Yes	2011		2008	2005
Sierra Leone	2004	DHS, 2013; MIS, 2013	IHS, 2011			2008	2002	2005
Singapore	2010	NHS, 2010		Yes		2011	2013	1975
Sint Maarten	2011			Yes				
Slovak Republic	2011	WHS, 2003	IS, 2012	Yes	2010	2010	2013	2007
Slovenia	2011 c	WHS, 2003	ES/BS, 2012	Yes	2010	2011	2013	2009
Solomon Islands	2009		IHS, 2005/06		2012/13		2013	
Somalia	1987	MICS, 2006						2003
South Africa	2011	DHS, 2003; WHS, 2003	ES/BS, 2010/11		2007	2010	2013	2000
South Sudan	2008	MICS, 2010	ES/BS, 2009				2012	2011
Spain	2011		IHS, 2010	Yes	2010	2010	2013	2008
Sri Lanka	2012	DHS, 2006/07	ES/BS, 2013	Yes	2013/14	2010	2013	2005
St. Kitts and Nevis	2011			Yes			2011	
St. Lucia	2010	MICS, 2012	IHS, 1995	Yes	2007		2008	2005
St. Martin								
St. Vincent and the Grenadines	2011			Yes			2012	1995
Sudan	2008	MICS, 2014	ES/BS, 2009		2013/14	2001	2011	2011
Suriname	2012	MICS, 2010	ES/BS, 1999	Yes	2008	2004	2011	2006
Swaziland	2007	MICS, 2014	ES/BS, 2009/10		2007d		2007	2000
Sweden	2011		IS, 2005	Yes	2010	2010	2013	2007
Switzerland	2010		ES/BS, 2004	Yes	2008	2010	2013	2000
Syrian Arab Republic	2004	MICS, 2006	ES/BS, 2004		2014	2005	2010	2005
Tajikistan	2010	DHS, 2012	LSMS, 2009		2013		2000	2006
Tanzania	2012	HIV/MCH SPA, 2014/15	ES/BS, 2011/12		2007/08	2010	2013	2002
Thailand	2010	MICS, 2012	IHS, 2011		2013	2006	2013	2007
Timor-Leste	2010	DHS, 2009/10	LSMS, 2007		2010d		2013	2004
Togo	2010	DHS, 2013/14	CWIQ, 2011		2011/12		2013	2002
Tonga	2006						2012	
Trinidad and Tobago	2011	MICS, 2011	IHS, 1992	Yes		2006	2010	2000
Tunisia	2014	MICS, 2011/12	IHS, 2010		2014/15	2010	2013	2001
Turkey	2011	TDHS, 2008	ES/BS, 2011	Yes		2009	2013	2003
Turkmenistan	2012	MICS, 2006	LSMS, 1998				2000	2004
Turks and Caicos Islands	2012			Yes			2012	
Tuvalu	2012						2008	
Uganda	2014	MIS, 2014	IHS, 2012/13		2008/09		2013	2002
Ukraine	2001	MICS, 2012	ES/BS, 2013	Yes	201213	2004	2013	2005
United Arab Emirates	2010	WHS, 2003			2012	2010	2011	2005
United Kingdom	2011		IS, 2010	Yes	2010	2010	2013	2007
United States	2010		LFS, 2010	Yes	2012	2008	2013	2005
Uruguay	2011	MICS, 2012/13	IHS, 2013	Yes	2011	2009	2013	2000
Uzbekistan	1989	MICS, 2006	ES/BS, 2011	Yes				2005
Vanuatu	2009	MICS, 2007			2007		2011	
Venezuela, RB	2011	MICS, 2000	IHS, 2012	Yes	2007		2011	2000
Vietnam	2009	MICS, 2013/14	IHS, 2012	Yes	2011/12	2011	2013	2005
Virgin Islands (U.S.)	2010			Yes	2007			
West Bank and Gaza	2007	MICS, 2014	IHS, 2011			2010		2005
Yemen, Rep.	2004	DHS, 2013	ES/BS, 2005			2009	2013	2005
Zambia	2010	DHS, 2013/14	IHS, 2010		2010d		2013	2002
Zimbabwe	2012	MICS, 2014	IHS, 2011/12				2013	2002

Note: For explanation of the abbreviations used in the table, see notes following the table.
a. Original chained constant price data are rescaled. b. Household consumption only. c. Population data compiled from administrative registers. d. Population and Housing Census.
e. Latest population census: Guernsey, 2009; Jersey, 2011 f. Vital registration for Guernsey and Jersey. g. Rolling census based on continuous sample survey. h. Reporting period switch from fiscal year to calendar year from 1996. Pre-1996 data converted to calendar year.

• **Base year** is the base or pricing period used for constant price calculations in the country's national accounts. Price indexes derived from national accounts aggregates, such as the implicit deflator for gross domestic product (GDP), express the price level relative to base year prices. • **Reference year** is the year in which the local currency constant price series of a country is valued. The reference year is usually the same as the base year used to report the constant price series. However, when the constant price data are chain linked, the base year is changed annually, so the data are rescaled to a specific reference year to provide a consistent time series. When the country has not rescaled following a change in base year, World Bank staff rescale the data to maintain a longer historical series. To allow for cross-country comparison and data aggregation, constant price data reported in *World Development Indicators* are rescaled to a common reference year (2000) and currency (U.S. dollars). • **System of National Accounts** identifies whether a country uses the 1968, 1993, or 2008 System of National Accounts (SNA). The 2008 SNA is an update of the 1993 SNA and retains its basic theoretical framework. • **SNA price valuation** shows whether value added in the national accounts is reported at basic prices (B) or producer prices (P). Producer prices include taxes paid by producers and thus tend to overstate the actual value added in production. However, value added can be higher at basic prices than at producer prices in countries with high agricultural subsidies. • **Alternative conversion factor** identifies the countries and years for which a World Bank–estimated conversion factor has been used in place of the official exchange rate (line rf in the International Monetary Fund's [IMF] *International Financial Statistics*). See *Statistical methods* for further discussion of alternative conversion factors. • **Purchasing power parity (PPP) survey year** is the latest available survey year for the International Comparison Program's estimates of PPPs. • **Balance of Payments Manual in use** refers to the classification system used to compile and report data on balance of payments. *6* refers to the 6th edition of the IMF's *Balance of Payments Manual* (2009). • **External debt** shows debt reporting status for 2013 data. *A* indicates that data are as reported, *P* that data are based on reported or collected information but include an element of staff estimation, and *E* that data are World Bank staff estimates. • **System of trade** refers to the United Nations general trade system (G) or special trade system (S). Under the general trade system goods entering directly for

domestic consumption and goods entered into customs storage are recorded as imports at arrival. Under the special trade system goods are recorded as imports when declared for domestic consumption whether at time of entry or on withdrawal from customs storage. Exports under the general system comprise outward-moving goods: (a) national goods wholly or partly produced in the country; (b) foreign goods, neither transformed nor declared for domestic consumption in the country, that move outward from customs storage; and (c) nationalized goods that have been declared for domestic consumption and move outward without being transformed. Under the special system of trade, exports are categories a and c. In some compilations categories b and c are classified as re-exports. Direct transit trade—goods entering or leaving for transport only—is excluded from both import and export statistics. • **Government finance accounting concept** is the accounting basis for reporting central government financial data. For most countries government finance data have been consolidated (C) into one set of accounts capturing all central government fiscal activities. Budgetary central government accounts (B) exclude some central government units. • **IMF data dissemination standard** shows the countries that subscribe to the IMF's Special Data Dissemination Standard (SDDS) or General Data Dissemination System (GDDS). S refers to countries that subscribe to the SDDS and have posted data on the Dissemination Standards Bulletin Board at http://dsbb.imf.org. G refers to countries that subscribe to the GDDS. The SDDS was established for member countries that have or might seek access to international capital markets to guide them in providing their economic and financial data to the public. The GDDS helps countries disseminate comprehensive, timely, accessible, and reliable economic, financial, and sociodemographic statistics. IMF member countries elect to participate in either the SDDS or the GDDS. Both standards enhance the availability of timely and comprehensive data and therefore contribute to the pursuit of sound macroeconomic policies. The SDDS is also expected to improve the functioning of financial markets. • **Latest population census** shows the most recent year in which a census was conducted and in which at least preliminary results have been released. The preliminary results from the very recent censuses could be reflected in timely revisions if basic data are available, such as population by age and sex, as well as the detailed definition of counting, coverage, and completeness. Countries that hold register-based censuses produce similar

census tables every 5 or 10 years. A rare case, France conducts a rolling census every year; the 1999 general population census was the last to cover the entire population simultaneously. • **Latest demographic, education, or health household survey** indicates the household surveys used to compile the demographic, education, and health data in section 2. DHS is Demographic and Health Survey, ENADID is National Survey of Demographic Dynamics, FHS is Family Health Survey, HIV/MCH is HIV/Maternal and Child Health, IrMIDHS is Iran's Multiple Indicator Demographic and Health Survey, KDHS is Kiribati Demographic and Health Survey, LSMS is Living Standards Measurement Study, MICS is Multiple Indicator Cluster Survey, MIS is Malaria Indicator Survey, NHS is National Health Survey, NSS is National Sample Survey on Population Changes, PAPFAM is Pan Arab Project for Family Health, RHS is Reproductive Health Survey, RMIDHS is Republic of the Marshall Islands Demographic and Health Survey, SPA is Service Provision Assessments, TDHS is Turkey Demographic and Health Survey, and WHS is World Health Survey. Detailed information for DHS, HIV/MCH, MIS, and SPA are available at www.dhsprogram.com; for MICS at www.childinfo.org; for RHS at www.cdc.gov/reproductivehealth; and for WHS at www.who.int/healthinfo/survey/en. • **Source of most recent income and expenditure data** shows household surveys that collect income and expenditure data. Names and detailed information on household surveys can be found on the website of the International Household Survey Network (www.surveynetwork.org). Core Welfare Indicator Questionnaire Surveys (CWIQ), developed by the World Bank, measure changes in key social indicators for different population groups—specifically indicators of access, utilization, and satisfaction with core social and economic services. Expenditure survey/budget surveys (ES/BS) collect detailed information on household consumption as well as on general demographic, social, and economic characteristics. Integrated household surveys (IHS) collect detailed information on a wide variety of topics, including health, education, economic activities, housing, and utilities. Income surveys (IS) collect information on the income and wealth of households as well as various social and economic characteristics. Income tax registers (ITR) provide information on a population's income and allowance, such as gross income, taxable income, and taxes by socioeconomic group. Labor force surveys (LFS) collect information on employment, unemployment, hours of work, income, and wages. Living Standards Measurement Study Surveys (LSMS), developed by the World Bank, provide a comprehensive picture of household welfare and the factors that affect it; they typically incorporate data collection at the individual, household, and community levels. Priority surveys (PS) are a light monitoring survey, designed by the World Bank, that collect data from a large number of households cost-effectively and quickly. 1-2-3 (1-2-3) surveys are implemented in three phases and collect socio-demographic and employment data, data on the informal sector, and information on living conditions and household consumption. • **Vital registration complete** identifies countries that report at least 90 percent complete registries of vital (birth and death) statistics to the United Nations Statistics Division and are reported in its *Population and Vital Statistics Reports*. Countries with complete vital statistics registries may have more accurate and more timely demographic indicators than other countries. • **Latest agricultural census** shows the most recent year in which an agricultural census was conducted or planned to be conducted, as reported to the Food and Agriculture Organization of the United Nations. • **Latest industrial data** show the most recent year for which manufacturing value added data at the three-digit level of the International Standard Industrial Classification (revision 2 or 3) are available in the United Nations Industrial Development Organization database. • **Latest trade data** show the most recent year for which structure of merchandise trade data from the United Nations Statistics Division's Commodity Trade (Comtrade) database are available. • **Latest water withdrawal data** show the most recent year for which data on freshwater withdrawals have been compiled from a variety of sources.

Exceptional reporting periods

In most economies the fiscal year is concurrent with the calendar year. Exceptions are shown in the table at right. The ending date reported here is for the fiscal year of the central government. Fiscal years for other levels of government and reporting years for statistical surveys may differ.

The **reporting period for national accounts data** is designated as either calendar year basis (CY) or fiscal year basis (FY). Most economies report their national accounts and balance of payments data using calendar years, but some use fiscal years. In *World Development Indicators* fiscal year data are assigned to the calendar year that contains the larger share of the fiscal year. If a country's fiscal year ends before June 30, data are shown in the first year of the fiscal

period; if the fiscal year ends on or after June 30, data are shown in the second year of the period. Balance of payments data are reported in *World Development Indicators* by calendar year.

Revisions to national accounts data

National accounts data are revised by national statistical offices when methodologies change or data sources improve. National accounts data in *World Development Indicators* are also revised when data sources change. The following notes, while not comprehensive, provide information on revisions from previous data. • **Argentina.** The base year has changed to 2004. • **Bahrain.** Based on official government statistics, the new base year is 2010. • **Bangladesh.** The new base year is 2005/06. • **Bosnia and Herzegovina.** Based

Economies with exceptional reporting periods

Economy	Fiscal year end	Reporting period for national accounts data
Afghanistan	Mar. 20	FY
Australia	Jun. 30	FY
Bangladesh	Jun. 30	FY
Botswana	Mar. 31	CY
Canada	Mar. 31	CY
Egypt, Arab Rep.	Jun. 30	FY
Ethiopia	Jul. 7	FY
Gambia, The	Jun. 30	CY
Haiti	Sep. 30	FY
India	Mar. 31	FY
Indonesia	Mar. 31	CY
Iran, Islamic Rep.	Mar. 20	FY
Japan	Mar. 31	CY
Kenya	Jun. 30	CY
Kuwait	Jun. 30	CY
Lesotho	Mar. 31	CY
Malawi	Mar. 31	CY
Marshall Islands	Sep. 30	FY
Micronesia, Fed. Sts.	Sep. 30	FY
Myanmar	Mar. 31	FY
Namibia	Mar. 31	CY
Nepal	Jul. 14	FY
New Zealand	Mar. 31	FY
Pakistan	Jun. 30	FY
Palau	Sep. 30	FY
Puerto Rico	Jun. 30	FY
Samoa	Jun. 30	FY
Sierra Leone	Jun. 30	CY
Singapore	Mar. 31	CY
South Africa	Mar. 31	CY
Swaziland	Mar. 31	CY
Sweden	Jun. 30	CY
Thailand	Sep. 30	CY
Tonga	Jun. 30	FY
Uganda	Jun. 30	FY
United States	Sep. 30	CY
Zimbabwe	Jun. 30	CY

on official government statistics for chain-linked series, the new reference year is 2010. • **Bulgaria.** The new reference year for chain-linked series is 2010. • **Congo, Dem. Rep.** Based on official government statistics, the new base year 2005. • **Côte d'Ivoire.** The new base year is 2009. • **Croatia.** The new reference year for chain-linked series is 2010. • **Egypt, Arab Rep.** The new base year is 2001/02. • **Equatorial Guinea.** Based on IMF data and official government statistics, the new base year is 2006. • **Gabon.** Based on IMF data and official government statistics, the new base year is 2001. • **India.** Based on official government statistics, the new base year is 2011/12. India reports using SNA 2008. • **Israel.** Based on official government statistics for chain-linked series, the new reference year is 2010. • **Kazakhstan.** The new reference year for chain-linked series is 2005. • **Kenya.** Based on official government statistics, the new base year is 2009. • **Korea, Rep.** The new base year is 2010. • **Kuwait.** Based on official government statistics, the new base year is 2010. • **Mauritania.** Based on official statistics from the Ministry of Economic Affairs and Development, the base year has changed from 2004 to 1998. • **Mozambique.** Based on official government statistics, the new base year is 2009. • **Namibia.** Based on official government statistics, the new base year is 2010. • **Nigeria.** Based on official government statistics, the new base year is 2010. Nigeria reports using SNA 2008. • **Oman.** Based on official government statistics, the new base year is 2010. • **Panama.** The new base year is 2007. • **Peru.** The new base year is 2007. • **Rwanda.** Based on official government statistics, the new base year is 2011. Rwanda reports using SNA 2008. • **Samoa.** The new base year is 2008/09. Other methodological changes include increased reliance on summary data from the country's Value Added Goods and Services Tax system, incorporation of more recent benchmarks, and use of improved data sources. • **São Tomé and Príncipe.** The base year has changed from 2001 to 2000. • **Serbia.** The new reference year for chain-linked series is 2010. • **South Africa.** The new base year is 2010. South Africa reports using SNA 2008. • **Tanzania.** The new base year is 2007. Tanzania reports using a blend of SNA 1993 and SNA 2008. • **Uganda.** Based on official government statistics, the new base year is 2009/10. Uganda reports using SNA 2008. Price valuation is in producer prices. • **West Bank and Gaza.** The new base year is 2004. • **Yemen, Rep.** The new base year is 2007. • **Zambia.** The new base year is 2010. Zambia reports using SNA 2008.

Statistical methods

This section describes some of the statistical practices and procedures used in preparing *World Development Indicators*. It covers data consistency, reliability, and comparability as well as the methods employed for calculating regional and income group aggregates and for calculating growth rates. It also describes the *World Bank Atlas* method for deriving the conversion factor used to estimate gross national income (GNI) and GNI per capita in U.S. dollars. Other statistical procedures and calculations are described in the *About the data* sections following each table.

Data consistency, reliability, and comparability

Considerable effort has been made to standardize the data, but full comparability cannot be assured, so care must be taken in interpreting the indicators. Many factors affect data availability, comparability, and reliability: statistical systems in many developing economies are still weak; statistical methods, coverage, practices, and definitions differ widely; and cross-country and intertemporal comparisons involve complex technical and conceptual problems that cannot be resolved unequivocally. Data coverage may not be complete because of special circumstances affecting the collection and reporting of data, such as problems stemming from conflicts.

Thus, although drawn from sources thought to be the most authoritative, data should be construed only as indicating trends and characterizing major differences among economies rather than as offering precise quantitative measures of those differences. Discrepancies in data presented in different editions of *World Development Indicators* reflect updates by countries as well as revisions to historical series and changes in methodology. Therefore readers are advised not to compare data series between editions of *World Development Indicators* or between different World Bank publications. Consistent time-series data for 1960–2013 are available at http://data.worldbank.org.

Aggregation rules

Aggregates based on the World Bank's regional and income classifications of economies appear at the end of the tables, including most of those available online. The 214 economies included in these classifications are shown on the flaps on the front and back covers of the book. Aggregates also contain data for Taiwan, China. Most tables also include the aggregate for the euro area, which includes the member states of the Economic and Monetary Union (EMU) of the European Union that have adopted the euro as their currency: Austria, Belgium, Cyprus, Estonia, Finland, France, Germany, Greece, Ireland, Italy, Latvia, Lithuania, Luxembourg, Malta, Netherlands, Portugal, Slovak Republic, Slovenia, and Spain. Other classifications, such as the European Union, are documented in *About the data* for the online tables in which they appear.

Because of missing data, aggregates for groups of economies should be treated as approximations of unknown totals or average values. The aggregation rules are intended to yield estimates for a consistent set of economies from one period to the next and for all indicators. Small differences between sums of subgroup aggregates and overall totals and averages may occur because of the approximations used. In addition, compilation errors and data reporting practices may cause discrepancies in theoretically identical aggregates such as world exports and world imports.

Five methods of aggregation are used in *World Development Indicators:*

- For group and world totals denoted in the tables by a *t*, missing data are imputed based on the relationship of the sum of available data to the total in the year of the previous estimate. The imputation process works forward and backward from 2005. Missing values in 2005 are imputed using one of several proxy variables for which complete data are available in that year. The imputed value is calculated so that it (or its proxy) bears the same relationship to the total of available data. Imputed values are usually not calculated if missing data account for more than a third of the total in the benchmark year. The variables used as proxies are GNI in U.S. dollars; total population; exports and imports of goods and services in U.S. dollars; and value added in agriculture, industry, manufacturing, and services in U.S. dollars.

- Aggregates marked by an s are sums of available data. Missing values are not imputed. Sums are not computed if more than a third of the observations in the series or a proxy for the series are missing in a given year.
- Aggregates of ratios are denoted by a w when calculated as weighted averages of the ratios (using the value of the denominator or, in some cases, another indicator as a weight) and denoted by a u when calculated as unweighted averages. The aggregate ratios are based on available data. Missing values are assumed to have the same average value as the available data. No aggregate is calculated if missing data account for more than a third of the value of weights in the benchmark year. In a few cases the aggregate ratio may be computed as the ratio of group totals after imputing values for missing data according to the above rules for computing totals.
- Aggregate growth rates are denoted by a w when calculated as a weighted average of growth rates. In a few cases growth rates may be computed from time series of group totals. Growth rates are not calculated if more than half the observations in a period are missing. For further discussion of methods of computing growth rates see below.
- Aggregates denoted by an m are medians of the values shown in the table. No value is shown if more than half the observations for countries with a population of more than 1 million are missing.

Exceptions to the rules may occur. Depending on the judgment of World Bank analysts, the aggregates may be based on as little as 50 percent of the available data. In other cases, where missing or excluded values are judged to be small or irrelevant, aggregates are based only on the data shown in the tables.

Growth rates

Growth rates are calculated as annual averages and represented as percentages. Except where noted, growth rates of values are in real terms computed from constant price series. Three principal methods are used to calculate growth rates: least squares, exponential endpoint, and geometric endpoint. Rates of change from one period to the next are calculated as proportional changes from the earlier period.

Least squares growth rate. Least squares growth rates are used wherever there is a sufficiently long time series to permit a reliable calculation. No growth rate is calculated if more than half the observations in a period are missing. The least squares growth rate, r, is estimated by fitting a linear regression trend line to the logarithmic annual values of the variable in the relevant period. The regression equation takes the form

$$\ln X_t = a + bt$$

which is the logarithmic transformation of the compound growth equation,

$$X_t = X_o (1 + r)^t.$$

In this equation X is the variable, t is time, and $a = \ln X_o$ and $b = \ln (1 + r)$ are parameters to be estimated. If $b*$ is the least squares estimate of b, then the average annual growth rate, r, is obtained as $[\exp(b*) - 1]$ and is multiplied by 100 for expression as a percentage. The calculated growth rate is an average rate that is representative of the available observations over the entire period. It does not necessarily match the actual growth rate between any two periods.

Exponential growth rate. The growth rate between two points in time for certain demographic indicators, notably labor force and population, is calculated from the equation

$$r = \ln(p_n/p_0)/n$$

where p_n and p_0 are the last and first observations in the period, n is the number of years in the period, and ln is the natural logarithm operator. This growth rate is based on a model of continuous, exponential growth between two points in time. It does not take into account the intermediate values of the series. Nor does it correspond to the annual rate of change measured at a one-year interval, which is given by $(p_n - p_{n-1})/p_{n-1}$.

Statistical methods

Geometric growth rate. The geometric growth rate is applicable to compound growth over discrete periods, such as the payment and reinvestment of interest or dividends. Although continuous growth, as modeled by the exponential growth rate, may be more realistic, most economic phenomena are measured only at intervals, in which case the compound growth model is appropriate. The average growth rate over n periods is calculated as

$$r = \exp[\ln(p_n/p_0)/n] - 1.$$

World Bank Atlas method

In calculating GNI and GNI per capita in U.S. dollars for certain operational and analytical purposes, the World Bank uses the *Atlas* conversion factor instead of simple exchange rates. The purpose of the *Atlas* conversion factor is to reduce the impact of exchange rate fluctuations in the cross-country comparison of national incomes.

The *Atlas* conversion factor for any year is the average of a country's exchange rate (or alternative conversion factor) for that year and its exchange rates for the two preceding years, adjusted for the difference between the rate of inflation in the country and the rate of international inflation.

The objective of the adjustment is to reduce any changes to the exchange rate caused by inflation.

A country's inflation rate between year t and year $t-n$ (r_{t-n}) is measured by the change in its GDP deflator (p_t):

$$r_{t-n} = \frac{p_t}{p_{t-n}}$$

International inflation between year t and year $t-n$ ($r_{t-n}^{SDR\$}$) is measured using the change in a deflator based on the International Monetary Fund's unit of account, special drawing rights (or SDRs). Known as the "SDR deflator," it is a weighted average of the GDP deflators (in SDR terms) of Japan, the United Kingdom, the United States, and the euro area, converted to U.S. dollar terms; weights are the amount of each currency in one SDR unit.

$$r_{t-n}^{SDR\$} = \frac{p_t^{SDR\$}}{p_{t-n}^{SDR\$}}$$

The *Atlas* conversion factor (local currency to the U.S. dollar) for year t (e_t^{atlas}) is given by:

$$e_t^{atlas} = \frac{1}{3}\left[e_t + e_{t-1}\left(\frac{r_{t-1}}{r_{t-1}^{SDR\$}}\right) + e_{t-2}\left(\frac{r_{t-2}}{r_{t-2}^{SDR\$}}\right)\right]$$

where e_t is the average annual exchange rate (local currency to the U.S. dollar) for year t.

GNI in U.S. dollars (*Atlas* method) for year t ($Y_t^{atlas\$}$) is calculated by applying the *Atlas* conversion factor to a country's GNI in current prices (local currency) (Y_t) as follows:

$$Y_t^{atlas\$} = Y_t / e_t^{atlas}$$

The resulting *Atlas* GNI in U.S. dollars can then be divided by a country's midyear population to yield its GNI per capita (*Atlas* method).

Alternative conversion factors

The World Bank systematically assesses the appropriateness of official exchange rates as conversion factors. An alternative conversion factor is used when the official exchange rate is deemed to be unreliable or unrepresentative of the rate effectively applied to domestic transactions of foreign currencies and traded products. This applies to only a small number of countries, as shown in *Primary data documentation*. Alternative conversion factors are used in the *Atlas* methodology and elsewhere in *World Development Indicators* as single-year conversion factors.

○ Front | ❓ User guide | ◉ World view | People | Environment

Credits

1. World view

Section 1 was prepared by a team led by Neil Fantom. Juan Feng and Umar Serajuddin wrote the introduction, and the Millennium Development Goal spreads were produced by Mahyar Eshragh-Tabary, Juan Feng, Masako Hiraga, Wendy Huang, Haruna Kashiwase, Buyant Erdene Khaltarkhuu, Tariq Khokhar, Hiroko Maeda, Malvina Pollock, Umar Serajuddin, Emi Suzuki, and Dereje Wolde. The tables were produced by Mahyar Eshragh-Tabary, Juan Feng, Masako Hiraga, Wendy Huang, Bala Bhaskar Naidu Kalimili, Haruna Kashiwase, Buyant Erdene Khaltarkhuu, Hiroko Maeda, Umar Serajuddin, Emi Suzuki, and Dereje Wolde. Signe Zeikate of the World Bank's Economic Policy and Debt Department provided the estimates of debt relief for the Heavily Indebted Poor Countries Debt Relief Initiative and Multilateral Debt Relief Initiative. The map was produced by Liu Cui, Juan Feng, William Prince, and Umar Serajuddin.

2. People

Section 2 was prepared by Juan Feng, Masako Hiraga, Haruna Kashiwase, Hiroko Maeda, Umar Serajuddin, Emi Suzuki, and Dereje Wolde in partnership with the World Bank's various Global Practices and Cross-Cutting Solutions Areas—Education, Gender, Health, Jobs, Poverty, and Social Protection and Labor. Emi Suzuki prepared the demographic estimates and projections. The new indicators on shared prosperity were prepared by the Global Poverty Working Group, a team of poverty experts from the Poverty Global Practice, the Development Research Group, and the Development Data Group coordinated by Andrew Dabalen, Umar Serajuddin, and Nobuo Yoshida. Poverty estimates at national poverty lines were compiled by the Global Poverty Working Group. Shaohua Chen and Prem Sangraula of the World Bank's Development Research Group and the Global Poverty Working Group prepared the poverty estimates at international poverty lines. Lorenzo Guarcello and Furio Rosati of the Understanding Children's Work project prepared the data on children at work. Other contributions were provided by Isis Gaddis (gender) and Samuel Mills (health); Salwa Haidar, Maddalena Honorati, Theodoor Sparreboom, and Alan Wittrup of the International Labour Organization (labor force); Colleen Murray (health), Julia Krasevec (malnutrition and overweight), and Rolf Luyendijk and Andrew Trevett (water and sanitation) of the United Nations Children's Fund; Amélie Gagnon, Friedrich Huebler, and Weixin Lu of the United Nations Educational, Scientific and Cultural Organization Institute for Statistics (education and literacy); Patrick Gerland and François Pelletier of the United Nations Population Division; Callum Brindley and Chandika Indikadahena (health expenditure), Monika Bloessner, Elaine Borghi, Mercedes de Onis, and Leanne Riley (malnutrition and overweight), Teena Kunjumen (health workers), Jessica Ho (hospital beds), Rifat Hossain (water and sanitation), Luz Maria de Regil and Gretchen Stevens (anemia), Hazim Timimi (tuberculosis), Colin Mathers and Wahyu Mahanani (cause of death), and Lori Marie Newman (syphilis), all of the World Health Organization; Juliana Daher and Mary Mahy of the Joint United Nations Programme on HIV/AIDS (HIV/AIDS); and Leonor Guariguata of the International Diabetes Federation (diabetes). The map was produced by Liu Cui, William Prince, and Emi Suzuki.

3. Environment

Section 3 was prepared by Mahyar Eshragh-Tabary in partnership with the World Bank's Environment and Natural Resources Global Practices and Energy and Extractives Global Practices. Mahyar Eshragh-Tabary wrote the introduction and highlights with editorial help and comments from Neil Fantom and Tariq Khokhar. Christopher Sall helped prepare the introduction, highlights, and about the data sections on air pollution with valuable comments from Esther G. Naikal and Urvashi Narain. Esther G. Naikal, Urvashi Narain, and Christopher Sall prepared the data and metadata on population-weighted exposure to ambient PM2.5 pollution and natural resources rents. Sudeshna Ghosh Banerjee and Elisa Portale prepared the data and metadata on access to electricity. Neil Fantom, Masako Hiraga, and William Prince provided instrumental comments, suggestions, and support at all stages of production. Several other staff members

Credits

from the World Bank made valuable contributions: Gabriela Elizondo Azuela, Marianne Fay, Vivien Foster, Glenn-Marie Lange, and Ulf Gerrit Narloch. Contributors from other institutions included Michael Brauer, Aaron Cohen, Mohammad H. Forouzanfar, and Peter Speyer from the Institute for Health Metrics and Evaluation; Pierre Boileau and Maureen Cropper from the University of Maryland; Sharon Burghgraeve and Jean-Yves Garnier of the International Energy Agency; Armin Wagner of German International Cooperation; Craig Hilton-Taylor and Caroline Pollock of the International Union for Conservation of Nature; and Cristian Gonzalez of the International Road Federation. The team is grateful to the Food and Agriculture Organization, the Global Burden of Disease of the Institute for Health Metrics and Evaluation, the International Energy Agency, the International Union for Conservation of Nature, the United Nations Environment Programme and World Conservation Monitoring Centre, the U.S. Agency for International Development's Office of Foreign Disaster Assistance, and the U.S. Department of Energy's Carbon Dioxide Information Analysis Center for access to their online databases. The World Bank's Environment and Natural Resources Global Practices also devoted generous staff resources.

4. Economy

Section 4 was prepared by Bala Bhaskar Naidu Kalimili in close collaboration with the Environment and Natural Resources Global Practice and Economic Data Team of the World Bank's Development Data Group. Bala Bhaskar Naidu Kalimili wrote the introduction, with inputs from Christopher Sall and Tamirat Yacob. The highlights were prepared by Bala Bhaskar Naidu Kalimili, Marko Olavi Rissanen, Christopher Sall, Saulo Teodoro Ferreira, and Tamirat Yacob, with invaluable comments and editorial help from Neil Fantom and Tariq Khokhar. The national accounts data for low- and middle-income economies were gathered by the World Bank's regional staff through the annual Unified Survey. Maja Bresslauer, Liu Cui, Federico Escaler, Mahyar Eshragh-Tabary, Bala Bhaskar Naidu Kalimili, Buyant Erdene Khaltarkhuu, Saulo Teodoro Ferreira, and Tamirat Yacob updated, estimated, and validated

the databases for national accounts. Esther G. Naikal and Christopher Sall prepared the data on adjusted savings and adjusted income. Azita Amjadi contributed data on trade from the World Integrated Trade Solution. The team is grateful to Eurostat, the International Monetary Fund, the Organisation for Economic Co-operation and Development, the United Nations Industrial Development Organization, and the World Trade Organization for access to their databases.

5. States and markets

Section 5 was prepared by Federico Escaler and Buyant Erdene Khaltarkhuu in partnership with the World Bank Group's Finance and Markets, Macroeconomics and Fiscal Management, Transport and Information, Communication Technologies Global Practices and its Public–Private Partnerships and Fragility, Conflict, and Violence Cross-Cutting Solution Areas; the International Finance Corporation; and external partners. Buyant Erdene Khaltarkhuu wrote the introduction and highlights with substantial input from Frederic Meunier (Doing Business) and Annette Kinitz (statistical capacity). Neil Fantom, Tariq Khokhar, and William Prince provided valuable comments. Other contributors include Alexander Nicholas Jett (privatization and infrastructure projects); Leora Klapper and Frederic Meunier (business registration); Jorge Luis Rodriguez Meza, Valeria Perotti, and Joshua Wimpey (Enterprise Surveys); Frederic Meunier and Rita Ramalho (Doing Business); Michael Orzano (Standard & Poor's global stock market indexes); James Hackett of the International Institute for Strategic Studies (military personnel); Sam Perlo-Freeman of the Stockholm International Peace Research Institute (military expenditures and arms transfers); Therese Petterson (battle-related deaths); Clare Spurrell (internally displaced persons); Cristian Gonzalez of the International Road Federation, Cyrille Martin of the International Civil Aviation Organization, and Andreas Dietrich Kopp (transport); Vincent Valentine of the United Nations Conference on Trade and Development (ports); Azita Amjadi (high-tech exports); Naman Khandelwal and Renato Perez of the International Monetary Fund (financial soundness indicators); Vanessa Grey,

Esperanza Magpantay, Susan Teltscher, and Ivan Vallejo Vall of the International Telecommunication Union and Torbjörn Fredriksson, Scarlett Fondeur Gil, and Diana Korka of the United Nations Conference on Trade and Development (information and communication technology goods trade); Martin Schaaper and Rohan Pathirage of the United Nations Educational, Scientific and Cultural Organization Institute for Statistics (research and development, researchers, and technicians); and Ryan Lamb of the World Intellectual Property Organization (patents and trademarks).

6. Global links

Section 6 was prepared by Wendy Huang with substantial input from Evis Rucaj and Rubena Sukaj and in partnership with the Financial Data Team of the World Bank's Development Data Group, Development Research Group (trade), Development Prospects Group (commodity prices and remittances), International Trade Department (trade facilitation), and external partners. Evis Rucaj wrote the introduction. Azita Amjadi and Molly Fahey Watts (trade and tariffs) and Rubena Sukaj (external debt and financial data) provided input on the data and table. Other contributors include Frédéric Docquier (emigration rates); Flavine Creppy and Yumiko Mochizuki of the United Nations Conference on Trade and Development and Mondher Mimouni of the International Trade Centre (trade); Cristina Savescu (commodity prices); Jeff Reynolds and Joseph Siegel of DHL (freight costs); Yasmin Ahmad and Elena Bernaldo of the Organisation for Economic Co-operation and Development (aid); Tarek Abou Chabake of the Office of the UN High Commissioner for Refugees (refugees); and Teresa Ciller and Leandry Moreno of the World Tourism Organization (tourism). Ramgopal Erabelly, Shelley Fu, and William Prince provided technical assistance.

Other parts of the book

Jeff Lecksell and Bruno Bonansea of the World Bank's Map Design Unit coordinated preparation of the maps on the inside covers and within each section. William Prince prepared *User guide* and the lists of online tables and indicators for each section and wrote *Statistical methods,* with input from Neil Fantom. Federico Escaler prepared *Primary data documentation.* Leila Rafei prepared *Partners.*

Database management

William Prince coordinated management of the World Development Indicators database, with assistance from Liu Cui and Shelley Fu in the Sustainable Development and Data Quality Team. Operation of the database management system was made possible by Ramgopal Erabelly working with the Data and Information Systems Team under the leadership of Soong Sup Lee.

Design, production, and editing

Azita Amjadi and Leila Rafei coordinated all stages of production with Communications Development Incorporated, which provided overall design direction, editing, and layout, led by Bruce Ross-Larson and Christopher Trott. Elaine Wilson created the cover and graphics and typeset the book. Peter Grundy, of Peter Grundy Art & Design, and Diane Broadley, of Broadley Design, designed the report.

Administrative assistance, office technology, and systems development support

Elysee Kiti provided administrative assistance. Jean-Pierre Djomalieu, Gytis Kanchas, and Nacer Megherbi provided information technology support. Ugendran Machakkalai, Atsushi Shimo, and Malarvizhi Veerappan provided software support on the DataBank application.

Publishing and dissemination

The World Bank's Publishing and Knowledge Division, under the direction of Carlos Rossel, provided assistance throughout the production process. Denise Bergeron, Stephen McGroarty, Nora Ridolfi, Paola Scalabrin, and Janice Tuten coordinated printing, marketing, and distribution.

World Development Indicators mobile applications

Software preparation and testing were managed by Shelley Fu with assistance from Prashant Chaudhari,

Credits

Neil Fantom, Mohammed Omar Hadi, Soong Sup Lee, Parastoo Oloumi, William Prince, Jomo Tariku, and Malarvizhi Veerappan. Systems development was undertaken in the Data and Information Systems Team led by Soong Sup Lee. Liu Cui and William Prince provided data quality assurance.

Online access

Coordination of the presentation of the WDI online, through the Open Data website, the DataBank application, the table browser application, and the Application Programming Interface, was provided by Neil Fantom and Soong Sup Lee. Development and maintenance of the website were managed by a team led by Azita Amjadi and comprising George Gongadze, Timothy Herzog, Jeffrey McCoy, Paige Morency-Notario, Leila Rafei, and Jomo Tariku. Systems development was managed by a team led by Soong Sup Lee, with project management provided by Malarvizhi Veerappan. Design, programming, and testing were carried out by Ying Chi, Rajesh Danda, Shelley Fu, Mohammed Omar Hadi, Siddhesh Kaushik, Ugendran Machakkalai, Nacer Megherbi, Parastoo Oloumi, Atsushi Shimo, and Jomo Tariku. Liu Cui and William Prince coordinated production and provided data quality assurance. Multilingual translations of online content were provided by a team in the General Services Department.

Client feedback

The team is grateful to the many people who have taken the time to provide feedback and suggestions, which have helped improve this year's edition. Please contact us at data@worldbank.org.